There's
MONEY
Where
Your
MOUTH Is

There's MONEY Where Your MOUTH Is

An Insider's Guide to a Career in Voice-Overs

ELAINE A. CLARK

BACK STAGE BOOKS

An imprint of Watson-Guptill Publications/New York

Senior Editor: Paul Lukas
Associate Editor: Alisa Palazzo
Designer: Areta Buk
Production Manager: Hector Campbell

First published in 1995 by Back Stage Books, an imprint of Watson-Guptill Publications,
a division of BPI Communications, Inc., 1515 Broadway, New York, N.Y. 10036

Library of Congress Cataloging-in-Publication Data

Clark, Elaine A.
    There's money where your mouth is : an insider's guide to a career in voice-overs
      p. cm.
    Includes index.
    ISBN 0-8230-7703-9 (pbk.)
    1. Television announcing—Vocational guidance. 2. Voice culture. 3.
Voice-overs. 4. Television advertising—Vocational guidance.
I. Title.
PN1992.8.A6C53 1995
791.45'028'023—dc20   95-17341
                                                    CIP

Printed in the United States of America

First printing, 1995

THIS BOOK IS DEDICATED TO ALL MY VOICE-OVER STUDENTS
AND TALENT AGENTS, THE INDIVIDUALS WHO HAVE TRUSTED ME
TO CAST AND/OR DIRECT THEIR AUDIO PROJECTS,
AND THE DIRECTORS AND PRODUCERS WHO HAVE SHAPED AND
MOLDED MY VOICE-OVER WORK OVER THE PAST 15 YEARS.

Contents

ACKNOWLEDGMENTS

A special thanks to Ed Hooks for convincing me to write this book and referring me to Paul Lukas.

To my former business partner, Andrew R. Ebon, for his sound business advice in establishing Voice One with me in 1986. Some of the scripts used in this book were previously cowritten by us for use in our voice-over classes. I thank him for his contribution.

To Joe Paulino, Denny Delk, Doug Lawrence, Steve Shapiro, Joan Spangler, Steve Tisherman, Steve Kaye, Wendy Yee, Bill Krauss, Beth Kaufman, David Platshon, J. S. Gilbert, and the National and San Francisco SAG and AFTRA offices for their help and input.

To my voice-over student, Rob Whiteman, for creating the title for my advanced voice over class, *Making It M.I.N.E.*

To Cliff Osmond for teaching me to "be a winner" and "go through the acting problem" and Mark Monroe for helping me to uncover my "subconscious" self.

For my parents who told me to always do my best and keep trying.

And especially, I thank my husband, Rob Clark, and daughters, Emily, Laura, and Elizabeth for their patience with me while I was glued to the computer writing this book. Rob's computer expertise was especially useful in helping me format some of the graphics.

Introduction

VOICE-OVER: The art of using the voice to bring "life" to written words. From the phrase voice-over-picture, *it refers to the voice behind the picture on television commercials, cartoons, industrial narrations, CD-ROM video games, interactive television, video trade show presentations, and infomercials. Radio commercials, books-on-tape, voice mail systems, computer software programs, multimedia, film looping (dialogue replacement for on-screen actors), A.D.R. (Automated Dialogue Replacement), and Walla (crowd noises in films and TV shows) also fall under this category.*

Until recently, voice-over performers were seldom thought of as *real* actors. Stage, film, and television actors held that esteemed spotlight. For some, being *seen* performing seemed much more prestigious than speaking into a microphone. This weary sentiment was expressed in the movie *Tootsie* when Dustin Hoffman pleaded with his talent agent to find him any kind of acting work . . . *even voice-overs!* This act of desperation sent a roar of laughter throughout the voice-over community. Obviously, Dustin Hoffman's character did not realize the benefits of being a voice-over actor.

Benefits? What are they? Besides the love of the art and the ability to use one's voice in a constructive and creative manner, the most obvious benefits are time and money. Voice-over actors are paid very well for the short period of time required in the recording studio. There is no time spent on memorization or blocking movements. During the session, very little time is wasted. The voice actor simply walks into the recording studio, receives a script, spends a couple of minutes studying it, comes up with an appropriate sound and characterization, incorporates the director's suggestions into the reading, and records the material. Voilà! The job is done; the check is in the mail. Since the work is fast and efficient, trained voice-over actors at the top of their field can easily bounce from one recording session to another, earning more money in a day, and in less time, than many on-camera and stage actors. (An enviable benefit, to say the least.)

As a voice-over actor, not being *seen* offers distinct advantages over on-camera and stage work. It means not having to spend a lot of time putting on make-up, futzing with hair, and selecting the perfect outfit. The only wardrobe-conscious decision the voice actor has to make is whether or not the clothes and jewelry make noise! (Crisp, starched shirts are best kept at home. Soft, quiet, comfortable fabrics are the preferred choice. Dangling necklaces, bangle bracelets, coins in the pockets, shoes that squeak, and electronic pagers and cellular telephones can ruin a "take.")

Remaining an anonymous voice actor also means that, the voice-over community and a few close friends aside, the majority of the population will not ask for your autograph when you go out in public. Only when you *speak* will a person with a trained ear suspect that your voice matches the one in the toilet bowl commercial or the in-store product display video. So, don't rush out and buy dark sunglasses. Wait at least until you land a job in a high-profile, prime-time cartoon series and are hounded by fans, reporters, and photographers.

For years, voice-overs were considered a closed field open only to the elite few who knew how to use a microphone properly and create a character voice in five minutes or less, rather than after a six-week rehearsal period. The "real person" sound currently in vogue in commercials and multimedia's growing need for outlandish characters and over-the-top acting performances in interactive games are changing the ground rules and allowing in more newcomers.

But why the sudden interest in voice-overs? Voice-overs, although a well-kept secret, have been around for years. They are fun, efficient, and *profitable,* which is just what Hollywood stars have discovered! Like never before, famous people are lending their voices to product endorsements. This influx of celebrity voices in commercials has heightened awareness of voice-overs and everyday people are clamoring to get in. In the past, only semi-famous actors whose careers were in decline or in need of a serious financial boost associated themselves with commercial products. Conversely, unknown aspiring actors used voice-overs as a stepping stone to pay off bills before their much anticipated stage or screen success. Now, the tide has turned. One might even get the impression that an actor has to become famous first, before voicing a commercial. Although not altogether true, celebrities, who in years past would have never considered appearing on a television commercial pitching a jar of pickles or a brand of ice cream, are stepping up to the microphone in swarms to lend their voices and "personalities" to advertisements.

Breaking into the voice-over business takes talent, skill, perseverance, and luck. When I backed my way into this career in 1981, I experienced most of what I learned by trial and error. Little did I know, as a theater major in college, that the part-time disc jockey position at the campus radio station would lead to a lifetime career in voice-overs. Upon graduating from college and moving to San Francisco, I attended my first voice-over class. The notion of freelancing with my voice had never occurred to me, but soon I was hooked. I put together my first commercial demo tape and mailed it out to about 50 advertising agencies and the leading voice talent agency in the city. Low and behold, I got my first job! Unfortunately, the talent agent whom I solicited was not as enthusiastic. I received a postcard of rejection. Three months later I assembled a second voice tape and mailed it out to about 100 advertising agencies. Desperate, daring, or awed by my talent, several producers hired me to voice some of their commercials. At last, I was making money. A talent agent must have sniffed the greenbacks, because when I called for representation the voice agent recognized my name and suggested I come in to register. Alas, it was still not my first choice of talent agencies. After submitting my voice tape to them a second time, that talent agency sent me a letter of rejection. Fortunately, this proved more positive than the postcard of rejection that looked as if it had fallen out of the typewriter several times. I was moving up in the world. Three months later, I assembled a third tape composed primarily of actual work and sent it to the voice-over agent I had my heart set on. Finally, I got signed! The next day the agent sent me out on a commercial print job. Go figure.

Since those humble beginnings, I have been registered with several talent agencies, have voiced hundreds of commercials, television promos, and industrial narrations, have taught professional-level workshops in voice technique and acting, and have cast and directed numerous books-on-tape, CD-ROM games, narrations, and commercial projects. As an actor who has *chosen* to become a voice-over expert, not only for the money but for the art, I devote this book to all the "hidden stars." May you enjoy many a day standing in a soundproof room talking endlessly into a microphone.

Levels of Learning

The primary focus of this book is on commercials, although industrial narrations, books-on-tape, and multimedia scripts are covered. I strongly suggest that you read it through once, then use it as a workbook. Practice the breathing and diction exercises and read the sample scripts out loud. Record your work and listen to your progress. Keep in mind that there are four levels of learning:

1. Unconsciously Incompetent
2. Consciously Incompetent
3. Consciously Competent
4. Unconsciously Competent

When you first picked up this book, did you assume that all you needed to make money in the voice-over business was a good voice? Were you cognizant of the technique, skill, and craft involved in delivering believable copy? If not, consider yourself a beginner in level 1, the *unconsciously incompetent* stage. By simply accepting the fact that learning how to do voice-overs requires time, commitment, understanding of copy, interpretation skills, breath control, and voice techniques, you can progress quickly to level 2: *consciously incompetent.* At this second level of learning, you may be able to hear your mistakes but not know how to fix them. That is where "perfect" practice fits in. If you follow the instructions in the book, practice all the drills, record your rehearsals, playback your recordings, analyze your delivery, and attempt to fix it on subsequent recordings, you should progress easily to level 3: *consciously competent.* This third stage has the greatest learning curve. The brain does most of the work. If you think about the copy and how you want to say the words, you can actually deliver the dialogue as you envisioned it in your mind. At this stage, you should consider enrolling in professional voice-over classes. Having a trained "second ear" will help balance out what you think you are doing with how the performance actually sounds.

Ultimately, the goal all voice actors want to attain is level 4: *unconsciously competent.* Like the professional tennis player who no longer has to stop and think whether to swing forehand or backhand as the ball approaches, the unconsciously competent voice-over professional looks at a script and knows reflexively what to do. This actor trusts his or her skills and allows the words to flow from the lips effortlessly, without the brain calling signals. Many voice-over actors never reach this final stage of professionalism. Consciously competent actors *do* get work. The financial and artistic rewards, however, are vastly more significant for actors who aspire to higher excellence. To get there, you must be patient and not expect brilliance to happen over night. Study hard and enjoy the work.

In learning a new skill, remember that perseverance (as well as talent) is the key to success. Show business offers no guarantees. Often, luck rather than intelligence is rewarded. If making money is your primary motivation for doing voice-overs, you are setting yourself up for failure. You must *love* the work in order to stay with it. The ones who don't succeed are the ones who either don't try or give up too early. Had I stopped pursuing a career in the voice-over business after receiving the talent agent's first postcard of rejection, I would not be sharing this book with you today and enjoying the benefits of working in the wonderful and exciting field called voice-overs.

Let the fun begin!

Chapter 1

Getting Started

Thomas Edison is credited with saying, "Genius is one percent inspiration and 99 percent perspiration." Upon entering the voice-over profession, one important factor should always be remembered: voice-overs are not only an art, they are also a business. Inherently, this work ethic separates the person who entertains family and friends with jokes, stories, and antics, from the professional who is hired and paid to breathe life into written words. Start wiping your brow, folks, because behind every good voice actor is a hard-working businessperson who must toil, sweat, and study to get to the top.

WHO GETS THE WORK?

To get a clearer idea of who gets the work, turn on the radio or television for 30 minutes and keep track of the voices you hear in the commercials. Depending on the station and time of day, you will probably hear somewhere between six to 15 commercials. How many men, women, and children are in each spot? Unless it is close to a major holiday or "back-to-school" time, you may not hear *any* commercials featuring a child's voice. In montage spots (commercials that feature numerous actors saying "one-liners"), chances are only one out of five voices will be female. Man-woman dialogue spots are often followed by a male announcer delivering the closing tag line. There may be several men-only spots, compared with only one or two female-only spots. When the 30 minutes is over, add up your talent roster. In most markets, the percentage of work breaks down as follows: 75 to 80 percent men to 20 to 25 percent women! Unfair as it sounds, the averages are moving in the women's favor. In the early 1980s, the work was 85 to 90 percent men versus only 10 to 15 percent women.

No matter which vocal bracket you fall into, good actors continue to get the majority of the work. (This is discounting radio commercials written and performed by radio sales reps.) The goal is to become the best. So until the tide changes—and it will—and the work becomes more evenly divided between men and women, women should realize that they might have to work a little harder on their craft to secure a stronger voice-hold in the industry.

A WORD ABOUT SAG/AFTRA

Screen Actors Guild (SAG) and the American Federation of Television and Radio Artists (AFTRA) are the two performing-arts unions that deal with voice-over actors. Although it is not absolutely necessary to be a member of one of these unions to get voice-over work, it is highly recommended.

BEGINNING YOUR CAREER

In recognizing the breakdown of work, I do not mean to discourage anyone from entering the business. I do, however, believe that people should know exactly what they are getting themselves into. The field of voice-overs is very specialized. Because of this, it is often perceived as being cliquish and hard to break into—although not impenetrable. To better understand this concept, consider the "San Francisco Chinese Restaurant Theory." San Francisco, a beautiful city noted for its multitude of fine restaurants, does not *need* another Chinese restaurant. But if a new Chinese restaurant opens that serves excellent food, people will inevitably dine there. The same is true with talent agents who represent a good stable of voice talent. Do they need new voice talent? Probably not, especially if adding new people dilutes their current talent pool, divides up the financial pie, and creates potential animosity among the clients. But if a new voice talent enters the market with something unique, special, and bankable, then the talent agent would be shortsighted in not signing that person.

On the creative hiring end, friendship, loyalty, and trust between producers and existing talent create a barrier that is sometimes hard to break down. It is human nature for people to stay with what they know, especially if the known talent is a friend, rather than gamble on the unknown. Therefore, it is common for a voice actor's first job to occur out of sheer desperation when the producer's first choice is out of town or ill. The unavailable actor's ill fortune becomes the new actor's bonanza. Talent payments do not reflect whether an actor is second, third, or forth choice—only that they did the job.

Denny Delk, a nationally recognized voice actor with agents in many cities across the country, tells the story of how he first got started in freelance voice. Having been recently laid off as a disc jockey at a local radio station, he called up a recording studio in San Francisco and asked if there was any work available. The studio, in its quest to stay abreast of new voice talent, scheduled a time for Denny to come in, meet the audio engineers, and perform a general audition. During the meeting the telephone rang. The office manager answered it and Denny heard, "I'm sorry. No, no. That's okay. I understand. Don't worry about it. I'll tell the client. Hope you feel better." Placing the phone down, the office manager turned to Denny and said, "Do you want to work?" It ended up being a thousand-dollar day! Denny recorded six spots for a major department store and went on to become their regular spokesperson.

THE RECORDING STUDIO

If dark, windowless, soundproof rooms make you feel warm and cozy, voice-overs is definitely for you. The recording studio is "home" to the voice-over actor. Architecturally, it is divided between two major areas: the control room and the soundproof recording booth. The engineer and director sit in the control room behind the mixing console, affectionately referred to as "the board," while the actor works behind the microphone and music stand in "the booth" or "studio." Between these two areas there is usually a double-pane glass window or a set of glass doors allowing visibility between the actor and the director/audio engineer team. The angled, double glass panes, convoluted foam padding, and absorption-treated walls in the studio help keep the room soundproof. Sometimes portable partitions, called "gobos," are also rolled into position around the actor if further absorption or reflection of sound is needed, or if a separate sound isolation area is required.

Once in the studio, the actor cannot hear what is going on in the control room unless the director presses the "talk back" button on the console. Conversely, unless the microphone is turned on in the control room, the director and engineer cannot hear what the actor is saying. At first, this "fish-bowl effect" may be disconcerting. Great words of wisdom may be lost on a deaf crowd, while comments not meant to be heard by the other party may come through loud and clear. (This is a good reason why actors should never make derogatory comments about the director, product, client, or engineer during the session.) With time and practice, the physical separation between actor and director becomes negligible, comfortable, and absolutely natural.

It cannot be stressed enough that, while in the studio, the microphone should never be touched. It is a very expensive piece of equipment, costing thousands of dollars. Unless told otherwise, let the engineer adjust the microphone to suit your height. (After all, making you sound good is one of the sound engineer's jobs!) Engineers like to turn the microphone off in the control room, run out into the studio, adjust the mic to suit the individual, run back into the control room, turn the sound back on, and have the actor speak into the microphone to test the "level." So, if you have a hankering to move that expensive piece of metal, ask first. Then, if the engineer allows you to touch it and you break it, it is the engineer's fault for permitting your clumsiness. If you must move something, let it be the music stand. They are hard to break, inexpensive, and easy to manipulate. Just put your foot on the bottom of the stand, grab hold of the long cylindrical tube trunk, and pull up.

Most professional recording studios come equipped with headphones. "Cans," as they are sometimes called, wrap around the top of the actor's head and fit snugly over the ears, allowing the actor to hear his voice the way other people do. Additionally, headphones allow the actor to hear direction from the control room, especially if the recording studio is not equipped with built-in wall speakers. Some actors find headphones helpful in keeping the voice consistent when creating difficult, new, or challenging characters. Earphones, as they are also called, allow the actor to keep close tabs on the voice and quickly adjust and avert inconsistency problems before they become apparent to the director or engineer. Headphones are also essential when two actors are recording a conversation from separate rooms. For instance, when one actor is on a "phone patch" (to sound as if on the telephone) or has to speak very loudly, the phone-filter effect or actor's loud volume can "bleed" into the other person's microphone. A sound solution is to place one actor in an isolation room, or "iso booth." Since the actors are in separate soundproof rooms and cannot hear (or possibly even see) one another, headphones must be implemented. Reading to sound—be it voice, music, or sound effect—also requires the use of headphones.

First time headphone users may find them disconcerting. People are used to hearing their voices rattling around inside their heads, not piped directly into their ears! Getting used to headphones takes practice. Take advantage of every opportunity to rehearse with them, but don't become dependent on them, as headphones can easily become a crutch. Many people hold back or direct themselves when wearing headphones. Subsequently, their voice quality sounds wonderful but the depth of their performance is jeopardized as emotional believability and reality become stifled.

Occasionally practicing with headphones is fine and is a good way to alleviate the discomfort and nervousness of on-the-job training. Some voice actors also worry that using headphones too often poses a risk of hearing loss. Many radio disc jockeys suffer from this ailment after years of hearing loud music and their voices hammered into their eardrums. Prolonged use of headphones is fingered as the culprit. So once you start working several jobs a day with great regularity, consider your options: not wearing them, telling the engineer to keep the level in the "phones" down, or placing only one "can" over an ear at a time, leaving the other can behind the exposed ear. (That way, you'll always have one good ear!)

WHAT IS THE VOICE-OVER ACTOR'S SCHEDULE?

Voice-overs are primarily recorded during the regular 9:00 A.M. to 5:00 P.M. work day. Within that time slot, 10:00 A.M. to 3:00 P.M. is the most cherished. Why is this midday time period so prized? Producers know that the voice functions better after it has had time to properly warm up. Early morning sessions do not always allow enough time for the actor to achieve a more resonant midday voice. Later in the day, the producer and engineer need time to edit the actor's recorded material and mix in the sound effects and music.

Obviously, if a job has to be completed by a certain date and time, the producer must make concessions. Recording studios, directors, and talent schedules often have conflicts. To accommodate this, some sessions have to start as early as 8:00 or 8:30 A.M., or go as late as 10:00 or 11:00 P.M. (Unless the client has a special arrangement with the recording studio, most producers avoid these early morning and late night sessions because of overtime fees.) Some studios make financial concessions with producers of long projects like books-on-tape and CD-ROM games. Recording sessions may start late in the day and continue long into the evening or be recorded on the weekend. On the whole, though, the usual business hours, Monday through Friday, 9:00 A.M. to 5:00 P.M, are the most likely times a voice actor will work.

HOW IS MY VOICE?

Having a good voice is a gift. Knowing what to do with it is the challenge. Just because a person speaks well does not mean that he can do voice-overs. In addition, just because a person can create an array of character voices does not mean that she can manipulate the voice to a director's satisfaction. Voice-overs require *eye-brain-mouth* coordination. The eyes have to be able to follow the lines on the page, the brain has to capably decipher the written words and retain the director's notes, and the mouth must be trusted to speak the words in the manner intended. If nervousness, insecurities, and mental blocks interfere with the delicate balance, the eye-brain-mouth transfer short circuits. Words become transposed, pronunciations and phrasings become garbled, and the actor's performance becomes a proverbial train wreck.

People perform best in familiar environments. As a freelance performer, this is not always easy. Work situations vary constantly, and engineers, directors, writers, producers, clients, and fellow actors change from session to session. Even recording studios have their own unique styles of operation, personnel, floor plans, and microphone brand and placement preferences. Naturally, the more an actor works, the more familiar he or she becomes with the people and situations. Performances progressively improve as comfort levels increase and industry track records are gradually established.

ACTING CLASSES

In order to compete with professionals who have decades of experience, actors must pay their dues. The best way to circumvent some years of dues-paying is by taking classes. Studying with a variety of teachers, rather than just one teacher or school, gives an actor a broader overview of the business. Each classroom experience allows the actor an opportunity to become better equipped in handling new and challenging situations.

Voice-over workshops and classes can be very specialized. They involve copy interpretation, acting skills, styles of delivery, phrasings, microphone techniques, timing ability, volume control, character development, and more. Voice-over classes are often more expensive than stage and on-camera classes. This is because, for optimum results, voice-over classes need to be held in recording studios where the hourly rate is typically much higher than the classrooms or open spaces used by stage, film, and television acting instructors.

When selecting teachers, feel free to inquire about their background. After all, what a student learns is a direct result of a teacher's experiences. In the beginning, especially, it is better to study with teachers who are voice actors rather than directors, producers, talent agents, and casting directors. Professional voice actors and teachers emphasize the *acting process*. Fundamentals of how to act on mic, get inside the skin of the character, interpret a script, and breathe new life into the written words are of primary concern to the voice actor and teacher. Directors, producers, agents, and casting directors, on the other hand, have a tendency to teach *end results,* because their desire is to hear a polished, finished performance. They know immediately what they do and do not like but offer little help in how to accomplish it. Both styles of classes are helpful, but it is better to build a firm acting foundation first before registering for a class that offers the possibility of being discovered and offered a job.

"But I just want to use my voice!" I cannot tell you how many times I have heard that sentiment expressed. We are not bodiless creatures, are we? We are not merely disembodied heads and mouths floating in space! No, we are complete, interesting people. Our mouths are just the orifice used to verbally express our feelings and emotions. Our words shake when we are frightened or cold; they soften when we speak to someone we love or who needs nurturing; they become excited upon hearing good news. Good acting incorporates the whole body, not just the voice. It begins in the toes and filters through the fingers and out the top of the head. Therefore, it is important to take not only voice-over classes, but stage and film acting classes and improvisation classes, as well. Scene study, monologue, and improvisation techniques help build a strong voice-over foundation.

General scene study and monologue acting classes teach ways to analyze a script and create action, while stimulating self-discovery and exposing vulnerabilities. Actors must learn to peel off layers of their own personality and replace them with character traits that are specified or eluded to in a script. Interesting acting choices require working *through* a problem rather than around it. Often, that is what separates good acting from normal life. Acting is a safe environment to express passionate love, consuming hate, outrageous stupidity, and supreme wisdom. When the scene or monologue ends, normal life resumes.

Improvisation classes develop an actor's self-trust, natural instincts, and ability to totally commit to an action or thought. In "improv," there is no room for a "judge" or "little voice" to sit on your shoulder and tell you what to do or not do because you might look stupid or fail. All preconceived ideas and inner judgmental negativities must be cast aside. Improvisation nurtures the show in *show business* by using the chance-taking, childlike, creative self. New characters, voices, body language, timing skills, humor, and poignancy can emerge from this experience.

When searching for reputable classes, talk to fellow actors to find out the best teachers and acting studios. Call local talent agencies and ask the receptionist for suggestions on classes offered in your area. Or, check the phone book for a theatrical bookstore in your neighborhood, and stop by to see if they carry any local show business magazines, newspapers, newsletters, reference guides, or periodicals. Many cities have publications that list auditions, classes, and show business news. San Francisco has a magazine called *Callboard* and a reference guide called *The Reel Directory;* Los Angeles has numerous publications including *Back Stage West, Dramalogue,* and *The Working Actor's Guide;* and New York has *Back Stage.* Colleges and universities are another resource for acting classes.

PRACTICING AT HOME

To make money, an actor must always be prepared for voice-over jobs and auditions! Getting the voice-over "chops" seasoned and ready for use requires a keen ear and dedicated practice. Reading this book, taking acting, improvisation, and voice-over classes are all excellent, but practicing at home ties the crafts together. Begin home practice by paying close attention to television and radio commercials. Listen for spots that are in your vocal range, are interesting or have unique script interpretations, and contain a voice you can emulate. (Beware! Your focus is going to shift dramatically from watching and listening to programs purely for entertainment, to listening to ads for their aesthetic value.) Next, start becoming aware of the various styles of delivery. This book provides a wide range of copy running the gamut from the hard-sell announcer to wacky character commercials, industrial narrations, books-on-tape samples, and multimedia scripts. Along with each piece of copy are some helpful hints on interpretation.

Once the material in this book has been thoroughly exhausted, you will need additional copy. For those taking voice-over classes or registered with a talent agency, you may be able to borrow some old scripts. Some advertising agencies oblige inquiries requesting scripts, although handing out old scripts is not a high priority request. Magazine ads, although meant to be looked at rather than read out loud, contain valuable copy point information that can be explored. Newspaper articles, books, catalogs, corporate training manuals, brochures, and junk mail provide additional practice material.

Dedicate a room or space at home to practice. Invest in a music stand to hold the scripts. Place the top of the stand at eye level, assuming that you will be standing most of the time. Either clip the script to the top of the stand or fold the top part of the paper over the top of the stand to keep the copy at eye level, prevent the chin from dropping and blocking the air passage, and the voice from going "off mic." Purchase a microphone and extension arm. Place the mic stand behind the music stand, secure the extension arm to the top of the mic stand, let it cross over the front of the music stand, and dangle the microphone in front of the music stand so that it is about six inches away from your mouth. You can check this by putting your thumb on your lower lip, spreading your fingers out, and touching your pinkie finger on the microphone.

Exact placement of the microphone depends on the type of microphone purchased. *Unidirectional microphones* pick up sounds from only the front of the microphone. They need to be pointed directly at the mouth so that the voice is recorded "on-axis." *Omnidirectional microphones* are sensitive to sounds from the front, back, sides, top, and bottom. Even though they collect sounds from all over, the sound pressure from the voice only acts on one side of the mic. Therefore, the mic's diaphragm should be placed frontward, facing the mouth. *Cardioid microphones* record in a heart-shaped directional pattern. They are most sensitive to sounds approaching from the front, and less sensitive to sounds approaching from the rear. Many of these microphones display a tiny, heart-shaped symbol. *Supercardioid microphones,* another type of unidirectional microphone, are more sensitive to voices recorded on-axis and less sensitive to sounds coming from the sides.

Professional-quality studio equipment is not essential for home practice. Adequate microphones can be purchased at music and electronic hardware stores for well under $500. Starting at about $75, they become qualitatively better as the price increases. Just inquire as to the type of microphones available. Some are multi-patterned and come equipped with a select switch so that the voice recording can be switched to various directional modes while other microphones have only one setting. Either type is fine for practice purposes. Some mics are better at recording musical instruments or singing than straight voices. If possible, try out the various microphones first before purchasing to find out which one makes you sound best. Some microphones are warm, bringing out the lower-range bass notes, while others are bright, enhancing the mid-range and treble tones. Budget in approximately $25 each for a basic floor mic stand, extension arm, and music stand.

Recording equipment is also needed. If you have an old reel-to-reel system buried in your attic or garage, drag it out and hook it up to your microphone. If you are fortunate enough to own a sound system with a cassette player, use that. Check first to see if there is a mic input connector on the back panel, as some systems do not allow for recording, only for playback. If that is the case, purchase a cassette recorder with microphone plug-in capabilities, voice recording, and playback. Cassette dictaphone machines are also good for practice recording sessions if they come equipped with controls to adjust the voice levels and a digital tape marker so that the recordings can be easily located. For those who keep up with the latest technology, a DAT (digital audio tape) recorder offers optimal benefits. The recorded sound is clean and the voice tracks are easy to locate. Ultimately, you will have to base your purchases on your budget.

Chapter 2
Voice-over Aerobics

At the risk of sounding like a cliché, your voice is your *instrument*. It needs to be properly warmed up before it can function at full capacity. Singers and musicians know that performing without an adequate warm-up is like playing a risky game of Russian roulette with the quality, pitch, and tone of the notes. Even if the bullet is dodged the first time and the performance is delivered flawlessly, a sour note still lurks in the chamber ready to go off at an inopportune time. Of course, failing to warm up is not suicidal, but it may catch you in an embarrassing or costly situation. Directors are not always forgiving. To avoid possible calamity, it is always better to overprepare than underprepare. Besides, warming up the voice is easy, fun, and only takes a few minutes.

Voice-overs require clean, clear, crisp enunciation. Daily speech is often sloppy and slurred. Vocal tones may rest in the back of the throat rather than in the front of the mouth cavity and the lips and tongue may barely move. To speak clearly and colorfully, voice-over actors need to exercise their mouth, tongue, and lips a little bit more than normal folks. Lazy facial muscles inhibit clear word delivery and audibility. The voice needs to be projected forward into the microphone, not be swallowed backward into the throat. The extreme volume necessary to be heard in the last row of a theater, however, is not required. Instead, the microphone should be treated like an ear. This draws a verbal bridge between the actor and the listener.

Overarticulation is not a desired trait in voice-overs. It results in a false, strained, and unrealistic sound that is choppy and hard to follow. The voice actor must find a happy medium between mumbling and over articulating that sounds natural and realistic. In the sentence, "I want to see Santa Claus," it sounds unnatural and overly staccato if all the *t*'s are pronounced. "I *wanna* see *Sanna* Claus," is the more fluid, natural way of saying the phrase. Listeners hear the words and automatically fill in the missing letters. So, in your quest for good speech, be careful that you do not overcompensate.

A common misconception about voice acting is that since only the voice is recorded, the only thing that needs to be warmed up is the mouth. What unconsciously incompetent thinking! True, the voice is the most important element in the voice-over equation, but to achieve optimum results, full body- and facial-muscle flexibility are needed. This chapter is devoted to teaching ways to warm up the face and body through stretches, resonance enhancements, articulation, and breathing. Practice each exercise as you read along. Then, when you get to the chapter workouts, incorporate the full body, face, and voice warm-up into your practice routine.

BODY WARM-UPS

Tension resides in the muscles, particularly in the shoulders and neck. This is especially true after a hard day of work. For a reading to sound relaxed and natural, it is important for the body to be free of tension. To begin, roll the shoulders forward in a circular motion to relieve tension in the shoulders and back. Feel the muscles stretch and relax. Reverse directions, maintaining a fluid, circular backward motion. Now lift the shoulders up to the ears and hold them there for a few seconds before releasing. Repeat this up and down movement two or three times. With the shoulders in a neutral position, drop your head down slowly so that the chin touches the chest. Hold and feel the neck muscles stretch. Now tilt the head back and hold. Next, roll the head to the right so that the ear is almost touching the shoulders. Hold it there and then drop the head, letting it roll in a semi-circular motion to the left shoulder. Hold, then reverse direction and repeat. Next, straighten the head, turning it side-to-side in a "tick-tock" motion as you look right and left. When ready, carefully rotate the head in a full circle to the right. Reverse direction and circle the head to the left. The neck muscles should now be looser and more flexible.

For upper body flexibility, put the hands on the waist and twist the torso right, then left, making sure that the hips stay stationary. Stretch the left arm up and over the head at an angle toward the right. Relax, and repeat the stretching motion in the opposite direction using the right arm and stretching it over the head to the left. Drop the arm and clasp your hands together behind your back. Bend forward at the waist and lift the hands up toward the ceiling so that the shoulder blades almost touch. Hold, then relax. Let go of the hands and shake out the arms. Next, lace your fingers together, palms down. Breathe in and lift the hands up over the head so that the palms face the ceiling. When you breathe out, drop the arms down, release the fingers, and touch your toes. Stand up straight and shake out your arms and legs. If you still feel residual tension, repeat the upper body exercises. Otherwise, move on to the face.

Warm up the facial muscles by opening the mouth as wide as it can go. In a grossly exaggerated circular motion, pretend to chew, taking five or six really big chews. Now extend the lips forward into an extremely grotesque kissing position, puckered far enough out so that you can see your lips just underneath your nose. Twist your lips to the right, and hold. Then twist them to the left and hold. Relax. Open the mouth wide, as far as possible. Hold and feel the mouth muscles stretch. Relax. Now, pull the lips downward so that the skin above the upper lip is stretched, the bottom jaw is dropped, and the lips form a small *o* shape. Hold for a couple of seconds, then reverse the action. Pull the teeth together and lift the lips up toward the nose. Relax. Now, jut the chin forward and feel the neck muscles stretch. Relax. Repeat the chewing motion, only this time add a verbalization. Say "yum, yum, yum" each time you chew. Repeat the "yum" chew eight or 10 times. Now open your mouth and stick your tongue out. Try to make it touch your chin. This stretches the back tongue muscles, allowing more freedom of movement. Finally, yawn as big as possible. Exhale and add a relaxing "ahhhh" sound.

DEVELOPING RESONANCE

Voice resonance is the result of vibrations in the facial bones, mouth cavity, teeth, and hard palate. It is what separates a thin, light, wispy voice from a tonally full, rich, commanding voice. Some people are blessed with resonance; others must learn to create it. When speaking, vibrations should resonate from the forehead, between the eyes, back of the nose, sinus area below the cheeks, under the jaw bones, and sides of the throat. As you practice the following exercises, use your fingertips to feel for vibrations in these areas.

1. Grab a good breath and say "hum." Hold onto the final "m" sound until the lips buzz uncomfortably. Sustain the buzzing "m" for 10 to 15 seconds. Feel the vibrations in the lips, nose, jaw, cheeks, sinus, and sides of the throat.
2. Make an "n" sound by opening the mouth and touching the tip of the tongue behind the upper front teeth. As the tongue vibrates on the back of the front teeth and the palate, a vibration should be felt in the nose bone, maxillary sinus area, jaw, and sides of the throat.
3. Alternate between the "m" and "n" sounds. Note how the vibrations change. The "m" sound stimulates the front of the face while the "n" sound shifts the focus backward, away from the lips.
4. Open your mouth, breathe in, and release the air as you verbalize an "ah" sound. Feel the vocal chord vibrations in the front of the throat as the sound reverberates in the larynx. Repeat this exercise several times. Each time, drop the pitch one note lower in the vocal register. (This is a good way to relax the voice and lower the natural pitch.)
5. Open the mouth wide and pull the lips back, stretching the neck and mouth muscles. Make an "ah" sound. Next, pull the lips forward into a small o shape and make an "oh" sound. Repeat several times, then segue the face movements and sounds together. Listen to how the sounds in the mouth cavity adjust to the shape of the lips and mouth.
6. Breathe in and make a long "e" sound. Hold the "e" until you feel the vibrations in the jaw bone, sides of the throat, and sinus.
7. Awaken your vocal chords by singing a rousing rendition of your favorite song a cappella or accompanied by a tune on your favorite radio station. Forget whether or not you are a good singer. Sing loudly and with gusto!

ARTICULATION

Part of a voice actor's job is to be capable of saying whatever words or combinations of words that are scripted. Being mush-mouthed or unintentionally stumbling over words is undesirable. Words and phrases such as "mileage may vary according to road conditions and driving habits," "regularly priced," and "February" can cause even the best voice talent to falter if not properly prepared. Since a voice actor seldom sees a script ahead of time, the performer must have versatility to quickly switch from a booming "voice of God," to a quick-talking game show host, to a soft-spoken real person, or a smiley retail announcer. The following exercises help combat sibilance, plosives, lazy tongue, and mouth problems.

Sibilance
Sibilance is the result of an exaggerated s sound, reminiscent of a leaky radiator, slithering snake, or radio station as it loses its signal. Minor sibilance distortions can

be corrected in the recording studio. By using a "de-esser," the audio engineer can reduce or de-emphasize the frequency at which the problem sound occurs. Strong sibilance problems, however, cannot be completely corrected or eliminated during the recording session. Obstacles such as dental problems (like missing teeth or loose dentures), nondifferentiation between the s, sh, and z sounds, and articulating the s sound too long can inhibit the quantity of jobs an actor books or can prohibit an actor from working altogether. With help—and possibly a dentist—an actor can learn to overcome major sibilance problems.

Begin by saying the word "yes." Hold onto the final consonant, and put your hand in front of your mouth. If the s is properly formed, you should not feel a rush of air. If you do feel air, adjust the mouth placement so that the teeth are closer together but not touching and the tongue is curved upward toward the roof of the mouth. Now, repeat the "s" sound eight to 10 times, making sure that each sound is short, crisp, and concise. Using that same quick and succinct s technique, say the phrase, "I kissed the silly salesperson who sold me this mattress for seventeen cents."

The sh sound cuts through the air like wind through a car window. The tongue accepts a neutral position and the lips protrude slightly forward, as evidenced in the words "hush" and "shush." Say the words and feel the placement of the lips on the final sound combinations as a steady flow of air rushes from the mouth. Now repeat the "sh" sound eight to 10 times so that it creates a short burst of sound. Notice how the lips protrude and retract at each verbalization. Using pronounced lip movements, read the following sentence aloud: "Josh, I surely wish you won't push people when you rush over and pay cash for Shirley's plush dish towel." Note that not all sh sounds are spelled that way. Example: surely.

People are often lazy when pronouncing the z because it requires more effort to execute than an "es" sound. The tongue needs to be awakened to the buzzing sensation. To form a "z," place the tongue in the s position then arch the tip of the tongue slightly backward on the roof of the mouth. Hold the "z" until a strong vibration can be felt in the tongue and teeth areas. Say the word "xylophone," holding onto the opening "z" sound until the vibration is felt. Using shorter spurts of sound, practice saying the "z" sound eight to 10 times, ensuring that each z has a vibration. Now read the following sentence two to three times, first slowly and then at normal speed. Feel each z buzz. "These sizzling hot sales days are yours and ours because winning a prize is always a breeze at Joe's Trailer Zone." (Note how sometimes the z sound is actually an s.)

To ensure differentiation between the s, sh, and z sounds, practice saying the popular tongue twister, "She sells sea shells by the sea shore." Remember the phonetics: SHe SellZ Sea SHellZ by the Sea SHore. Now try a more apropos tongue twister: "Voice-overs are sheer joy when the s's sound sexy." VoiSe-overZ are SHeer joy when the Esses Sound Sexy.

Plosives

A plosive is a sudden explosion of air as it hits the microphone's diaphragm. The result is a loud pop or distortion that renders the recording unusable. "Pop" is another word for a plosive, as in, "You popped your 'p.' We need to do it again." Hard consonants such as b, k, p, and t are the usual culprits. If you place your hand in front of your mouth as you say these letters, you will feel a sharp rush of air as it hits your hand.

Pop filters and windscreens are used in studios to help alleviate some of the problem; the engineer dangles a stretched piece of nylon in front of the microphone or fits a foam ball snugly over the microphone's grill, diverting some of the air flow. If the popping problem persists, the actor needs to do one of two things: change position relative to the microphone or smile. Since the pop is caused by air directly hitting the mic's diaphragm, the actor can talk across the axis of the microphone at a diagonal. By shifting positions slightly, the air stream no longer strikes the microphone "dead on," causing the distortion, but instead glances off at an opposing angle from the location where the actor is standing. This becomes evident if you hold your hand directly in front of your mouth and say "p." The air bounces off the hand and ricochets back to the face. If you tilt your head an inch or two to the right and repeat the sound, you will feel the air hit the middle of the hand, graze past the left side of it, and disperse.

Smiling, or stretching the lips, is yet another way to soften the air expulsion. When the lips thin and no longer protrude on the plosive consonants, the air movement is reduced. Shifting the primary focus of the word to an accompanying vowel sound also creates a softer, less plosive sound. Experiment with this sensation by holding your hand in front of your mouth again and saying the word "pop." Alternate between the hard, violent action as the lips pucker outward and the softer sound resulting from the stretched, smiling, thinned lips. Now focus on the *ah* vowel sound in the middle of "pop" as you repeat the word rather than on the beginning and ending *p*'s.

Vowels and Consonants

When words are strung together in a sentence, they resemble a song. There is a *tempo, rhythm,* and *melody* to speech. Tempo sets the speed or pace of the words. Rhythm is defined by a cadence that adds measured movement to the words. Melody adds voice fluctuation, usually within a seven- to 10-note musical range. Without these three elements, words become boring, lifeless, and monotone. The words in a voice-over script are like a musical score, defined by quarter notes, half notes, whole notes, and sixteenth notes linked together in an interesting fashion. Consonants wrap around the single sustained vowel, enhancing the sound by adding rhythm and melody. Letters, such as *l, m, n, r, v, w,* and *z,* lend tonal vibrations similar to string instruments like the violin, cello, double bass, mandolin, and guitar. Harder consonants, such as *b, d, g, k, p, q,* and *t,* have rhythmic attacks that add a beat similar to the snare drum, timpani, bass drum, and bongo. To create better vocal variation and understanding of word structure, try the following exercises.

1. Slowly repeat each letter of the alphabet a minimum of four times starting with the letter *a.* Listen to where the sound originates, how it is formed, and the location and speed at which the air is released. Note the specific functions of the tongue, lips, and teeth.
2. Say the alphabet again, only this time elongate the vowel sounds. Open and close the mouth and lip opening to find optimal resonance. Notice how consonants like *b, c, d, g, p, t, v,* and *z* can be sustained into a final "e" sound, *j* and *k* form a long "a," and *q* and *w* form a "u" sound.
3. Using the following commercial example, create two entirely different reads by shifting focus between the vowels and the consonants. The first time, focus on the vowel sounds so that every time an *a, e, i, o,* or *u* is encountered, the mouth is

opened wider and the vowel sound is stretched out. The second time, focus on the consonants by stretching them out and shortening the vowels.

> Okay, all you movie fanatics. Here's your chance to own your own movie theater! Don't believe it? It's the affordable new giant-screen TV by Dynovision. You heard it right—Dynovision. The leader in video technology. Check out the six-foot diagonal screen. The resolution and sound are so superior, you'll swear I'm standing right in your living room. The new big-screen TV by Dynovision makes you feel like you're in the movies! The only difference is *you* have to pop the popcorn.

While reading the script with separate attention on the vowels and consonants, did you accidentally stumble onto two distinctly different voices? Often, elongating the vowels creates a happy, enthusiastic character, while concentrating on the consonants develops a sinister, slimy persona. Understanding the value of melody and rhythm in the vowel and consonant "notes" helps enhance one's natural speaking voice in addition to aiding in the performance of foreign dialects, accents, and cartoon voices. Read the commercial a third time, mixing and matching the long and short vowel and consonant sounds. A new tempo, rhythm, and melody should unfold.

Verbal Weight-Training

"Verbal weight-training" is to the mouth what ankle weights are to the runner. When weight or resistance is removed, the targeted area feels light and easily maneuverable. Begin the training by putting your upper and lower teeth together. They do not need to be clenched, only touching slightly. Without separating your teeth, recite the following passage several times as clearly and distinctly as possible. Be prepared; the tongue and lips must work overtime to compensate for the lack of jaw movement.

> How much curry can a great chef add if the kitchen is all out of curry? Not enough curry to satisfy the chef who must have curry in a hurry.

Now separate your teeth and recite the passage again. With full mobility, the words should sound clear and round as they trip easily off the mouth, lips, and tongue. This exercise should be performed before every audition or job using this saying, a favorite verse or tongue twister, or the actual script copy. It is especially useful when copy is overwritten and speed and clarity are of utmost importance.

BREATHING

Breathing—you do it all the time. What's the big deal? You breathe in, you breathe out. What more is there to know? If you don't breathe, you're dead, right? Well, partner, if that's what you think you might as well hang up your proverbial voice-over spurs and look for employment elsewhere. Breath control and support can either make or break a read. It is not something to be taken for granted like horns on a bull. Without knowing how to control and utilize the breath to its fullest, an actor can easily sputter out of control, crash and burn, and fail miserably at a recording session. If copy is particularly demanding, an actor without proper breath control may even have to be picked up off the floor and offered mouth-to-mouth resuscitation.

To illustrate this point, the following commercial section is written so that the actor must read the entire piece in one breath in order to bring the copy in "on time." It should sound effortless, comfortable, and natural, not strained, gaspy, or defused. Get a good breath and read this section out loud.

> Twenty-percent savings on lawn chairs, barbecue grills, patio furniture, sun umbrellas, birdbaths, gazebos, fountains, above-ground swimming pools, sun decks, spas, swing sets, planters, garden tools, pink flamingos, and outdoor sprinkler and lighting systems.

Did you make it? If so, pat yourself on the back. If not, all you have to do is develop your lung capacity and breath support.

Reading a marathon set of words requires the same focus, relaxation, and breath support as preparing to swim the complete length of the pool underwater. Without a thoroughly expelled cleansing breath, followed by a few deep breaths to "tank up," and a final holding breath, the swimmer sputters for air only seconds after diving into the water. The same result occurs in voice-overs. Without proper breath support, somewhere in the middle of the copy the actor's breath becomes strained, runs out, and stops. Read the commercial example again following these three basic rules:

1. Take a deep, cleansing breath in, then exhale. Make sure the breath does not get stopped in the chest, but is totally released. This rids the body of stale air and helps facilitate relaxation and focus.
2. Put your hands on your waist and take two deep, inhaling preparatory breaths. Drop your jaw and let the air flow in quietly and unobstructed. Feel your rib cage expand and contract with each breath and exhalation. Your shoulders should not move up and down. That is a sign of a shallow "chest" breath.
3. Take a third and final deep, base breath. Hold it in for one or two seconds before beginning. This allows the breath to stabilize and gives the read a firm, attention-grabbing attack on the opening word.

Life teaches us many bad breathing habits. We learn that sucking in our stomachs makes us appear thinner, stooping our shoulders makes us feel shorter, and puffing out our chests makes us feel stronger and more attractive. Protective body posturing often prevents or inhibits the natural and healthy flow of air into the lungs. Getting a good breath does not involve moving the shoulders up and down or puffing the chest out unnaturally. This is only a signal that the breath is locked inside the chest or throat, and the result is a shallow or halted breath. Good breathing habits involve very little shoulder and chest movement. Instead, the primary action should be located in the diaphragm and rib areas. The diaphragm, located just below the rib cage, expands and contracts with each breath. This becomes apparent if you place your hands at the bottom of your rib cage. Face your thumbs to the back and fingers towards the stomach, then open the mouth, relax the throat, and gently inhale. As the air flows in, a pyramid effect results. Breath expands from the throat into the lungs, and pushes the rib cage out. When the breath is exhaled, the ribs return to their natural resting place. Sideways expansion of the ribs, rather than up and down movement in the shoulders, signifies proper breathing agility.

Some actors at auditions or jobs deal with the anxiety and stress by holding their breath or blocking it shallowly in their chest and throat. Tension, fear, and shakiness creep into the breath making the words sound unnatural and obstructed. Therefore, it is important to remember to execute the three simple steps to good breathing and breath support: cleansing breath, deep preparatory breaths, and full-base breath that is held slightly to create stability before beginning.

USING THE BODY

Full use and flexibility of the body is essential to achieving voice-over excellence. Unfortunately for some, this is not always easy. Being left alone in a soundproof room, and taking direction from unfamiliar people, can trigger an actor's innermost insecurities. Instinctively, the actor seeks protection from this new and uncomfortable situation in the form of body carriage. Unwittingly, actors puff up their chests to appear strong and impenetrable, some try to disappear by either clasping their hands in front or behind their backs, some behave like deer staring into the headlights of an on-coming car and let their arms dangle lifelessly at their sides, while still others feign casualness and self-confidence and sink their hands deep into their pockets. The "attention," "fig leaf," "at ease," "dead arms," and "pocket" poses are all inhibiting.

An actor stepping behind a microphone is much like a baseball player stepping up to the plate. Both professions require that the performer be ready to respond to whatever pitch is thrown their way, be it a fast ball, curve ball, knuckle ball, or spit ball. For the voice-over actor to put some kind of spin on the copy, the body has to be prepared for the impact. The tense, rigid *attention* posture almost guarantees that the actor will strike out with a stiff vocal delivery and detached sound. Rather than swinging with ease, he hits the words right back into the director's mitt without any bravado or finesse, when ideally the copy should soar out of the ball park. Then, following the reading, the *attention* persona tends to shift into an at ease position. The pseudo-casual legs spread and hands behind the back create a defensive shield. Like a foul ball, the words bounce off the chest, out-of-bounds, without feeling, direction, or emotional grounding.

The *fig leaf* position is a sign of weakness. Stoop-shouldered, demure body styling projects an image of being wimpy, insecure, or shy. The voice that follows implies, "Please don't hurt me!" An easy player for the director to strike out, the actor then retreats into soft quietness and the mind subconsciously blocks the relationship between the actor and listener.

Stiff *dead arms* on an actor are a sign of defeat. Even before the actor starts talking, it is obvious that the read is going to be uninteresting. The team doesn't stand a chance of winning if the actor stands soft-shouldered, arms and hands dangling lifelessly by his sides, with energy dripping off his fingers and puddling on the floor. There must be "life" in the arms! Even in a soft, intimate spot, the hands can be held close to the face to help create a soothing, caressing sound. Copy that requires an intensity or "punch" screams for the muscles to flex and the hands and arms to be active.

Many people tuck their hands in their pockets when they get in front of a microphone. Some use this restraining technique to make them appear more relaxed and casual—*at ease*. Others naturally place them there because for years they have been unduly criticized for talking with their hands. In either case, the helpfully descriptive hands are forced out of commission. The result is either elbows flapping around like a chicken trying to fly or hands attempting to wedge themselves out of pockets that appear filled with cement. Even if the hands do manage to break free, the friction of the release from the pockets can cause a noise loud enough for the microphone to pick up. Therefore, it is better to keep the hands free and ready for action.

Voice-overs require a tremendous amount of physical energy. It starts in the toes, surges through the legs, extends through the stomach and shoulder blades, and is released through the top of the head and fingertips. With the exception of the mouth, which should remain relatively close to the microphone throughout for recording purposes, the rest of the body is free to move. It can twist, stretch, jump, caress, shake, rattle, rock, and roll.

Body posturing and movement can create defining character traits. Alternately lifting your heels off the floor to simulate walking adds authenticity to a scene in which people are talking as they walk down a road together. Quickening the pace, bending the elbows and swinging the arms forward and back, and adding rhythmic exhales of breath creates the illusion that a person is running or exercising while talking. Making a fist and holding a make-believe telephone up to the ear simulates involvement in a private phone conversation. Shifting weight onto one leg and looping thumbs through belt loops adds a hometown, country flair.

Hand and body motions augment our daily speech. When asked to describe a spiral staircase, the index finger automatically springs to action and points upward as it swirls around and around in circles. When asked to describe a spiral staircase without the use of hands, the eyes automatically project upward toward the ceiling to help verbally illustrate the unique design. Without prior thought or mental taxation, hands lend descriptiveness and "color" to words. Hands stretch outward as far as they can go to emphasize something BIG and move close together to demonstrate something LITTLE. The voice naturally corresponds to the size, weight, speed, and motion of the hand gestures. In fact, if you lift your right hand and say the word "right" and then lift your left hand and say the word "left," you can hear a pitch change as the voice moves right and left. The same concept holds true with many other words and phrases. With the words "back" and "forth" and "up" and "down" the voice corresponds to the locale. The same is not true if you point up but say the word "down." The brain comprehends the discrepancy and interferes with the natural word flow.

In this manner, hand and arm movements augment physical location, size, shape, and crucial copy points (to be discussed later). Relying solely on the voice and head to stress words results in an unappealing style that is often punchy or choppy. Trusting the body to do half the work not only makes voice-overs easier, it contributes to a more authentic sound. Standing lifelessly while speaking into a microphone will not make the director and client jump up and down in ecstasy at your wonderful interpretation, nor make customers rush to the store to buy the product. To hit a home run in the voice-over major leagues, you have to use the whole package: body, heart, and voice.

Chapter 3

Copy Basics

This chapter presents the technical nuts and bolts of voice-over acting. In chapters 4 and 5 you will learn how to disguise these techniques so that they sound natural and real, rather than wooden and mechanical. Before that all-important creative spin is placed on the word delivery, it is necessary to understand how to interpret the copy so that the copywriter's message stands out and how to clarify the client's and producer's concept.

Advertising agencies and production companies jump through hoops before a script lands in an actor's hands. The creative director meets with the client and gleans as much information about the company and product as possible. The information is then tossed around and discussed by the people in the creative department. If all goes well, a new and improved sales approach is agreed upon, and the copywriter begins developing the script. Once completed, the script undergoes additional changes initiated by other members of the agency, the client, and the legal department. Sometimes it is tried out in focus groups to test the public's reactions, and more changes are made. Finally the script is approved, often bearing little resemblance to the original draft.

The actor walks into the recording studio at the final stage of the script's evolution, when she is handed the copy. Tensions run high. Will the copy actually work? Can it sell the product? Is it creative and award-winning? The actor walks into the soundproof room and places the copy on the music stand. The director and producer exchange feigned glances of delight. They are glad as hell to be out of the office. The long hours of script dissection fall now on the talent's shoulders. Drum roll, please.

With that much pressure riding on your every word, it is important to first get inside the writer's head and figure out his intention. It is not enough to read the words and expect listeners to "get it" on their own. Who has time for that, especially if you are listening to the car radio while driving down the highway at top speed with cars darting in and out of traffic? Actors have to look at a script, understand the concept, and convey the desired message. The purpose for advertising a new product may be purely to introduce it to the market and create name recognition. Some products boast speed and reliability, while others emphasize slow, "time-honored" processes and customer satisfaction. Still others compete directly with rival brands. There are clues throughout the script to help you determine the primary intention. As you read the example below, see if you can decipher the copywriter's intention.

(Music under: nostalgic dance music from the 1950s)
Remember when bobby socks were keen and circle skirts had poodles on them? When going to the hop on Saturday night was a way of life? And boys carried girls' books home from school. And no one ever locked their doors? A lot has changed

since then, but luckily one thing hasn't . . . Bobby Sox Diner. The original jukebox cranks out the same great tunes from the '50s. Burgers and shakes are still made the old-fashioned way and taste even better than you remember. And everyone who works there is *neat!* So grease your hair back (or pull it up in a ponytail) and hop on down to the Bobby Sox Diner for a delicious burger, fries, and milk shake while you bop to your favorite tunes. Relive the past at Bobby Sox while you enjoy the present. Just lock your front door on your way out. Bobby Sox Dinner, located at 5th and Grant, across from the Tower Building. Who says you can't go back again?

The script is obviously based on nostalgia. It states that a lot of things have changed since the 1950s but Bobby Sox Diner remains the same. Therefore, dining at Bobby Sox Diner is essential to reliving the glorious past. Bobby Sox Diner = '50s-style enjoyment.

COPY POINTS

What exactly are copy points and why are they important? Copy points are the essential elements contained in a piece of copy. They include the client's name, key phrases, slogans, sales items, dates, times, locations, and other crucial client information. The essence of the script's success lies in the listener's ability to remember the copy points and the actor's ability to make them stand out. Here is a simple copy point check list:

Who is the hero client?
What is the client selling?
Why does the consumer need this product?
When do customers use the product and/or when can the product be purchased?
Where is the product or client located?
How is the product used?

The copy points are illustrated (and underlined) in the following script.

(Background sound effect: Young children playing)
Welcome to Kiddie School, for four- and five-year-olds. Where the walls get messy quick! Now J-19 has a wall cleaner that handles the challenge. New J-19 Wall & Window Cleaner. J-19 dissolves crayon marks, messy handprints, and sticky, built-in food goo. In fact, it's three times as effective on slimy messes as the top-rated wall cleaner . . . even tougher than little Herbert, here. When it comes to dirty handprints, J-19 is the best. New J-19 Wall & Window Cleaner. Available at grocery and drug stores in cities where four- and five-year-olds live.

The copywriter chose a children's setting to illustrate the power and necessity of the product. Further analysis plucks out these copy points:

Who is the client? J-19
What is the product? Wall & Window Cleaner.
Why is it necessary? Walls get dirty, especially when small children are around.
When should the consumer use it? When walls are messy with handprints and goo.
Where can J-19 be purchased? Grocery and drug stores.
How does J-19 work? It dissolves dirt three times as effectively as the top-rated
   cleaner.

IDENTIFYING THE PRODUCT

It is imperative that the "hero" product be identified. Read the script and find out what is being sold, introduced, or promoted. Underline the appropriate word or phrase. The product name is called the "key" or "money" word. Make sure you know how to pronounce it. Do not leave anything to chance. Time and time again, actors share stories about how they booked a job because they were the only one at the audition who knew how to pronounce the client's name properly. Sometimes even familiar product names can be deceptive. Chevron, for instance, is pronounced differently in California and Texas, with Texans favoring a final "on" sound, while the California preference is a short "un." Next, check to see if there is a catchy slogan to go with the product. This is a phrase that describes the type or quality of service offered by the product, store, or restaurant. For example, a furniture store may have the slogan "Because we're wooden." A department store might emphasize a particular sale like "Sales Assistant Day." Or, a restaurant may call itself "The family restaurant." If you see that a product does indeed have a slogan, underline it. These descriptive words are equally important as the product name.

Once you have underlined the key words and phrases, treat the markings as a visual cue to slow down. Advertisers pay big bucks to have their name broadcast. Telling the story and then "throwing away" the brand name defeats the purpose of the commercial. This common directorial term, "throw it away," simply means to not linger on or emphasize the words. Potential customers have to know where to spend their hard earned dollars, and it's your job, as the voice talent, to tell them.

Have you ever told someone about a clever or amusing commercial, only to discover you don't remember what it was for? That is an example of unsuccessful advertising. Advertisers would strap audiences to their seats and force them to listen to the product name repeated a zillion times if possible. Instead, advertisers must cleverly disguise or "package" their product sales pitches within short stories. No matter how involved or inane the copy, the ultimate goal in advertising is for the listener to remember the product and make the client's cash register ring. You must shape the words in a manner that is effective, meaningful, memorable, and motivating.

Just as arm movements can help your delivery, smiling on the key words and phrases, in addition to slowing down, gives additional emphasis to the product. Smiles should sound friendly, accessible, and truthful, not forced or false. Pride in ownership, impressed satisfaction, and gleeful amazement are only a few ways to impact a truthful, believable smile. The voice actor must enthusiastically embrace the money words and dispel any negativisms (such as hatred for animals if selling dog food or dislike for shopping if pitching a department store). Before the audience can believe in a product, *you* must first believe that the product is wonderful.

Yet another way to add focus to the product is by adding a millisecond pause before and after the key word and phrase. The pause should not be long enough for a freight train to run through; instead, it should be almost nonexistent. Dead air, especially in radio, brings a commercial to a grinding halt, and, even worse, signals the listener to switch to another station. When used properly, the ever-so-slight pause before and after the key name holds the listener's attention and gives the brain time to retain the information. The consumer's subconscious mind is awakened to real or implied questions pertaining to the product as the voice talent draws attention to the product name. Without that millisecond pause, the anticipation and thrill of recognition is gone. As a reminder to pause, mark your script with a slash both before and after the key word. Here are some examples of script markings:

The perfect getaway. / Pleasant Pacific Cruise line, / for the time of your life.

Note the slashes before and after the underlined product name and the line underneath the slogan, "for the time of your life."

It's time to enjoy the great outdoors, / and what better place to get equipped / than Marine Outdoors.

As you can see, there is no hard and fast rule that says the slash has to immediately precede the key name. Placing the slash after the word "than" creates awkward phrasing. Pausing before the word "than" is more effective. It sets up the answer to the question, "What better place to get equipped?" Also, a slash can be used at commas and periods as a reminder to make a phrasing change.

I'm the manager of a Yellow Belly Catfish Restaurant. / It's my job to make sure all the seafood served / at Yellow Belly / is fresh and prepared to your liking.

In this ad, the first slash is placed after the restaurant name. It also signals the end of the sentence. Since the script calls for a real person talking, it would sound very unnatural and artificial to pause before the key name. Pausing after the name gives the listener time to reflect on the dining establishment. The second slash is placed before rather than after the word "at" because it answers the question, "Where is all the seafood served?" Pausing after "at" makes the sentence sound disjointed. Remember: look for the phrases!

As you learn, and become more proficient at voice-overs, you may no longer need to make visual cues on your script. The techniques will become second nature. Until that auspicious event occurs, trust your eyes rather than your brain and mark your script. Be careful, though, that the marked words and phrases do not result in choppy or technical sounding reads. These markings are merely visual stimuli to help you easily assimilate and respond to the various copy points.

LISTS

In almost every piece of copy there is a list. These lists may involve singular words, series of phrases, or strings of sentences. All these lists, no matter how long or how short, need variety. Each item on the list should sound different from the preceding item. In musical terms, each item in a list of three should move up one or two notes (C-D-E or C-E-G).

This stair-stepping method is the most common form of three-list variation. It is also an effective way to set up the product, especially at the beginning of the commercial. Example:

What comes in *chocolate chip, macadamia nut, and oatmeal?* Mr. Garland's cookies, of course! They're baked fresh every day.

Stair stepping the list downward is an excellent way to end a spot. It adds finality and reassurance that the product is superior to its competitors.
Example:

For a *deep, rich, golden* tan, buy Miami Tan.

An alternate version of the three-item list is to vary the musical notes. Start low on the first item, move high on the second, and split the pitch difference on the third (C-E-D or C-G-E). For variation, also read this commercial through starting on the higher note, moving to the bottom note, and ending on the middle note (E-C-D).
Example:

Are your muscles sagging? Does your body look like a carton of cottage cheese? Does putting on a bathing suit make you burst into tears? Maybe it's time to shape up at Buffo Health Club.

When the list involves four items, the stair stepping method tends to make the actor's voice strain or "top out" on the highest note of the four-note scale. So these lists should be varied either in a zigzag fashion (C-E-C-E) or with the first three notes moving up or down the scale and the final note returning to the location of the first or second note (C-D-E-C or E-D-C-D).
Example:

Tony's Tune-Up will *rotate your tires, tune up your engine, change your oil,* and *smog check your vehicle.*

Unlike regular, spoken language, commercials and industrials often emphasize the conjunctive word "and." This tells the listener that in addition to all the other wonderful things the company or product achieves, it also offers something extraordinary. You can experiment with this concept by reading the commercial example listed above. This time, when you reach the word "and," stretch it out. It then gives added importance to the final item. Visual note: Look in the mirror when you read this. Your eyebrows may go up when you say the magic word "and."

Five or more listed items are considered a *laundry list.* Stair stepping the notes up the scale is out of the question. Not only is it tedious to listen to, it could be downright impossible. Instead, randomly place each item on a different note in the musical scale. It is most effective if you use your hands while doing so. Alternate each item from one hand to the other, moving your fingers or entire arms, whichever you prefer. Movements help you position the items on varying notes of your invisible scale and give the list much needed variety.
Example:

Latimer's is having a close-out sale on *socks, slips, panties, boxer shorts, cotton briefs, T-shirts, pajamas, pants, dresses, dress shirts, skirts, blouses, belts, wallets, purses, shoes, sheets, towels,* and *more.*

Remember, the rule of thumb with lists is variety! If all the items are read continuously on the same musical note, the listener hears only *one* item. Additionally, if two items in a list of three are read side-by-side on the same musical note, it sounds like only *two* items. Variety in the reading separates the items and simplifies the listener's job.

COMPARATIVES

Comparing products is advertising's way of waging war. Millions of dollars are spent each year trying to prove that one cola is better than another. Car rental companies fight over the right to claim that they are number one. Burger chains duke it out over who has the best-tasting or lowest-priced food. The consumer is caught in the middle, watching the allegations and comparisons fly over them like mortar fire. Who will win the battle? Advertising executives, holding tightly to their jobs, pray to the almighty consumer that it will be them.

In this day of dime-a-dozen lawsuits, comparisons have to be based on concrete information. Advertisers cannot slam another product as being inferior unless there is substantiating evidence to prove this point beyond a reasonable doubt. But when product preference is subjective, psychological warfare has to be waged. In voice-over terms, you must make your client's name sound wonderful while appearing deaf, dumb, and blind to the competition and its benefits. Nothing *negative* needs to be said about the other product that could give due cause for legal recourse. On the other hand, nothing *positive* should be said either.

Let's think about this for a minute. Say you want to go out to dinner at that cute little restaurant with the pink awning that you pass every day on your way to work. It looks kind of expensive and money is tight, so you want to make sure the food is excellent before you plop down a ton of dough. You ask around at work to see if anyone has eaten there. Joe Watercooler says, "Yeah, I've eaten there. It's okay." "Okay?" you say. "It's fine," says Joe, "but have you tried that new place on Second Street? Sally and I went there last week. Best steak we ever had!" Now which restaurant would you go to? The place with the pink awning or the recommended place with the great steaks? Unless you are a vegetarian, you will probably choose the restaurant on Second Street—the one that sounds good.

There is a definite art when comparing opposing products: *smile* while you say the client's copy points and *drop the smile* when you talk about the competition. Frowning on the negative information isn't necessary, simply don't smile. A smile adds warmth and reassurance. Not having a smile psychologically suggests that the product is merely okay, but not great. Legally, nothing bad has been said. The client just offers the consumers a comparative choice. Which would you choose? The product that is wholeheartedly endorsed by the pleasant, smiling voice or the ho-hummer? Now add a timing differential. Slow down when you say the positive information. Speed up when you say the negative information. Psychologically, the listener hears and retains the positive information and doesn't hear, or quickly forgets, the negative information. In essence, you are "throwing away" the negative information.

Try reading this short retail ad. Remember to slow down and smile on the client's information, and speed up and throw away the competition's information. To make your job easier, the positive copy points have been italicized. Use a pencil and mark your script. Underline the client's name and slogan and put vertical slashes at places where you want to pause slightly.

> *Half-Price Clothing Store brings you designer clothing for half the price.* Brand A Store has the same designer clothing, but sells it at a premium. Why spend more at Brand A, *when you can get the same quality at half the price? Half-Price Clothing Store, where looking great doesn't have to cost an arm and a leg.*

Making facial gyrations as you smile and drop the smile may feel strange and unnatural at first. Get used to it. Effective voice work often requires the adeptness of a rubber face.

PACING

Every piece of copy has its own meter. Some spots are fast. Others are slow. Within that meter, to use a musical metaphor, there are whole notes, half notes, doted thirds, triplets, sixteenth notes, and so on. Treating every word like a quarter note is boring and monotonous. The listener, provided he hasn't been lulled to sleep, quickly tunes out because the word delivery is predictable. There is no sense of anticipation, and the element of surprise is missing.

In the previous segments, you learned to throw away the competitor's information and to slow down and linger on your client's name and slogan. These techniques not only help the advertiser's message stand out, they make the spot more interesting. Without these pacing changes, the audience has to work hard to figure out who to root for and what to buy. Don't leave anything to chance. Spoon feed the information to the listener so they know exactly what you are talking about and why this piece of information is so delectable. A common error for new voice-over actors, especially those with theatrical training, is to slow down on the exciting storytelling information and speed up on the client copy points. It's time for a mental readjustment! Tell yourself that the purpose of advertising is to talk about the product. The story is merely the glue that holds the important client information together. Make this your mantra. From now on, remember that the purpose of the story is to share with the listener the wonderful benefits of the client's product, company, or service.

The following script is an example of a story line in which an actor could easily fall victim. Remember that, within the story, the product is the star. It is the motivating factor for telling the story. Pace the script accordingly: slow down on the copy points and add less importance to the non-product related information. Mark your script if necessary.

I'm drivin' down the road mindin' my own business, when out of nowhere this angel appears on my steering wheel. I think, "Man, you shouldn't have had that leftover burrito for breakfast." I rub my eyes in the hopes that it'll go away. No such luck. It says, "Do you love your mother?" "Sure," I say, "But what's my Mother got to do with you?" "Did you buy her flowers?" "Why?" I say. "Check your calendar. It's Mother's Day." "Today?!" I shriek. "Don't worry. There's still time to order flowers," says the angel. "Pick up that nifty car phone of yours and call 1-800-PETUNIA." ANNOUNCER TAG: Be an angel, call 1-800-PETUNIA today to order your Mother's Day flowers.

The first few lines, although amusing, are the *set-up*. There is no reference to the client until the very end of the copy, therefore the first half of the spot should be read slightly faster than the bottom half. The first mention of flowers is the signal to slow down and resolve the problem established in the beginning of the script.

SCRIPT CONSTRUCTION

Most commercials follow a definite pattern or formula, recognizing the formula will help you deliver the words more effectively. Start by imagining the script as a three-course meal. There is the salad plate, followed by the main course, and topped off by the dessert. Occasionally, the dessert is topped off with an after-dinner mint.

The salad is the initial *set-up,* the attention-getting device, which whets the appetite for the more substantial information to follow. The set-up can be, for example, the announcement of a particular type of sale as described by an enthusiastic announcer, or a series of "slice-of-life" sentences read by a "real person," establishing a problem that the hero product can easily solve. Then comes the *body.* This section is the meat and potatoes of the commercial meal, designed to hold the listener's attention by answering the important who, what, why, when, and how questions posed in the set-up. "Real person" commercials feature both the solution to the problem and a rationale for using the product, while announcer-type spots state specific item and price information.

Finally, there is the dessert-like *resolve.* Crucial information is stated for the final time. This piece of information is designed to linger forever on the brain (not the hips). The resolve has more fat grams than the other parts of the script because it is the final time the product name and major copy points are mentioned. It tops off the meal and leaves a sweet, lasting impression. The occasional after-dinner mint is called a *button.* The button is a throw-away line that clinches a commercial. Descriptive copy information is generally not given out at this time. The function of a button is to add cleverness, humor, and finality to the end of a spot, and it can be either a single word or an entire phrase or sentence. Some buttons are scripted in, others are ad-libbed by the actor and included in the final mix.

The following example is of the announcer genre with each section identified as either set-up, body, or resolve. When you read the copy, make sure there is a definite transition between each of the sections. One way to ensure a vocal transition is to shift weight from one foot to the other; the voice changes slightly when the body shifts. Just make sure you don't move off mic when you make this adjustment. Another way to ensure a transition is to cock your head to another position or alternate focus from one hand to the other. Keeping those tips in mind, try working on your transitions.

SET-UP
It's that time of year again. You guessed it—winter! Time to drag out the warm clothes, clean out the furnace, and cozy up with a loved one by a roaring fire. What better way to take the chill off of winter than with Burn-A-Log.
BODY
Burn-A-Log is the fast, clean, easy way to have a fire. Just place Burn-A-Log in your fireplace and light it. There's no need for messy starter fluid or kindling. One match is all it takes to start Burn-A-Log.
RESOLVE
So the next time you want a romantic evening, or could use a fire to stay warm on those cold winter nights, try Burn-A-Log. Guaranteed to start with only one match.

Once again, the sections in this next spot are separated for your practice reading pleasure. As you read it, imagine that you are relaxing on a cruise ship.

SET-UP
Let me have your attention for a minute. How'd you like a chance to win $200,000? "$200,000," you must be saying to yourself. "Of course I want $200,000! Who

wouldn't? I could buy a new house, new car . . . heck, a fleet of new cars, college for the kids, some nifty vacations, all kinds of stuff for the house."

BODY

Well, that's exactly what you could win if you enter the Keno Lottery. Just pick three numbers out of 49 and the average top prize is over $200,000. That's right, $200,000! Spend a buck, win a chance at $200,000. Look at me, I won and now I'm enjoying a luxury cruise around the world! Best of all, you don't even have to be present to win. The Keno Lottery people find you and give you the cash, no matter where you are . . . on the high seas, or in your living room with that tattered furniture. Right now I'm waiting to see if my latest three-number pick wins. There's no limit to the amount of times you can win. So why stop?

RESOLVE

The Keno Lottery—it's a chance to make your dreams come true. So, cruise on down to your local Mom and Pop shop, plop down some cash, and enter your winning threee numbers. It's the easiest 200,000 bucks you could ever make.

BUTTON

Say, pass me that suntan lotion, will ya?

COLORING THE ADJECTIVES

Every word in a piece of copy has been carefully selected and scrutinized. Whisking right past the adjectives without adding coloring or shading is an insult to the copywriter—have fun with them! They bring additional life to the script. Be careful, though, not to overly elongate or unduly emphasize the adjectives so that they overshadow the copy points. The balance is delicate. Years ago my talent agent played me a demo tape that she had recently received from a new voice talent seeking representation. The poor woman's tape had us in stitches every time she milked the words "j—uuu—ccc—ie" and "ch—eeww—ie." Each word must have gone on for at least five seconds.

Adjective coloring should be quick and effective, without losing perspective of the overall copy intention. A squiggly line drawn underneath the word or phrase is a good mental reminder to play with the words. Pick up your pencil, and practice this marking technique on the following script example.

We Brits love our bonbons, chocolates, and caramels. But there is one thing you Americans have that we don't—Toffee Bar Delights. Toffee Bar is a delicious vanilla ice cream bar covered in mouth-watering toffee and drenched in real milk chocolate. When I bite into a Toffee Bar Delight, I feel like . . . well, (crunch) a Yank!

Did you put a squiggly line under *delicious, mouth watering,* and *real?* If so, put your perky pencil down and give yourself a firm pat on the back.

DOLLARS AND PERCENTAGES

When the price of the client's product is mentioned, it should sound very small. This is easily achieved by saying the price quickly and matter-of-factly, as if the money is small and insignificant. Unconsciously, the listener comprehends the financial investment as reasonable. Often the words "only" or "just" precede the dollar amount, lending further credibility. Conversely, when comparing prices with the hero product, the competitor's prices should be stretched out to sound unreasonably expensive. Try this experiment. Shrug your shoulders and smile when you say the first sentence of the following example. Drop the smile and take more time when you mention the dollar amount in the second sentence of the example.

Our product is only $9.95. Theirs is $9.97.

Of course, advertisers typically base their selling strategy on more than a two-cent price differential, but this example demonstrates the psychological impact of price comparisons. The listener hears the positive attitude placed on the hero product as compared to the negative imagery dumped on the competition. It is not until the spot is totally scrutinized by the listener that the true financial difference becomes glaringly apparent. Hopefully by then the consumer has already purchased the hero product and feels that it was a good deal.

Dollar amounts usually appear numerically in scripts and are preceded by the dollar symbol (for example, $9.95 or $15). Although it is the director's call as to whether or not the actual words "dollars" and "cents" need to be verbalized, these words are sometimes omitted from the actor's dialogue because the listener comprehends that the subject matter pertains to money without being reminded. In some scripts, these words are omitted because they take up valuable airtime, and some directors believe that tossing off the numbers without adding financial references softens the sticker shock. The word "dollars" is used more often when the money is an even amount, as with $15, and very rarely is the word "cents" used. So check with your director first before you talk money.

Contrary to dollar amounts that are intended to sound small, percentages are expected to sound large. You can stretch out and add pride to the words "five percent" and the listener comprehends BIG savings. It is not until the words are seen in writing that the actual percentage amount sinks in. For comparison, read the following example out loud. Smile and stretch out the first percentage amount and make it sound fabulous; drop the smile and speed through the second half of the second sentence where it contains the competitor's measly percentage savings.

Save 40% on designer-name clothes! Bargain Clothes saves you more dollars every day than the 2% savings advertised by our competitors.

TARGETING THE LISTENER

Advertising is targeted to various sex and age demographics. It covers men, women, teenagers, children, and the combined sexes in the 18 to 24, 24 to 36, 25 to 49, 49 to 65, and 65-and-over age categories. Media buyers buy time on local and national television and radio stations across the country that meet their desired criteria. Household cleaning products are pitched more heavily during the day to target a higher female audience—thus the name "soap" opera. Beer is touted during sports programs due to the large male audience. Toys are pitched relentlessly during Saturday-morning cartoons so impressionable youths will persuade their parents to buy them the latest toy, doll, or gadget.

Understanding the product's intended market helps the actor in his or her quest for ultimate effectiveness. Necessary vocal choices can be made based on this valuable demographic information, but unfortunately, many actors are stumped by this concept. They do not consider *who* the target audience is, and so they don't know which voice to pull out of their verbal "bag of tricks." Should the voice be loud and crazy, soft and intimate, or real and natural sounding? The copy offers some clues, of course, but sometimes the vocal choices and interpretations are more subtly based on audience. If the client is pitching bubble gum, the ad is probably intended for a young audience, and the freedom to be wacky, crazy, and fun takes precedence. The same approach does not work for an ad touting gum that does not stick to dentures. The older demographic dictates a more natural and sensible interpretive approach. (Although, consciously choosing to read "against type" can still be an option if the director is open for an amusingly different read.)

Industrial narrations are also targeted to specific audiences. There is a different sound for scripts that appeal to beginning clerical workers versus those intended for CEOs of major corporations. It is of primary importance to find out the level of product knowledge, business savvy, and formal education within your audience. Trade buzzwords should roll off the tongue (even if you don't know their meanings) when addressing individuals in the industry. Names and uses of new products are voiced more deliberately or excitedly when introduced and described for the first time.

Video, computer, and CD-ROM games also have varying demographics. Find out if the game is targeted to small children, teenagers, or adults. Games geared toward teenage boys often contain heavy monster voices that can scare away a young child who prefers light, friendly, goofy voices, while adult computer programs and games are more realistic. So if you don't know the target audience when voicing a project, ask the director! The information can help you approach the material more effectively.

Chapter 4

Hiding "the Sell"

Radio is often referred to as the "theater of the mind." Words bring the picture to life. They add color, clarity, and depth of meaning. *How* you say something is just as important as *what* you say. Voice-overs, regardless of whether they are commercials, industrial narrations, CD-ROM programs, or cartoons, need to create that same sort of action or life in the targeted listener's mind in order to sell the product. The information has to be relayed in a manner that can easily be absorbed and appreciated.

The current trend in advertising is to hide the sell. This requires acting ability. The more you understand about yourself and your emotional life, the better job you can do. The technical aspects previously described in chapter 3 are voice-over building blocks. Each block is stacked on top of the other as the copywriter's intention is discovered, phrasings are negotiated, and key words are stressed. Now it is time to color those building blocks so that they no longer sound bland or glaringly obvious. No one should ever be aware of technique, it should just facilitate understanding of the copy.

Spend a lot of time on this chapter. As you will soon discover, there are many ways to hide the sell and bring the copy to life. Depending on the demands and complexities of the script, you may be required to use all of these acting tricks at once or only a few. Fully understanding these concepts means the difference between booking the job and the casting director saying, "Nice voice, but can't act." Everyone has life experiences that are unique. It is your job to use your experiences to bring the words to life and create a real and engaging dialogue with the audience.

CREATING A DIALOGUE WITH THE LISTENER

In order to create a dialogue with the listener, an intimate, one-on-one relationship needs to be established between the actor and the audience. There needs to be a bridge linking the two together. It should sound as if the voice talent is talking directly to each individual listener, regardless of whether or not a person is in the car, living room, board room, or video arcade. This link is achieved by *personalizing the message,* which is to say that the actor says the scripted words as if he or she is talking to a familiar person, someone whom the actor has encountered during their lifetime.

In other words, you substitute the image of a person you know for the cold metal microphone dangling in front of you. The person you choose as a substitution should not be a vague generalization or a random choice, but a person who stirs in you the specific emotion needed to enhance the script. It could be a parent, spouse, family member, coworker, sales clerk, or even a movie star about whom you've fantasized.

Just thinking about this person should open up your heart and make you emotionally alive and accessible. If you are really "present" and "in-the-moment" you will be aware of this new emotional life. Breathing patterns, pulse, voice, and body position change as you react to people's images. You become a *whole* person that someone can relate to, rather than a stick figure who does not possess any feelings.

Choosing a substitution may be difficult at first. The tendency is to look at the copy and say, "I'm going to talk to a person working in a store who is wearing a blue shirt and ragged blue jeans because that is what the script calls for me to do." Or, "I'm going to use a friend's experience because I do not have any of my own involving a professional pizzamaker, cutting up meat and veggies." Or better yet, "I'm going to talk to a bunch of guys standing on the corner wearing cowboy boots and ten-gallon hats because I think that would be different and interesting." These are not true substitutions. Instead, they are brain traps, meaning that, intellectually, the substitutions make sense, but emotionally, they are useless. There is no brain-heart transfer if you don't use people you have known. Unless remembering a bunch of guys standing in the street wearing cowboy boots and ten-gallon hats evokes some kind of feeling in you, the scenario will not work. A "generic" story cannot stimulate an emotional charge. Describing clothing colors doesn't work either because, once again, it is an intellectual choice that does not create any feeling.

Take time now as you read this section to learn how to truly evoke *genuine* feelings. If you have a microphone and recording equipment, get them ready now. Stand up and put your hand on your heart, feeling it pumping new blood through your system. The soothing rhythm should be a relaxing experience. Breathe in and out a couple of times. Verbalize a sigh if it helps you relax. As you do this, your breath should slow down and become deeper. This hand-on-heart technique is a grounding process used to help elevate your awareness of your current emotional state. Check and see how you are feeling at this moment. Are you happy or sad? Nervous or afraid? Your current emotional state is your initial starting ground. If you do not feel anything at this moment, your body may have "checked out" temporarily because it is confused about this process. Try the exercise again, refraining from any unnecessary, distracting movements that may prevent you from becoming grounded and emotionally aware. Otherwise, emotional energy will be dispelled rather than allowed to course through your body. Turn your thoughts inward by feeling the heartbeat.

Now begin the personalization process. Think about a pleasant experience with your mother, father, or someone else from your past with whom you have had a powerful emotional bond. Sink into your memories as you imagine that special moment and the feelings between the two of you. Smell the air. Is bread baking in the oven? Are you enjoying cookies and milk after school? Remember the sounds in the room at the time of your memory. Are cars whizzing by? Are birds chirping lightly in the background? If you truly connect with this wonderful moment, a gentle, natural smile should cross your lips. Now, stay in this moment as you turn on your microphone and tape recorder and record the following phrase from a fictional commercial:

Because all bread should taste like it's homemade.

Rewind the tape and listen to the recording. If you were really present in your experience, the vocal chords should sound relaxed, warm, and caring. There will not be a cold or strained sound in your voice. Can you hear the feeling of love and affection emanating from the tape? Congratulate yourself if you can! That is the essence of the actor-audience emotional link. This feeling of genuine concern for your listener—the almighty consumer—is what sells the product. Movie stars and professional actors are hired not only for their high profile, but for their ability to readily access their emotions. But even if you are not famous (yet), you need to be able to do this.

As we mature into adulthood, we learn tricks that help us to survive and live in society. For some, the brain takes over and guides them on their journey into adulthood. Others are more emotional, wearing their hearts on their sleeves. Good actors—unconsciously competent actors—blend a unique understanding and interpretation of the written word with a trust in the ability of the body, voice, and heart to give life to the mind's reading of these words. For the brain-heart transfer to occur, the actor must let go of these learned behaviors and allow the moment to unfold naturally. For many, this is difficult. Perhaps a bad moment has crept into your memory that blocks your emotions. Maybe outside pressures prevent you from concentrating. Possibly, you do not trust this process and how it works. Undoubtedly, there is something preventing you from visualizing and experiencing the loving moment from your past. Releasing the brain's hold on the idea and allowing the moment to happen is a scary and incomprehensible concept to the person who has used intellect to survive. The key to this brain-heart transfer is **trust.** Truly believable, real, and heartfelt acting is recognized and praised throughout the world, regardless of the medium—be it on stage, television, cinema, or behind a microphone.

Choosing a personalization automatically affects the emotions placed on the written words. In real life, we speak differently to strangers than we do to friends, and the same is true of how we speak to children versus adults or to someone who is ill versus a healthy person. In voice-overs, it is imperative that the space surrounding the mic be replaced by a personalization that evokes the emotional overtones needed to drive the story forward. Due to the speed in which voice-overs are recorded, all personalizations must be easily accessible to the voice actor.

Make a list of your strongest personalizations and the emotions and attitudes that you can automatically evoke. Remember to be specific. Perhaps thinking about an old friend makes you feel young and mischievous. Imagining a phone conversation with your grandmother may make you feel guilty for not taking more time out of your busy schedule to visit her. Speaking with your boss may make you feel angry. Remembering how you kissed and tucked your child into bed at night may bring back a flood of warm, loving feelings. Arguing with your teenage son may make you feel frustrated and tense. All feelings are legitimate if they are genuine. Remember, there are no right or wrong feelings, as long as they are truly yours.

Using a personalization is traditionally an actor's trick. Most voice-over directors are unfamiliar, and unconcerned, with the process the actor goes through to enhance a script so it meets with client approval. That is why you, the actor, are hired in the first place! Presumably, the actor knows how to bring the words to life. Otherwise, the director, client, or an office worker could voice the commercial themselves without your help. So as a mental note, it may not be in your best interest to discuss this personalization process with the director while working on an actual voice-over job, as it may add confusion to the mix. Instead, take note of the emotion the director wishes to convey, and just select the appropriate personalization from your past experiences to conjure up the desired emotion. The director will hear the natural feeling in your read without you giving away any of your acting secrets!

Once you have mastered the concept of personalizations, you will find that your work improves immensely. You should become more dexterous in your ability to find, on cue, the appropriate emotional links required by the director and the script. New voices will emerge from your subconscious. There will be a greater sense of play and less of a feeling that you are working. The more in touch you become with your own life and the experiences it generates, the better you will sound. You will elevate the script to a higher level. The brain-heart transfer will have been achieved.

BUILDING A CHARACTER

There are five basic principles to building a character: *Who are you? Where are you at this moment in time? What are you doing? Why are you there? When is the action taking place?* In this section, we will delve more deeply into the voice-over acting process to learn how to develop a complete and well-rounded character. The person you create needs to be alive, breathing, and, most importantly, real. Within these parameters, the clearly defined character can range anywhere from the average next-door-neighbor type to the outlandishly zany and crazy kook living in your refrigerator. Regardless of the extent of character polarity, each voice needs to be believable so the listener can easily relate to it and, therefore, to the product. Also, it is important to decide if the character is intended to be humorous or straightforward. Using the five W's will add insight and depth to this artistic process.

Who Are You?

First of all, you need to decide *who* you are. There are clues within the copy to help you make this decision. The manner in which the dialogue is written, for instance, adds keen insight into the character's background. Extreme regional character traits, such as British, southern, Boston, Brooklyn, and New York accents, are easily identifiable, as is the Canadian use of the term "eh." Check for intentional grammatical errors, slang words or colloquialisms, overtly proper or precise use of the language, frequency of buzzwords and technical terminology, and dialects. This will tell you whether you are a white-collar or blue-collar worker, a foreign person or a "local," intelligent or dim-witted, or young or old. You should also try to discern whether or not the character is shy, uncomfortable, and vulnerable or bold, straightforward, and brash. Slang, like the use of the words "a grand" versus "one thousand dollars," is a signal that the reading requires a casual rather than formal delivery.

Television scripts often contain visual descriptions that provide additional clues about the character. If the visual picture is funny, this should be reflected in the voice. If the picture on the screen depicts beautiful beaches and tropical scenery, the voice should capture that alluring charm. On-camera voice-over scripts are often accompanied by a complete character breakdown. For example: male, age 30 to 40, witty and intelligent, very "real" and not announcer-y or cartoon-y. On occasion, a reference is made at the top of the copy to act like a specific television character or movie personality. *Storyboards,* a series of rough sketches depicting the action to be filmed, contain valuable information.

Dialogue is typed below the corresponding sketch, alerting the voice talent to the action on the screen and to how the words should be delivered so that the final presentation makes sense when the sound and picture are put together. *Animatics,* primarily used for nonbroadcast applications such as pitching accounts and testing ideas, follow this same general concept. Storyboard sketches are strung together on film or video tape to simulate action. The recorded voice-over is used to enhance the accompanying pictures.

In addition to the writing style, copywriter's notes, visual descriptions, and pictures, the script's title is another source of information. If the title is "Relaxing Getaway," the spot probably sells a vacation retreat, and the voice should sound soft, friendly, and relaxed. Conversely, if a script is titled "Amazing Blowout Sale," the voice probably needs to be big and animated. The medium on which the spot airs also tells the actor whether to be big or understated. Radio commercials require the actor to draw a complete, strong picture of the character in the listener's mind without using a visual image. Television voice-overs use the actor's voice to enhance the image on the screen, and can be subtler.

Actors are constantly in a tither because directors, casting directors, and agents have a tendency to pigeonhole actors even when they understand and know how to utilize these clues and devices to create a variety of personae. If a script calls for humor, the casting person is most likely to call in a comedian or a voice actor with a naturally quirky or funny voice rather than someone who has to manufacture that trait. If the part is written for a man, there is a 99.9-percent chance that a woman will not get the part. If the script requires a low, sexy voice and the actor's natural speaking voice is high and guileless, that person will probably be omitted from the casting. Therefore, realizing who you are in your real life helps in understanding who you can play.

Some people make a living in voice-overs by just being themselves. They establish an understanding of their vocal depth and age range and use it to their best advantage. Attitudes and situations change but the same general voice filters through. If the acting ability is there and the natural voice is in demand to fill a certain niche, that person will work often. Other actors are hired because of their wide range of vocal abilities. People with multiple voice talents are sure bets at auditions or jobs. They "fill out" an audition and are able to cover all the bases during the job, especially when the client doesn't have a specific idea or voice in mind. No matter what twists or turns the copy and direction take, that multi-talented person can utilize a "rubber" throat to suit the script and changing directorial demands.

Since not all actors are able to change their voice to suit the demands of a wide assortment of scripts, *type-casting* is implemented. This is where a person possessing similar characteristics to the written character is considered for a specific part. The closer the actor is to the role, the more likely the recording will sound the way it was intended. On the whole, this is not a bad concept. After all, the operative word in the phrase is casting, and type-casting is merely a way of singling out the most logical and appropriate actors for a specific job. Character types change from one job to the next, allowing a wider range of actors to acquire work. Rather than getting mad at the thought of being "typed," spend some time exploring who you are and the personal assets you have to offer. Make a list. It may be that your voice is low, genuine, and humorous or that it is young, quirky, and charming. By recognizing your individuality and voice personality, you will separate yourself from the rest of the voice-over pack. This will help you understand why you are called, or not called, on certain auditions and bookings and give you the option to either fix and expand your range or live with your current voice. Understanding your voice and who you are will also help you eliminate bad choices when given a script. If you have a beautiful, resonant baritone, don't squash it and make it high and nasal. Use your assets.

Deciding who you are in a given script is like playing a game of connect-the-dots. If you write your personal attributes on the left side of the paper and the character's description on the right side of the page, you can draw lines between the two, and determine which areas are similar. This enables you to see how many of your own personal, naturally-occurring assets can be used to enhance the character. And you will understand some of your own uniqueness! After all, actors are selected when they have something special to offer.

Where Are You?

In daily life, we behave differently according to our locale. The freedom and ease enjoyed while vacationing luxuriously on a tropical beach is far different from the pressure-filled lifestyle of a demanding work environment. Dining out at a fancy restaurant is much calmer and more relaxing than wolfing down a fast-food hamburger in the car. Talking on the telephone at home is not nearly as challenging as carrying on a conversation at a local pay phone situated on the corner of a busy intersection. *Where* we are has dramatic impact on our actions, thoughts, and demeanor.

"Slice-of-life" radio commercials rely heavily on the establishing of a specific location. If the action takes place outside on a cold winter day, the actor needs to sound chilly. If a scene takes place in a restaurant, the voice actor (or actors) needs to respond to such things as looking for a table, being seated, getting the waiter's attention, talking across the table, ordering a meal, chewing food, hearing dishes crash, and paying the check. If the script calls for the actor to look for a salesperson in a large, cavernous warehouse, the actor must adjust to the voluminous size of the room.

Sound effects add the crowning touch on these types of commercials. Most recording studios offer a large range of prerecorded sound effects on compact disc that are readily accessible to the engineer and production team. After the actor has finished recording the dialogue, the sound effects (SFX) are mixed in with the voice. In the example about a cold winter day, the sound of a brisk winter breeze could be added underneath the dialogue. The restaurant scene would have the obligatory sound of silverware clinking in the background. The lonesome actor tromping through the imaginary warehouse would have a technical effect, such as an echo or reverberation, added to the voice during or after recording to make the room seem enormous and empty.

The sound effects and the actor work together to establish the scene. Without the actor's input, the SFX would sound completely out of context. Therefore, it is important to look at a script and establish a definitive location so that the appropriate action, attitude, or response can occur. There are tricks an actor can use to establish locations. For instance, if the scene takes place in a kitchen where cookies are being baked, take time to inhale and smell the sweet air. Then, add an "mmm" sound as you exhale. Have the "mmm" sound blend into your next word. If there is a noticeable break between the "mmm" and the word, the illusion is broken. The audience immediately knows that the "yummy" sound is contrived. Also keep in mind that, with time limitations always looming over the voice-over actor, belaboring the "mmm" will detract from, rather than add to, the reading. There are other stereotypical sounds that establish time, place, and action. A yawn, if used in a scene occuring early in the morning or late at night, establishes that the person just woke up or is sleepy. Adding an "ahhh" sound as the breath is exhaled confirms the character's state of ecstatic relaxation and ease.

Television commercials and video presentations are somewhat different from radio commercials in that they have the luxury of showing the viewer exactly where the action is taking place. The voice behind the picture does not have to work hard to define the locale since it is presented to the viewer visually. Of course, the voice must still react to the on-camera actors, their on-screen location, and the unfolding action. For example, the following television commercial features a dog flopped on the floor, bored with his food. When the hero product is poured into his bowl, the dog's ears perk up, he jumps up, smells the food, and hurriedly gobbles it down. Then the dog smiles, licks his chops, trots over to the closet, rummages through it, and pulls out a leash which he promptly drops in his master's lap. The startled owner awakens from his snooze and attaches the leash just in time to be whisked out the front door. In the next shot, we see the dog dragging his owner down a quiet suburban street and into the distance. The camera pans back to the bag of miracle dog food.

> Is your dog bored with the same old dog food? He must not be eating Miracle Dog Food. It's specially formulated to give your dog all the vitamins and minerals he needs to make him happy, healthy, and energetic. Maybe it's time for you to switch to Miracle Dog Food.

The words in this commercial have to complement the action on the screen. Raising a cocked eyebrow adds a feeling of levity to the voice. Gently smirking or adding a twinkle in the eyes adds a humorous understanding of the owner's plight.

Voice-overs for commercial and industrial on-camera use are recorded one of two ways: to picture or to time. Reading "to picture" takes discipline and training. The actor has to read the script and watch a video monitor while the accompanying visual is playing. (It's sort of like patting your head and rubbing your stomach.) The actor acknowledges the scene changes out of the corner of the eye, and as the eyes follow the script, the peripheral vision picks up color and light changes. Although this technique can put the fear of cardiac arrest into the pounding heart of a voice actor who's never done it before, it is much easier than it sounds. Typically, the actor is given a chance to see the video once or twice before the recording process begins, to become familiar with the scene changes and timing requirements. If the reading is flubbed, the tape is rolled back and the recording process begins again.

What Are You Doing?

Now that you know who and where you are, you need to decide *what the heck you are doing!* Just because the scene is set in an office, does not necessarily mean you are sitting in a cushy chair behind a large mahogany desk sharpening pencils. In any given situation, there are a dozen actions from which to choose. So don't always stop at the first or most obvious choice, but dig deep and explore the full realm of the script. If outside, decide if the person is jogging, power walking, strolling, skipping, standing still, jumping rope, being interviewed by the press, hiding from someone undesirable, chatting with a friend, or just picking his nose. The more creative the choice, the funnier, more unique, and more real the spot will become.

Some commercials have clues or descriptions of character assignments and actions. Given these parameters, the character has varying degrees of achievement. If the script states that you are a secretary filing important papers, you can choose to be extremely efficient at the job, a bumbling idiot, or somewhere in between. When choosing your action, remember to take note of the character's relationship to the product. The hero product should always be portrayed in a positive manner, otherwise what's the point of spending money to promote it? Insubordinate, dim-witted, or rude actions should be confined to the characters who represent the competition.

Why Are You There?

Understanding *why* you are in a given situation adds another degree of realism to the script. Without a purpose, the character will sound stilted and artificial, and undoubtedly you have heard spots like this on the radio. Two people pretend to sound excited as they banter banal copy information back and forth. For example:

Voice 1: Boy, that soup smells good. Can I have some?
Voice 2: Sure, help yourself.
Voice 1: It tastes great!
Voice 2: Thank you. I opened the can myself.
Voice 1: You sure have a way with metal.
Voice 2: It's the new can opener from Can-O-Matic. And watch! See how easy it is to use?
Voice 1: It's heavy!
Voice 2: That's right. It's the heavy metal can opener from Can-O-Matic—the only one with tiny transistor radio built right into the handle.

Beginning voice actors are often cursed with scripts as lame as this one. It takes a creative voice actor to make it sound good, and more than ever, the *who, where, what,* and *why* need to be implemented. The two actors must establish where they are. The obvious choice is in a kitchen, but what if it is at an on-sight store demonstration, where Voice 2 is cooking soup for customers to taste while they shop? That scene selection would then elevate Voice 2 to the position of a product demonstrator and Voice 1 could then be the hungry shopper, client, friend, or business associate. Defining the relationship between Voice 1 and 2 as boss-trainee, husband-wife, or customer-sales person is necessary. Next, a level of expertise should be established. Is the product demonstrator a beginner, an intermediate, or an old pro? The *why* is needed to tie the scene together. Is Voice 1 there to squelch a case of starvation, to taste a promoted product, or to supervise the new employee? Is Voice 2 making lunch, or selling soup or Can-O-Matics? If a salesperson, does Voice 2 like or dislike the job? Is Voice 2 annoyed by or appreciative of Voice 1's presence?

Tension, friction, and conflict grows out of the *who, where, what,* and *why* choices. An otherwise dull and lifeless script becomes interesting when relationships develop and sparks start flying. Voice actors who are gifted with the ability to execute strong, interesting, and in-depth character and situation choices are hired regularly for that very reason. The spot sounds good because the actor knows how to fill in the blanks in the written draft. Well-written scripts are a delight because interesting and thorough characters, locations, and situations are scripted in; the actor just has to take the provided information and expand it slightly. Scripts that are not as well-written rely heavily on actors to make them engaging.

When Is the Action Taking Place?

Knowing or deciding *when* the action takes place is the crowning touch on the five W's. People's actions change throughout the day. Some are grumpy when they just wake up, while others feel chipper the minute they jump out of bed and their feet hit the floor. Some feel energetic and ready to party at midnight, but others lie on the couch exhausted and watch television with one eye open. Is the action occurring during the day while the character is at work, or on the weekend when the character is relaxing by the pool? Seasons are another aspect that affect a person's gait and attitude. Is it a beautiful spring morning that puts a bounce in the step or the third consecutive week of torrential rain? Mealtimes often trigger a response that can be used to develop a character. Is it close to the breakfast, lunch, or dinner hour? Has the character just started work or is she starving because she's just ending a 10-hour stretch on the sales floor.

Given the example from the "Why Are You There?" section above, wouldn't Voice 1 and Voice 2 behave differently depending on the time of day the action occurred? Voice 1 would probably appear hungrier if the scene was positioned during lunch or dinner. Voice 2, in turn, would be affected by the length of time on the job. Maybe the long, ten-hour work shift made the character's feet ache, causing him to be tired and agitated.

There is a cause and effect to almost everything a person does. Eliminating the realities of life from the voice creates a flat, two-dimensional character. Things that are taken for granted in daily life—such as who and where you are, what you are doing, and why and when you are doing it—need to be implemented in the acting process. Rich, well-defined characters result, and, when added to the carefully crafted words, they make the copy points stand out and the voice-over job a success!

Chapter 5
Making It M.I.N.E.

Truly understanding and perfecting the mental, physical, and vocal aspects of voice-overs is much like learning a second language. Follow the rules, and you will learn to properly conjugate the sentences, but as time goes on, the rules multiply and change as exceptions are discovered. The student realizes that a language which initially appeared simple and straightforward has hidden nuances and complexities. The same is true with voice-overs. Time and practice are required to make the dialogue and script interpretations reflexive and effortless. "Copy Basics" (chapter 3) laid the fundamental voice-over foundation. We learned the importance of the client's name and key words and that the listener must always understand how, when, and where to spend their hard-earned dollars. "Hiding 'the Sell,'" (chapter 4) provided a little more depth, explaining how to add interest and imagination to basic copy information by incorporating fun and realism into the script.

Now, learning to make the words uniquely yours is the advanced stage in voice-overs. It involves putting the *how* into the read by digging beneath the surface of the script and bridging the gap between yourself and the character. A Ph.D. in voice-overs is given when the two above-mentioned areas of learning—plus "Making It M.I.N.E."—are fully assimilated into the performance, because it is at this point that the voice actor becomes unconsciously competent. Within minutes, the voice-over artist has a strong handle on how to effectively read the dialogue. Words appear to leap off the page with effortless ease—it seems the person behind the microphone isn't working at all! The true voice-over genius is born.

WHAT DOES "MAKING IT M.I.N.E" MEAN?

The M.I.N.E. in "Making It M.I.N.E." stands for Motivations, Intentions, Needs, and Emotions. It is the manner in which an actor becomes "emotionally alive," "present," and "in the moment." Either consciously or unconsciously, the actor's complete, multifaceted persona is transferred into the scripted character, and current events or past experiences that shaped the actor's life are incorporated into the specific events of the material even though they do not have any immediate bearing on the actor's emotional life. Rather than the words sounding cold, unreal, and detached because they do not personally affect the actor, a genuine feeling is generated. A rainbow of human colors is exposed that lends a subtlety and brilliance to the words.

Every person has an emotional "wound." It is this dark side that colors our actions. Recognizing, tapping into, and exposing the soft spot reveals a person's deepest vulnerability. The incessant joke-teller who monopolizes the conversation has a need for attention. Friends who constantly ask if you like something have a need for approval. Obviously, a person's needs justify his actions, and getting needs met is a way of exposing our humanness and vulnerability as we experience life. Creating or emulating perfection by only exposing our strengths, on the other hand, keeps people at a distance and creates a barrier between the flawed universe and the "perfect" you. Finding the true need is not always easy. Surface needs often hide the deeper, more fundamental needs underneath. Gifted voice actors expose their personal needs in their acting. They recognize the character's need and connect it with their own so that the two become intertwined. The actor disappears, and instead, a real person takes his place.

MOTIVATIONS

Motivation gives an actor a purpose for saying the words or a force behind the character's action. It is the prior event that explains why the present action occurs in a specific manner, and it gives the aura of a past or present history. It provides some logic and context for the action. For example, many people are motivated to go to work beyond obvious monetary reasons. The motivation to go to work could stem from enthusiasm, self-satisfaction, power, obligation, camaraderie, or some other source. People change jobs—or think about changing jobs—when they lose their motivation. The actor's motivation is the direct result of a prior experience. Rather than the character's life beginning and ending with the words written in the copy, there should be a feeling that the scene is a "slice" taken from that person's life. The prior situation fuels the story and the character is given a purpose and sparked with energy. The order of events in finding the character's motivation is as follows:

1. The actor finds clues to the character's behavior in the script. It could be happy, sad, angry, exhausted, energetic, frustrated, bored, determined, anxious, relaxed, and so on. From that behavioral choice, the mental and physical condition is established.
2. She then determines why the character feels that particular way. A simple, prior history, or "pre-life" scenario, is developed to reinforce the desired feeling so it will enhance the story. This provides the reason for speaking at this point in time and in this particular manner. For instance, if the actor is required to sound frustrated, she would then search to understand the reason for this frustration. The reason would either be inherent in the script or mentally fabricated. Perhaps this frustration stems from an earlier confrontation with the dry cleaners who lost the character's favorite shirt.
3. Within the pre-life scenario, the actor checks to see if the character's motivation is connected to her own personal feelings or experiences. Does thinking about the foul-up at the dry cleaner actually stimulate a real sense of frustration or is it just a silly story? If the actor does not relate to the imaginary experience on a gut level, a new pre-life situation must be created. The actor selects one that rings true. If the very thought of misplacing the car keys makes your palms sweat and breathing shallow, that is a sign of genuine connection. A spontaneous physiological change occurs as the body experiences the moment without the brain interfering and placing judgment. This is the scenario to use.
4. The chosen pre-life is then used to move the story forward. The motivation from the scenario creates believable actions within the text. Natural tones within

the actor's voice exposes her vulnerabilities. The intrigue of human successes or failures draws the listener into the scene. Best of all, the actor does not have to act anymore. The process of interpreting the copy is simplified when instinct takes over. The power of dynamic subtleties replaces the need to overact. The actor surrenders to the structure rather than constantly controlling the situation.

INTENTIONS

An *intention* is the tactic used to "meet the need" of the character within a script. This need remains constant; never changing, it is the "through line," or driving force, for the actor, running from beginning to end of the voice-over spot. On the other hand, the intentions can change as often as necessary. Selecting a specific intention, like "to harass" or "to provoke," gives purpose to the scripted words. The voice alters as it adapts quickly to each of the chosen intentions, and the audience understands what is happening in the scene due to these vocal shifts.

For clarity, you should be able to define the intention in one word. Following is a string of possible intentions; feel free to add to it. As you read each intention aloud, try to portray its meaning in the tone of your voice. Preface each word with, "I intend to . . ." I *intend to* beckon, beg, challenge, charm, command, criticize, dazzle, demand, embarrass, encourage, flatter, intimidate, patronize, plead, seduce, tease, urge. Keep in mind that, within a given script, there can be one or several intentions. As tactical approaches currently employed become worn-out or ineffective, the intention should be changed. This is referred to as a *transition.*

Subconsciously, throughout our daily lives, we use intentions to try to get exactly what we want. When the current intention no longer works in our favor, we change our approach. A child who wants a new toy intends *to flatter* his mother by saying, "I love you. You're the best mommy in the whole world." When the mother responds, "No. You're not getting that toy," the child must make a transition. The new course of action may be *to bargain:* "I'll clean up my room for a week, if you let me have that toy!" If the response is still "No," the child must decide whether to accept the defeat or choose yet another intention. When all else fails, the child may resort to something more drastic—a temper tantrum perhaps—and the situation continues and escalates.

No one likes to lose, and conflict ensues when neither participant backs down. Each party stands their ground in an effort to "win." Intentions are merely measures used to ensure a win. So even if the mother refuses to buy the toy, the child will make the mother wish she had!

NEEDS

A *need* is the desire to fill a void within oneself. It is the basic and fundamental reason why individuals behave in their own unique manner. As a person grows into adulthood, his experiences serve as a mold that shapes his behavior, and a basic, subconscious need becomes embedded in his psyche. It could be a need to be loved, acknowledged, or accepted. Need becomes the "through line" of a person's life. As an actor, the ability to recognize and use your need as a through line becomes a valuable tool in the personification of a character.

Before you can recognize the needs of a scripted character, you must first be able to acknowledge and embrace your own needs. That means searching your past to find out what makes you tick. This step is important, because it will eventually add more depth to your performance. Rather than walking into an audition or job with only half your personality accessible, you can recognize the weaknesses in your own character that might detract from parts of your being. It will also serve to bridge the gap between what is real and what is fake, between you and the voice role. Through careful backtracking, good and bad experiences that shaped your life will become exposed. Process these thoughts. The subconscious mind will unleash the hidden need inside you and expose the vulnerability to the conscious mind. Then you can use this knowledge of yourself in your interpretation of the copy.

Good acting is reflected in the actor's ability to ask probing questions about the characters to identify the deep-rooted need. By continuing to ask "What?" and "Why?," the underlying meaning is eventually divulged. In a commercial touting facial cream, the actor might run through a litany of questions something like this:

Why am I here? To buy the product.
What will the product give me? Younger-looking skin.
Why do I want to look young? Because I want to feel confident and good about myself.
Why must I feel good about myself? Because I want to increase the chance of someone liking me.
What will I get if someone likes me? Love.

The series of questions ends with the recognition of the basic need. In this case, to be loved.

EMOTIONS

An *emotion* occurs internally. It is the product of a human "condition," and can be neither right nor wrong. Instead, emotions have their own freedom. They take on lives of their own and are capable of instantaneous change. This change is especially evident in small children who have not yet learned the adult art of *hiding* emotions. In a matter of seconds, a child can drift from ecstatic leaps of joy to convulsive tears of sadness, or from strong aggression to forthright love. Adults, on the other hand, often strive for "perfection" and a supreme sense of order and control. In so doing, a person risks losing touch with her emotions, which are the very essence of acting.

In voice-overs, as in other forms of acting, it is necessary for a voice actor to regain some of that childlike emotional verisimilitude. After all, emotions add depth, realism, and life to scripted words that are merely a skeleton to which the actor adds flesh and substance. Thirty percent of the success of the copy (and the sell) is in the script, the other 70 percent is in the acting!

Begin by familiarizing yourself with your own emotional life. Take note of how you feel at different moments of the day. Does your body become rigid during an argument? When you are anxious, does your stomach do flip-flops? If someone frightens you, does your breathing become shallow? Do you throw things when you are angry, or do you curl up in a ball and start crying? An emotion is the result of a personal situation, or unique life experience. The very act of waking up in the morning can be exhilarating to the person who is anxiously anticipating an exciting event, or depressing to someone who must pick up the pieces of the previous day's disaster. As the day progresses, events either enhance or worsen the condition. So memorize your emotions and their causes at each given moment, and try to replicate them. It is one of the steps in becoming consciously aware of your unconscious behavior.

Happy and *sad* are the emotional extremes. Between them falls a vast spectrum of emotional conditions. What follows is a partial list of emotions to help you begin. Incorporate the corresponding emotion into your vocal tone as you read the words aloud: anger, anxiety, embarrassment, boredom, confidence, confusion, depression, disgust, ecstasy, exhaustion, fear, guilt, hope, hysteria, loneliness, love, shock, shyness, suspicion. By simply selecting an emotion or series of emotions within a script, the voice-over gains its purpose. The audience quickly perceives the purpose of the words. They no longer dangle meaninglessly in midair, but are grounded in truth.

Of course, commercial voice-overs are seldom designed to reflect the truly hideous side of human nature. Whenever a product is sold, it is usually accompanied by an element of fun. The energy has a positive upward motion, rather than a negative energy dragging the whole spot down. No listener wants to hear a voice talent whining or viciously arguing, because these unpleasant emotions are too real and scary. They can alienate the listener and send the client into bankruptcy. If a script involves an argument, it must be performed playfully or in an outrageous manner that is intentionally "over the top."

Many voice actors get tripped up in the belief that all scripts require a huge, smiling delivery. Although a pleasant attitude needs to be reflected in the hero product and its services, there is a whole gamut of emotions at one's disposal. If one part is a set-up that reflects a competitor's product, more emotional latitude is available to poke fun at the competition. Corny, provocative, and funny approaches are all highly successful in advertising.

PUTTING IT ALL TOGETHER

Now it is time to make sense of everything by putting it all together. Below is a 60-second radio script. The main character is required to have an introspective attitude, as if the listener is hearing the person's inner thoughts. Depending on the actor's sex, an appropriate gender selection of *he* or *she* should be made. Following the commercial is an analysis. It is divided into three sections: recognition of basic copy information; personalizing the message and developing the five W's; and digging deeper to expose the motivations, intentions, needs, and emotions.

I was sitting in this café, drinking a double espresso when this gorgeous blonde walked in. My heart skipped three beats. Could I be having a heart attack? No, it must be the sudden influx of caffeine. I let out a quiet sigh of relief as I grabbed a handful of Nutty Crisps. (CRUNCH) Mmm, they sure taste good. (CRUNCH) Nutty Crisps, I thought, are the perfect complement to this double espresso. (CRUNCH) It was then that I noticed it. The gorgeous blonde sitting in the corner didn't have any Nutty Crisps! She would miss out on the deliciously crunchy taste of Nutty Crisps. (CRUNCH) How unsatisfying. (CRUNCH) My hand shaking, I lifted my bowl of Nutty Crisps off the table. Putting one determined foot in front of the other, I walked over to her table. "Hi," I said. "Hi. I noticed you had Nutty Crisps at your table," she said as I stood there trembling like an idiot. "Yeah," I said intelligently, "Would you like some?" "The bowl's empty," she said. "Oh, no!" I thought, "I must have eaten the last Nutty Crisp!"

ANNOUNCER: Nutty Crisps. The crunchy snack you can't quit eating.

COPY BASICS

Client: Nutty Crisps.
Key Words: Taste good; perfect complement; deliciously crunchy taste.
Slogan: The crunchy snack you can't quit eating.
Set-up: First three sentences.
Body: Begins with the fourth sentence and builds in intensity until she says, "The bowl's empty."
Resolve: The narrator's final thought, followed by the announcer tag.

HIDING "THE SELL"

Some of these elements involve using your imagination, so your personal choices may differ from those listed below.

Personalization: Telling a close friend or confidante—or reliving the events in your own head.
Who are you?: Single, yuppie hypochondriac. Information based on the descriptive language used in the copy—café, double espresso, gorgeous blonde, fear of heart attack, nervous eating pattern, and need to use Nutty Crisps as an ice breaker.
Where are you?: In a café.
What are you doing?: Drinking designer coffee and eating Nutty Crisps.
Why are you there?: To relax.
When is it?: Saturday afternoon.

MAKING IT M.I.N.E.

This is only one way of incorporating the motivations, intentions, needs, and emotions. See if you can connect with other choices.

Motivation: Ended a serious relationship, creating a need to get away and think.
Intention: Initially, the intention is to please oneself. Later, it changes to "to impress" the gorgeous blonde.
Need: Love.
Emotion: First, the person is depressed because of the break-up in the pre-life scenario. Second is fear of having a heart attack. Third is relief at the realization that the coffee and blonde combination caused the heart to flutter. Fourth is satisfaction at the unique taste sensation of coffee and Nutty Crisps. Fifth is surprise that the blonde doesn't have any of the hero snack. Sixth is empathy for her lack of the snack. Seventh is nervousness at meeting the goddess-like beauty. And, finally, there is embarrassment at having eaten the last morsel.

The role of the gorgeous blonde can be dissected in the same manner. Although the copy basics remain the same, the other selections must reflect an entirely different personality.

HIDING "THE SELL": More choices are left to the imagination. The major decision is whether or not to be attracted to the narrator.

> **Personalization.** Heartthrob or nerd.
> **Who are you?:** Attractive single person.
> **Where are you?:** In a café.
> **What are you doing?:** Drinking coffee and craving Nutty Crisps.
> **Why are you there?:** To meet people or to quietly enjoy Nutty Crisps.
> **When is it?:** Saturday afternoon.

MAKING IT M.I.N.E.: Due to the lack of strong copy information regarding the gorgeous blonde, it is important to create full and imaginative choices. Of course there are other ways of playing the character besides the one listed. See how many other ways you can develop the character.

> **Motivation:** A date for the evening.
> **Intention:** To seduce the narrator.
> **Need:** Attention.
> **Emotion:** The first word, "Hi," is confident. The second sentence is coy and smug. Finally, there is disappointment on discovering that the bowl is empty.

Tying the whole spot together is the closing tag. An announcer must convey the various fun elements, from the product's addictive taste to the humorous dilemma portrayed in the scene. Confident satisfaction enters into the announcer's voice at the final mention of the product. The concluding slogan is divided into two parts, the description and the connecting phrase. Following the product description "crunchy snack," the announcer effectively connects the parting thoughts with the scene by stretching out and/or hesitating on the words "you can't quit eating."

SUMMARY AND SELF-EVALUATION

Understanding and using the concept of "Making It M.I.N.E." requires personal exploration. It is only after you come to terms with your *own* inner character that this crucial step can be implemented. Take time now to make a list of what you perceive to be your own personal assets and frailties. In one column, note your pluses—for example, your sparkling personality, creativity, good sense of humor, ability to sight-read easily, skill at using the microphone as an "ear," talent for imitating voices, excellent sense of timing, strong acting abilities, flexible voice, and your ability to make techno-babble sound natural and effortless. In the other column write your minuses. While this information isn't nearly as pleasant, it is very enlightening, so try to be honest with yourself. Examples might be: you are shy and get nervous at auditions, sometimes talk too fast, swallow the final consonant of some words, lose part of your personality when asked to perform behind a microphone, sometimes are too busy to practice behind the mic, and have a tendency to transpose words.

Holding a mirror up to yourself and examining what lies beneath the surface is very courageous. Take pride in this ability, too, as well as in your pluses. It will give you the strength and courage to change or compensate for the minuses. As the dualities in your life are minimized and eliminated, you will have a better chance of living up to your full artistic potential.

Chapter 6

Tags, Donuts, and Promos

Now that you understand the fundamentals to voice-over acting from both a technical and an acting standpoint, it is time to practice putting the two concepts together. We will begin here with tags, donuts, and station promotions (promos) and proceed to announcer, spokesperson, real person commercials, and characters, multiples, industrial narrations, multimedia, and books-on-tape in following chapters. These sections are designed to help you grasp the subtle differences inherent in each writing style.

Please note that there are differentiations between radio and television voice-overs. As a general rule, television commercials are read at a slower pace than radio commercials, and the picture enhances the product and concept, thus eliminating the need for lengthy verbal descriptions. Radio commercials, without this visual tool, must build product recognition through the use of words, sound effects, and music. In many cases, an amazing amount of words are folded into a tight 15-, 30-, or 60-second spot, forcing the voice actor to delve into the copy and utilize the full capabilities of his lungs for consistent breath support.

Tags are short one- or two-line sentences at the ends of commercials that add final punctuation to the selling points mentioned earlier in the copy by another actor or set of actors. *Donuts* are tags that occur in the middle of a commercial; the body of the commercial "wraps around" the announcer "hole" that is scripted into the middle of the copy. It is not uncommon for commercials to have both a donut and a tag.

Local and network television stations use *promos,* spots on both radio and television that draw awareness to upcoming programming. Nielson and Arbitron surveys are used to track audience viewership, and, obviously, the larger the audience, the more the station can charge for this commercial airtime. This explains the million-dollar cost to place an ad during the Superbowl. There are basically six rating surveys throughout the year: January, February, May, July, October, and November. Of these, February, May, and November are the most important. (The other ratings periods are disregarded, largely because sports and other specials supersede regular broadcasting and skew the numbers in a manner less representative of regular programming.) During the ratings periods, the promotions departments produce various versions of the promotional pieces: one for next week, one for tomorrow, another for the actual day of the event. This covers all the bases as the countdown begins to the airing of the program. Promo segments are produced "just in time" or two to three days prior to airing. Typically, a promo campaign runs for five weeks, starting one week before the four-week rating period. Repetition provides a greater opportunity for viewers to watch the promo and, hopefully, tune in to the program. Although the talk shows still provide a bit more sensationalism during these "sweeps" than during the nonratings periods, there now seem to be fewer topics like "transvestite yodelers who like to skydive" than in the past. Most of the promos created by television stations are cut from news pieces. As time permits, HFR (Hold for Release) promos are used. These are stories that feature current but not headline-driven news.

PRACTICE MAKES PERFECT

Throughout this chapter and the next eight chapters, an assortment of practice scripts are provided so you can learn-by-doing. Set up your recording equipment and read each commercial aloud several times, then record your progress. Directorial advice is provided above the script with voice-over acting reminders given below it. There is also a reference as to whether the script is for television or radio. Use this information to make stylistic choices. The recording length is furnished to help you develop a sense of timing so practice with a stop watch. Create your own unique interpretations using the techniques learned in chapters 4 and 5.

California Tomatoes
TV/10 seconds
An array of animated cartoon tomatoes dance on top of a dinner table. One tomato is very strong and muscular, another sports a sombrero, and a little cherry tomato wears a diaper. At the end of the spot, on the word "fresh," they jump into a basket and become "real."

Whether your meal calls for a beefsteak tomato, a Mexican-style tomato, or a cherry tomato, make it a tomato grown fresh in California.

Product: fresh, California tomatoes. Additional key words: meal, beefsteak, Mexican-style, and cherry. The voice has to reflect a fun, festive quality. The list of tomatoes should have variety. This can be achieved by physically altering the body to reflect the shape and personality of each type of tomato, or simply by stair stepping (see chapter 3).

Golden Fields Bread
TV/8 seconds
An all-American family sits around the breakfast table as the sun filters through their kitchen window. The mother smiles lovingly at her children as she places the tray of hot, buttered toast on the table. With obvious delight, the family grins contentedly at one another as they eat the delicious bread.

Tomorrow morning, start your day with Golden Fields whole wheat bread. Golden Fields. What mornings should taste like.

Product: Golden Fields. Slogan: What mornings should taste like. Key phrases: tomorrow morning, start your day, and whole wheat bread. They address the questions of when to serve the bread and what type of bread it is.

This commercial typifies the harmonious family that never argues, never spills their milk, and never crams food into their mouths as they rush out the door. The product,

Golden Fields bread, is the reason for their contentedness as they sit around the breakfast table. Therefore, the desired effect on the consumer, should they choose not to purchase this product, is guilt. Don't buy Golden Fields and your life will undoubtedly fall apart. Golden Fields = happiness. Possible intentions are to challenge, impress, convince, or inspire. And, luckily, if the viewer failed to serve Golden Fields this morning, the problem could easily be rectified tomorrow.

Truform Underwire Bras
Radio/5 seconds
This commercial falls under the retail category. It is targeted to a specific buying audience that wants to feel good about its appearance. Every bit of information is important, so word clarity and meaning are of the utmost importance. The muscles around the lips have to work overtime.

> New Truform underwire bras, for the full-figured woman. Available now in fine department stores everywhere.

Product: Truform underwire bras. Key words: new, fine, underwire bras, available. The key word "now" answers the question, "When is the product available?" while "fine" describes the type of department store where the product can be purchased. Incorporation throughout of a proud smile adds additional product focus. And a lilt in the words "full-figured woman" will create a personal tone, making each listener feel the product was intended specifically for her.

Marking the script is particularly helpful in retail ads. Put quotes around the word "new." Words like *new, improved,* and *free* are frequently used to draw attention to a product. As a general rule, always add emphasis and excitement to these words. Also, underline the name of the hero product and stretch it out—in this case, the word "Truform." Put a squiggly line under the product description, "underwire bras." Product clarity is achieved here through a change in inflection. Place two arrowed lines under the last sentence. The first should arch upward to the word "now." The second should begin at "fine," descending to the final word "everywhere." Musically, the voice rises and falls in the direction of the arrows. The final sentence should be read faster than the first, which contains the major copy information, because, presumably, this will maintain focus on the key descriptive sentence.

Kitty Menu Cat Food
TV/10 seconds
In this commercial, a beautiful, long-haired, white cat with a diamond collar stands beside her 14-karat gold food bowl. The cat is finicky about her food, until a can of Kitty Menu is opened. Satisfied, the cat eats all the Kitty Menu and contentedly licks her lips.

> Kitty Menu cat food comes in four delicious flavors—chunky chicken, tuna supreme, liver pâté, and turkey tetrazzini. Kitty Menu, for your gourmet cat.

Product: Kitty Menu. Slogan: for your gourmet cat. Key words or phrases: cat food, four delicious flavors, chunky chicken, tuna supreme, liver pâté, and turkey tetrazzini. This spot caters to cat owners who are willing to spend a little more money to feed their precious animal. The voice should reflect an aura of elegance. Vocally, a low, sultry sound is more desirable than a high, quirky one. A low voice accentuates the gourmet appeal.

Jumbo Deluxe Van

Radio/8 seconds
This tag ends a humorous radio commercial that features a husband and wife loading an endless supply of camping equipment into their Jumbo Deluxe Van. At the end of the spot, they search for their son who is found playing happily underneath the debris.

> The Jumbo Deluxe Van. EPA estimated mileage 17 city, 21 highway. Mileage may vary according to road conditions and driving habits.

Since the product name includes three words, use the first two words to describe the type of van being advertised. You can do this by stretching out and billboarding (emphasizing) "Jumbo Deluxe," then dropping the pitch slightly on "van." This technique helps the listener remember the brand name. The next two lines are the disclaimer. Legally, this information must be included in the commercial. Both sentences in the disclaimer should be read progressively quicker than the first sentence, which states the name of the hero product. In musical terms, the first sentence is like whole notes, the second is like quarter notes, and the last is like sixteenth notes. Draw an angled, arrowed line under the second sentence. Have it peak at the word "city" and descend on the number "21." The pitch of the voice should follow the rise and fall of these arrow cues. Make sure the mileage amounts stand out clearly—put a dot under the numbers if this helps you to remember.

Pay careful attention to the periods and commas. Pencil in two slashes after the word "van," denoting a strong pause, and punctuate the product name so it stands out clearly and distinctly from the rest of the copy. (In voice-overs, remember that pauses are measured in *milliseconds*.) Add one slash after the word, "highway," so that you will remember to make an attitude transition. Then, enclose the final sentence in parentheses. Using parentheses is a notice to drop the pitch of the voice and speak much quicker. Even though this information is necessary, the advertiser doesn't want the listener to dwell on driving variables.

News Center News Magazine

TV/10 seconds and 5 seconds
This is a television promo designed to boost viewership during the crucial Arbitron and Nielson rating sweeps periods. It is a time sensitive topic, requiring a vocal style that commands attention, peaks curiosity, and ultimately delivers audience. There are four variations: each spot should be recorded twice, once using the word "tonight" and again substituting the parenthetical word "tomorrow."

> Do ghosts exist? We'll talk to people who claim they have ghosts living in their homes. Is it a hoax or is it real? Find out tonight (tomorrow) on News Center 13, at 11:00.

> Meet a family with ghosts, tonight (tomorrow) on News Center 13, at 11:00.

Product: News Center 13. Key Words: tonight (tomorrow), at 11:00. The set-up is used to perk the listener's curiosity. Put a slash before the word "find." Make sure there is a definitive transition between the topic/problem and the program/solution. The key words delineate date and time.

Again, promos are time sensitive. The listener must tune in to a particular time slot or that time is lost forever. Here, perhaps more than any other type of commercial, the use of *intentions* is crucial, and there are several choices from which to choose: to tease, to intrigue, to mystify, to impress, to provoke, and to titillate. All enhance the material. Explore how the body and voice change with each intention.

Reliable Bank
Radio/5 seconds
This spot requires a firm, intelligent voice of authority. There also needs to be an element of warmth in the delivery.

> Reliable Bank. For all your banking needs. Member FDIC.

Product: Reliable Bank. Slogan: for all your banking needs. Key words: all, banking needs. The key words should stand out. Put a squiggly line under the word "all" and a dot under the words "banking needs." In some instances the director may choose to stress the word "your." That is an optional interpretation based on the other parts of the copy.

Financial institutions rarely display humor in their advertisements. Money is considered far too serious a matter to be taken lightly. Deep male voices that lend an air of security are the typical choice in bank spots (although some banks are beginning to give women an opportunity). The intention in this commercial is to cajole the listener into believing that the hero product, Reliable Bank, is far superior to its competitors, and the very name of the bank connotes this vocal need for reliability. Confidence and satisfaction should filter into the voice as these words are spoken. The final sentence is a quick legal disclaimer. Place parentheses around the words "member FDIC" and *throw it away.* Place no additional importance or inflection on this phrase.

Creekside Vino
Radio/60 seconds; Donut/8 seconds; Tag/4 seconds
This spot includes a donut and a tag. Romantic music plays in the background as the scene is established.

> **Man:** At last, a night without the kids.
> **Woman:** The baby-sitter!
> **Man:** She has all the numbers, and I alerted the fire department like you told me.
> **Woman:** Jamie's diaper! Let's go home.
> **Man:** Relax, I changed her diaper before I put her to bed.
> **Woman:** Tommy's homework!
> **Man:** I gave the sitter explicit instructions.
> **Waiter:** Can I bring you something to drink?
> **Man:** A bottle of Creekside Vino, please.
> **Waiter:** Excellent choice. I'll be right back with your Creekside Vino.
> **Woman:** We're staying?
> **Man:** You deserve some time off. The kids will be fine. Besides, I just ordered Creekside Vino.

Woman: That's quite a treat. I feel like an adult again. Listen to me, I'm speaking in sentences longer than three words!

Man: That calls for a celebration!

DONUT: Creekside Vino is a delicious, sparkling wine suitable for any occasion. Even if you're just celebrating a night out without the kids.

Man: Cheers!

Woman: I love you . . . and this Creekside Vino is delicious.

Man: We should go out more often.

Woman: I'll reserve the baby-sitter.

TAG: Make every occasion a special one with Creekside Vino.

Product. Creekside Vino. Key words or phrases: sparkling wine, delicious. Put a squiggly line under the word "delicious" for emphasis. Shrug your shoulders and toss away the expression "for any occasion." This gives the product a practical, matter-of-fact quality, suggesting that the wine can be consumed on any occasion. In the tag line, make sure the words "every" and "special" stand out. End the spot with the reassurance that Creekside Vino is the best by either shrugging the shoulders and giving the product a clear, "we're-the-best" feel or, more effectively, letting the breath relax and the voice deepen.

The announcer donut acts as a scene changer. It interrupts the action to advertise the product. When the scene resumes, time has elapsed. For this style of writing to work, it is important for the announcer to match the emotional intensity of the scene. In this case, the donut section follows the man's jubilant intent—to celebrate—and the announcer should build on this excitement. The second sentence in the donut refers to the parental discussion about breaking away from home and the kids. This kind of remark is an aside, and no pertinent copy information is given. Instead, there is a feeling that the announcer relates to the couple's dilemma. It also indicates a bit of humor in the situation. The tag line reflects the couple's romantic tendencies. Consequently, the tag should demonstrate an alluring quality. The intention would be to charm.

Commonly, in commercials such as this, the scene and announcer sections are recorded separately. Each section has an estimated time allotment. In this case, the opening section until the donut is approximately 38 seconds; the donut times out to eight seconds; the closing scene is eight seconds; and, the tag is four seconds. This totals 58 seconds, which allows two seconds for sound effect ambiance and scene change cuts between the couple's dialogue and the announcer. Whoever records their section last may have to adjust to time shortages or overages.

You may want to use this commercial to practice reading interactive dialogue with a friend. Remember to keep the conversation light, and devoid of any overt whining. Also, try to overlap the ends of lines or begin speaking immediately following the other person's line. This adds a bit more realism to the scene and keeps the action flowing. Lengthy pauses of dead air between actors kill the spontaneity and interaction.

Minitoys

TV/10 seconds

This tag is a sponsorship. Aired on a noncommercial station, it concludes an educational television program. The voice needs to be warm, friendly, and brimming with company pride.

This program was brought to you by the makers of Minitoys. Minitoys, a globally responsible company that has united environmentally conscious children in laughter for the past 25 years.

Product or sponsor: Minitoys. Key phrases: this program, brought to you by, makers of, globally responsible company, united environmentally conscious children in laughter, and last 25 years. Due to the efficiency of words, two possible intentions are "to charm" and "to impress." Since the sponsor's name is spoken twice, one time right after another, it is crucial that the second "Minitoys" sound different than the first.

Since the sponsor is only mentioned at the conclusion of the program, clear and crisp enunciation is essential. For some, the word combinations may pose a tongue twisting problem. If so, take a deep breath and relax as you let the air escape. Use this as a grounding process before beginning. Notice that there are a lot of words to fit into ten seconds. Never should the spot sound rushed. Stumbling on words is a signal that the phrases are not properly delineated and that the breath is not settled completely in the body. The sentences can be broken up a number of ways. Take full advantage of the musical scale by adding high and low notes as a means of accentuating the key points.

Explosion City
TV/5 seconds
This tag line is for a new action movie. It requires a tough, earthy, guttural vocal approach.

Explosion City!! Coming this Friday to a theater near you.

This tag line is part of a movie trailer. Best clips from the film are edited together in a manner designed to peak audience interest and convince them to pull out their wallets and plop down hard-earned cash at the box office in aroused expectation.

Take time to say the name of the movie. Keep in mind that it is a tough action flick. Draw two slashes after the client name as a reminder to make a transition into the *when and where* sentence: "Coming this Friday to a theater near you." The second sentence should read quicker than the first, in hopes that the listeners will retain the movie name. Intention choices could be to impress, to excite, or to command.

Chapter 7

Announcer

Announcer copy is the most traditional style of commercial. There is no clever dialogue to fool listeners into believing they are overhearing a real, slice-of-life conversation. Nor is there the feeling that the person speaking is associated in any way with the company. Rather, an understanding is established between the audience and the announcer, clearly delineating their roles: the announcer is hired, without pretense, to sell the product; the listener is there to accept the information as a potential consumer. No attempt is made to create a special bond between announcer and listener. Instead, all pertinent information is spelled out directly, efficiently, and candidly by the announcer voice from "nowhere."

As a genre, announcer copy can be quite creative. However, it is typically associated with commercials that feature an item and its price. Radio disc jockeys are often heard reading such announcer-style ads. Presumably, radio personalities have a built-in following that sells product. It is also assumed that, since they use their voices every day, they can bring ad copy in on time. Therefore, many advertisers with small- to medium-size budgets save time and money by having radio DJs at the various stations read their copy live over the air. They can also prerecord it using a station's recording facilities and staff announcers. The procedure minimizes or eliminates expensive production and talent costs. While radio announcers appear to be likely candidates for freelance commercial voice work, the crossover is not always easy. The very style of announcing that proves successful during on-air programming and station-made ads, is not desirable in freelance voice work. There, the focus is on higher production standards, acting ability, vocal variations, versatility, and being able to deliver a wide range of delivery styles rather than on the station-specific familiarity between DJ and listener.

Announcers are plentiful, not just within the radio business, but throughout the whole voice-over field. This delivery style is considered the easiest to achieve because personal exploration and emotional disclosure are at a minimum. Instead, the dominating factor is delivery style. There are *hard-sell announcers* who relentlessly bark copy information, *soft-sell announcers* who add subtlety and grace to the words, *youthful announcers* who lend effervescence to the product, and *zany announcers* who pump energy and humor into the copy. These stylistic differences open the door to freelance announcer work for voice-over talents from other areas, and so radio announcers who are accustomed to reading a lot of copy on the air "hit a wall," meaning freelance voice actors are hired over radio announcers because of their ability to bring written words to life. They add nuances and a psychological selling impact that radio announcers may not be able to achieve. The words become the stars rather than the voice being the main area of focus. When advertising agencies call for dialogue subtleties from an actor, and high production standards from a recording studio, money no longer is an issue, so the need to use radio announcers is substantially decreased.

Announcer commercials can be very lucrative, because, once a client chooses an announcer for a product, repeat business generally ensues. And, unlike talent in on-camera commercials, unseen voice-over actors can record commercials for competitive companies provided the same, recognizable voice is not used or an exclusive contract has not been signed by the actor, prohibiting the recording of ads for similar products or companies.

ANNOUNCER COPY

Announcer copy is usually unmistakable. There are no personal pronouns like *I, me, we,* or *us* that would allude to closeness and familiarity with the company. There is no sense that the speaker will be there at the store waiting on customers as they enter or that the listener even expects this preferential treatment. Instead, the overwhelming feeling is that the voice is a slightly detached third party who is probably just what he or she appears to be—an announcer paid to say the words. Excitement and interest are not minimized, but there is a sense that the announcer doesn't know any more about the inner workings of the business or product than what is written in the script. A microphone is not treated as an ear, but is placed in front of the announcer's mouth for the sole purpose of recording scripted material.

Keeping up with announcer trends is an important element of voice-over tracking. The tone of announcer voices changes according to the country's political, economic, and military situation. For example, the deep, booming, male announcer voices, which were not in vogue in the 1980s, returned briefly during the Persian Gulf War. In a time of crisis, advertisers pitching product must appear sympathetic to the present situation or be lambasted for their blatant disregard for life and country. Goofy, satirical voices that were successful prior to a crisis would seem out of place and insensitive. Any flamboyant commercial advertising should be mindful of the darkened state of affairs.

If you are not already doing so, pay attention to the various styles of both radio and television announcers. Note when a male voice is used as opposed to a female one. As of this writing, male voices are utilized more often for products and services involving financial institutions or items carrying a high price tag, such as luxury cars. As mentioned previously, women's voices seldom pitch banks and brokerage firms, and are just now starting to creep into economy and family-oriented car commercials. Sporting events, believed by advertisers to be a male-oriented affairs, are dominated by male announcers. Cleaning and baby supplies are the dominion of the female announcer, with a few male voices representing the occasional househusband. In general, stereotyping male and female roles is the norm in advertising. Also note that advertising trends tend to lag behind real life trends by several years. So, as you see the world changing around you, realize that you may have to wait awhile before it is reflected in the commercials you voice.

As you rehearse the announcer commercials in this chapter, keep the targeted customer and the product price tag in mind. Voices selling upscale products are usually slower and more luxurious-sounding than those pushing inexpensive items. Urgency is a factor on time-limited items, and food commercials should make your mouth water. Pretend you are the advertiser and decide whether the commercial works most effectively with a male or female voice. Base this information on the copy and the current market trends.

Goldwater's

Radio/30 seconds

This is a retail spot for a moderately upscale department store. The announcer should have a strong smile in the voice and a feeling of excitement rooted in the stomach area. Do not blast or punch the words. Doing so cheapens the store's reputation and appeal in the moderate-to-upscale market. Make sure all the words are clear and well enunciated.

> This weekend Goldwater's is having a Midnight Warehouse Sale to make room for fall. Choose from furniture and accents, carpets and rugs, bed and bath linens, and VCR and stereo equipment. All at prices reduced as much as 50%. Plus, with the Goldwater's Midnight Warehouse coupon from this Friday's newspaper, you'll receive an additional 10% savings. Goldwater's is open 'til midnight this Friday, Saturday, and Sunday. The Midnight Warehouse Sale at Goldwater's, 24th and Auburn Street in Camden.

Retail ads punctuate the *who, what, why, when,* and *where* facts. Stressing the copy points so they stand out clearly and distinctly from one another is one reason your mouth must move more efficiently and definitively. The first sentence contains four of the crucial pieces of information within the five *W*'s category. By placing the most important elements first, the copywriter and voice talent work together to inform their listeners. When: this weekend. Who: Goldwater's. What: having a Midnight Warehouse Sale. Why: a special sale to make room for fall merchandise. Where: Goldwater's at 24th and Auburn Street in Camden. Instantly, the listeners understand the sale and are unconsciously given the option to continue listening or tune out. No elaborate story is needed to lure clients to the store. Instead, the information is given forthrightly.

Immediately following the set-up sentence is a list of sale items used to show product diversity. Here the items are grouped in pairs, a writing technique that shows further variety within the store's departments. When reading a group of two items, experiment with hand movements; moving your hands from right to left and vice versa lends effortless movement to your voice and suggests a huge product range stretching from "here to there" and from "this to that." In addition to the lateral vocal movement between each two items, there needs to be vertical vocal movement between the four pairs. Vocal variety highlights merchandise variety. And remember, lists should be read more quickly than other parts of the copy. After all, the mind doesn't need much time to decipher the meaning "carpet" or "VCR."

When you reach the third sentence, you will need to change the tempo again. The spot opened with a slow, "milked" attention-getter followed by a quickly read list. Now, the spot needs to slow down again to draw focus to the price reductions. Stretch out the words "50 percent."

"Additional 10% savings" is the alerting factor written into sentence four. All words in this sentence should entice the buyer to save additional money by bringing in a coupon. Emphasizing the word "plus," awakens the audience to the possibility of the added savings, while the words "bring in," "coupon," and "Friday's newspaper" tell the audience *how* to receive them.

The repetition of some of the copy points, in sentence five, ensures that no information is missed (the actual days "Friday, Saturday, and Sunday" are spoken just in case someone does not know what constitutes a weekend) and then the final sentence is grandiose. It is the last time the type of sale and the name of the store are repeated. These elements should stand out and linger in the minds of the listener. The address at the end of the sentence should be thrown away. Read it faster than the first part of the sentence so as not to distract from the client, Goldwater's.

As you can see, retail spots are relentless. There is no down time. Energy needs to surge out of your fingertips and down through your toes. It may help to keep your hands close to your face and emphasize with your fingers. This adds clarity to the read by stretching out important words, giving more punch to key copy points, and cleaning up any slurring and diction problems that may arise. Really use the muscles surrounding your lips. Your mouth should feel a bit fatigued after an hour of recording retail material.

Heartbeat Way
TV/10 seconds
This is a public service announcement. Photos of people in dire need are flashed on the screen. The message strongly, yet sensitively, suggests that people support a worthy cause by making a donation to this tax deductible charity. Soft compassion should be vocally expressed.

A gift to Heartbeat Way can make a difference. Why not touch the lives of people around you? Give part of yourself. Give the Heartbeat Way.

Spots like this are based on guilt. Its effectiveness stems from the compelling need people have to donate money, feel good about themselves and their actions, and avoid guilt pangs. For this to work, the talent must be completely relaxed and self-assured. The voice should be low, resonant, and caring. A strong personalization should be used to open up the heart and expose the actor's need for help, love, nurturing, acknowledgment, and compassion. Take your time saying the words. Add as much texture and subtlety as you can muster to really connect with your listener.

The opening sentence confirms that individuals can make a difference in the world. Next, it suggests that the listener take some sort of action. Finally, the ease of giving is expressed. Closing the spot is the desired action, showing how a person can give of themselves and get some emotional good in return.

Wonder Insurance
Radio/30 seconds
This commercial should be delivered in a tongue-in-cheek manner. Be careful not to mock the client while striving for that glimmer of humor, and take full advantage of your pearly-white smile while reading the body of the spot.

You insure your car, your house, your life, and your health. But do you have smile insurance? Your teeth will last a lifetime with good habits and regular dental care. Smile Insurance, from Wonder Insurance, helps you maintain that gleam. That's because Wonder Insurance takes the pain out of seeing the dentist with low monthly premiums. This keeps Wonder Insurance clients smiling! So stop putting off that visit to the dentist. Protect those pearly whites. Get smile insurance. It's something new from your friends at Wonder Insurance.

Consumer fear is the tactic used in this commercial. You take care of the other parts of your body and your environment; shouldn't you take care of your teeth? It exposes a weakness in the listener's insurance habits, which can be protected by extending the insurance policy.

Use the list to set up the lack of smile insurance. Confirm the belief that everyone needs to take care of their teeth in the second sentence. The transition into the body of the commercial begins on the third sentence. It is at this point that a smile should begin to form and become readily apparent on the word "gleam." Have a twinkle in your eye when you say, "This keeps Wonder Insurance clients smiling!" The resolve begins immediately following that line. Use the following three sentences, starting at the word "stop," to build momentum for the client. Play with the final line. Make sure the audience understands that the policy is new and that the people behind the insurance are their friends.

Sofa Connection
Radio/60 seconds

This spot requires an energetic and excited "in-your-face" announcer style. Be careful that it does not become obnoxious or irritating. It should sound fun and easy. Make sure the energy level stays consistent throughout the spot and does not start to fade after 20 or 30 seconds.

This could be your big chance to win! So, listen carefully. First, hurry down to Sofa Connection and try out their huge assortment of love seats, sectionals, futons, and sofa beds. From traditional to modern, contemporary to classic, and fluffy to firm, Sofa Connection is sure to have a sofa that's right for you. Then, enter the Sofa Connection Big-Seat Sweepstakes. If your name is selected at the Big-Seat drawing on June 1st, you'll receive a 26-inch color television! That's right, a new color TV to watch while you're sitting on a comfortable, new sofa from Sofa Connection. All you have to do is fill out the sweepstakes form when you come to any Sofa Connection. And you don't have to be present to win. But time is running out. Don't delay. Stop by Sofa Connection today and enter the Big-Seat Sweepstakes. After all, doesn't your seat deserve a little extra padding?

Understanding the construction of this spot will help to build intensity and interest in a long reading. The first two sentences are set-ups used to grab the listener's attention. After the initial excitement of the first sentence, drop the pitch since no important copy points are mentioned in the second sentence. Dropping the vocal pitch also sets up the listener's job—to go to Sofa Connection.

The body of the spot contains a list. From a conceptual standpoint, the commercial is designed to boost foot traffic within the store, sell furniture, and build a mailing list.

In exchange, the customer is tempted with the chance of winning a color television set. Note that there are several sentences in between the major list items that can throw off the commercial "through line." In fact, there is a series of two additional lists between the first instruction—"hurry down"—and the second—"then, enter." Use vocal variety to punctuate the store's large selection. The listener hook occurs right after the second instruction. It is the payoff for shopping at Sofa Connection and the reason why people will continue listening to the commercial. As you work through the spot, increase your intensity and vocally ascend a note for each list item. Make "you don't have to be present to win" sound easy by shrugging your shoulders and lifting your hands. Smile on "friendly sales people."

The resolve is filled with urgency since this is a time-limited opportunity. The urgency factor helps steadily drive the intensity forward through the end of the spot. It is not until the final line that the actor has time to relax. Use this time to play and tease the audience. After all, sweepstakes should be fun!

Fly High Airlines
Radio/30 seconds
This spot calls for a slick, smooth, soothing mid- to low-range voice.

> Fly High Airlines now has low fares to Mexico. You can visit Los Cabos, Guadalajara, Puerto Vallarta, and Mazatlán. And, Fly High Airlines has complete vacation packages that are affordable, too. Reservations are easy. Just pick up the phone and call 1-800-FLY-HIGH. That's 1-800-F-L-Y-H-I-G-H. Shouldn't your next vacation be to Mexico? Call Fly High Airlines today, and fly high with us.

Since the spot is selling relaxation, the voice needs to reflect a sense of ease and anticipated pleasure. Each city should have a different spoken feel whether it be exotic, luxurious, exciting, or peaceful. Take advantage of the word "and" to set up Fly High's vacation packages as even better than their airplane flights. Add action to the voice to reflect how easy it is to pick up the phone. Gesturing with the hands toward yourself adds an invitation and simplicity to the words. Group "1" and "800" together to create "one eight hundred." Add a beat before saying the remainder of the phone number. Spell out F-L-Y-H-I-G-H when the number is repeated. The dashes between the letters are a signal for the actor to say the individual letters rather than the actual words. Plant the seeds of adventure as you tell the listener how to spend her next vacation. The final sentence should inspire action (call today), and you end with the slogan "Fly high with us."

Sparkle Ease
TV/30 seconds
Visually, this commercial parodies a happily married couple who spend their quality time bending over a smelly toilet bowl, trying to get it sparkling clean. There is a light, whimsical air to this poetic commercial. A good sense of rhyme and rhythm is required.

> This is the story of John and Sue.
> They had a toilet that always smelled P-U.
> They'd scrub all day with cheap detergent,
> But nothing worked. Even though the need was urgent.

Then one day they discovered Sparkle Ease.
They poured it in, and sure as you please . . .
The smell went away.
For them, it was a red-letter day.
And that is the story of John and Sue,
An ordinary couple from Yippididoo
Who discovered the joy of Sparkle Ease
And lived happily ever after, no longer on bended knees.

For both the story and the rhyme to work clearly, you should emphasize a few key words; in order, they are: story, John, Sue, toilet, P-U, scrub, cheap detergent, nothing worked, urgent, Sparkle Ease, poured it in, please, smell, away, red-letter day, that, Sue, ordinary couple, Yippididoo, discovered, Sparkle Ease, happily ever after, no longer, bended knees.

Also it is important to note the three sections of the story: the problem, the discovery of the miracle product, and the happy resolve. The "discovery" section (lines five through eight) encompasses the body of the poem. Read each of these lines a bit slower than the preceding one. Allow a beat or two before beginning the resolve, and then quicken the pace up until the end. This resolves the odoriferous dilemma of John and Sue who . . . thanks to you . . . no longer go hoo-hoo. So what if it's corny . . . it's bound to be true.

Steak Wagon
Radio/30 seconds
The read, coupled with the sound effects of steaks grilling and people eating, should make the listener's mouth water. There is a ruggedness associated with the restaurant that should also be reflected in the voice. A Texas twang is optional; read the spot both with and without it. Disregard the numbers. They will be used afterward to reference notes pertaining to the interpretation of the copy.

> (1) How do you like your steaks? (2) Red and juicy on the inside, or dark and crispy on the outside? (3) Some restaurants have a hard time delivering what you really want. (4) Fortunately, the chefs at the Steak Wagon understand how to cook steaks. (5) First, they hand select the best cuts of beef. (6) Then, they marinate them overnight in their special sauce. (7) Finally, they cook them right at your table. (8) Just say, "when," and the steaks are taken off the grill and placed in front of you, sizzling hot. (9) Steak Wagon steaks are always thick and delicious. (10) That's what brings the customers back for more! (11) Enjoy a steak cooked your way, at the Steak Wagon.

I'm going to use this script to illustrate transitional beat changes. To prevent listeners from becoming bored and disinterested, intentions need to change every five or 10 seconds. Whenever a spot becomes stagnant and predictable, people naturally stop paying attention, and in advertising there is too much money on the line for this to happen. Variety adds interest and intrigue to a read. Take time now to mark your script. Remember that a slash indicates intention changes. Next to each section, write down your choice of intention prior to your read. (Refer back to chapter 5 if necessary.)

After reading this section, double check your work to see if your choices were valid. Often, people associate different words for the same intention. Keep in mind that there are many ways to read a commercial so your choices may be different from the following example.

1. The first two sentences inquire.
2. Sentence three stands alone. It provokes the listener into remembering a bad dining experience.
3. "Fortunately," the fourth sentence comforts the potential diner.
4. Cooking instructions, which are described in sentences five, six, seven, and eight, are used progressively to dazzle, please, and impress.
5. The ninth and tenth sentences are used to entice.
6. Finally, sentence 11 urges the listener to experience the ultimate steak dining pleasure.

In addition to these intention changes, the spot should also sound tasty. Imbue key food words with delicious, yummy feelings or sounds. Remember, you want to make the listener hungry and start drooling. Of course, due to the tightness of the spot length, you'll have to refrain from luxurious multi-second word "milkings." Here's a list of mouthwatering key words: steak, red, juicy, dark, crispy, best cuts of beef, marinate, special sauce, sizzling hot, thick, delicious, enjoy. Adding vocal action to phrases like "cook them right at your table," "taken off the grill," and "placed in front of you" contributes immensely to drawing a more complete, tantalizing auditory picture.

What should you do if you hate steak or are a vegetarian? You can always refuse the gig. Otherwise, you can use a substitution. If chocolate makes you slobber lustfully, think "chocolate" and "sweet, delicious, gooey goodness" every time you say "steak" and the other key words. File through your sense memory to find your most favorite food item. The love of food has to shine through on these types of spots. We've all driven out of our way to grab a burger or burrito after hearing a fast-food restaurant spot. Listen closely to food advertisements on the radio and TV, and judge their success by how they affect your hunger or eating habits.

Baloney's Banquet
TV/30 seconds
Hey dudes and dudettes, this crazy spot is for an interactive CD-ROM game. It requires a big and exciting read. Experiment with outrageous animated cartoon voices. Teenage boys are the target audience. Remember, there is no such thing as "too big!"

> Jumpin' Jack! Highway Baloney is back . . . bigger and better than ever. Now he's in Baloney's Banquet! The ultimate food fight of the century. Smashing things hasn't been this much fun since Highway Baloney ran over furry animals in Baloney's Road Kill. (SFX: *squish*) Duck flying tomatoes. (SFX: *splat*) Avoid pies in the face. (SFX: *plop*) And watch out for the killer garbage disposal. (SFX: *grinding noise*) Highway Baloney is at it again in Baloney's Banquet from Zippo! (SFX: *Zippo*, echoes four times) Simply outrageous!!

The best way to work on a spot like this is to read it out loud at least five distinctly different ways. This will free your mind from thinking you have only one vocal choice.

Try being a super hero, weight lifter, bug on a wall, exceedingly excellent dude, or squished mutant animal. Make up your own characters. Refrain from judging your voice or putting any restrictions on it. Instead, play, have fun, and push the limits. Stretch out words, twirl them around in your mouth, explore strange vowel sounds and combinations. Make your own sound effects if it helps open up that playful part of yourself. Or, pause, without losing energy, for one or two seconds at each sound effect notation. Finally, read the spot again, blending the best parts of all the reads into one. Your growth from take one to take six should be truly . . . outrageous!

Precious Darling

TV/30 seconds

Spots like this air in the middle of Saturday-morning kiddie cartoons and on other cartoon-oriented networks and time periods. The voice should be very animated, cute, and smiley. The targeted audience is three- to seven-year-old girls. Don't hold back. At the completion of the spot, ultimate success will have been achieved if you feel bright and cheerful. Think *cute* and *adorable!* Remember that this is a television commercial and that you can take your time. The visual features a charming five-year-old girl hugging and playing with the product.

> Who's the cutest girl in town? It's Precious Darling, that's who. She's adorable. She's huggable. And she's so real, you won't want to put her down. Pull her string and she talks. (Cut to doll saying, "I love you.") Pat her back and she burps. (Girl burps doll.) Put her on her knees and she crawls. (Doll crawls then girl picks her up and hugs her saying, "Precious Darling, I love you.") Precious Darling, by Semko. Batteries not included.

This spot may be a stretch for you if you haven't explored the sweeter ranges of your voice. Spend some time watching children's programs, and you'll soon learn that there is no limit to how precious the advertiser expects a voice talent to sound just to pitch a child's toy. Set up the situation, announce the arrival of the doll, and describe her multifaceted abilities. This should emphatically remind young viewers which doll they should ask their parents or grandparents to buy. Make "by Semko" sound like "of course, we're the best, you can trust us." Throw away the battery disclaimer by reading it quickly and without emotion. For fun pretend you are the doll *and* the little girl. See what new voices you can create!

Skizzer

TV/60 seconds

Little did we know years ago that this type of ad would eventually transmogrify into the modern-day infomercial. Yes, this amazing product slices, dices, and even does your laundry! The voice is actually a parody of an announcer.

> It's the amazing Skizzer from Cutterby. Tired of scissors that don't cut? Fed up with dull, chipped blades? Don't get upset. Now there's the amazing Skizzer! It's the only kitchen scissors that never requires sharpening. At long last, a scissors that works time and time again, and never gets dull. Don't believe it? Watch how easy Skizzer is to use. It effortlessly cuts through chicken bones! Smoothly slices this metal coat hanger in two. Crisply chops this piece of celery. Ordinary scissors

would dull and chip, but not Skizzer. It even passes the amazing paper-cutting test. Yes! Skizzer works every time. No kitchen should be without one. Avoid the headaches, throw out those old scissors, and get Skizzer! To order your amazing Skizzer, call 1-800-S-K-I-Z-Z-E-R. Don't delay, call 1-800-SKIZZER today! Operators are standing by. And if you order now, you can receive a free origami kit.

As you undoubtedly surmised, the primary intention in this spot is to amaze. Unless your head has been buried in the sand for the last 30 years or you're a mere tyke in diapers, you should be able to figure out how to read this spot. If not, turn on the television and you'll soon hear a similar type of commercial. It shouts! It astounds! And most of all, it builds, builds, builds, builds! Need I say more?

Chapter 8

Spokesperson

A spokesperson is someone who is hired on a repeat or contractual basis to represent a product or company. Celebrities and sports figures are often hired for this purpose. Their image or sound is used in the hopes of generating increased sales and greater product recognition. Sophistication, humor, sex appeal, intelligence, stupidity, and agility are just a few qualities that influence image choices. Associating this person and their style, grace, or wit with the company and the product is considered an advertising coup. Their personality or famous attribute can either mirror the company image or be in direct opposition to it. Casting someone 180 degrees against type is useful in humorous spots because it further highlights the contradiction.

Of course, famous people are not the only spokespeople on television and radio. In fact, many successful "no-name" spokespeople remark that their association with a product is so strong that people often stop them on the street to inquire what's on sale this week! They project such personal appeal that, when coupled with a genuine sense of understanding and caring, people can't help but trust them.

SPOKESPERSON SPOTS

Scripts are rarely marked as *announcer, spokesperson,* or *real person.* Instead, it is the talent's job to glean this information from the script and choose the proper vocal and stylistic approach. Spokesperson spots are fairly easy to recognize. More often than not, they contain possessive clues like "us" and "our," and the pronoun "we," which insinuate that the voice talent is part of the company. This writing style is used to create a familiarity and close personal relationship between the audience and the speaker. "We" wouldn't tell you anything untrue. Join "us" this weekend for uproarious fun. "Our" store policy is to treat the customer with courtesy and respect.

There are three levels of expertise in spokesperson scripts: customer, employee, and owner. Understanding the spokesperson's perspective adds natural, authentic layering to the role. How you approach the script and relate to the audience is directly attributed to your position with, or relationship to, the company. It means that you either treat the audience as an equal, approach them from a slightly elevated "helper" level, or talk down to them, offering guidance from a highly informed authoritative position.

Customer is the first level. This role treats the audience as an equal. The only difference is that the spokesperson is a more careful shopper. She knows so much about the store that she feels compelled to relay this firsthand shopping information to the listener. It is a consumer-to-consumer approach, implying, "Take it from me, your friend. I've shopped around and found that this is the best product on the market."

The spokesperson-customer's enthusiasm and belief in the company is shared respectfully with the audience-customer through personable one-on-one charm.

The second level of expertise is *employee*. Here, helping the customer is the primary focus. Employee spokespeople take personal pride in their job. They admire the company and feel honored to sell such wonderful products. Employees care deeply about their customers and want to help them. The underlying message is, "You came to the right place. Our company and product are the best. Relax, we'll help you every step of the way. You won't be disappointed." The employee spokesperson's character has just enough experience to reassure the listener he is making a wise decision.

Ownership is the third level of expertise. The spokesperson relates to the listener from an administrative, upper management position. The voice looms over the audience as the undisputed authority. It is a little more formal. "Trust us," it beckons, "We've worked hard to create the best, most reliable, and enjoyable product or service on the market. Everyone knows that we're the greatest." Ever-present is the feeling that the owner stamps his personal seal of approval on every product and ensures that all employees cater to the customers.

Again it is time to practice these personas. Try and infuse your own personality and style into the spots. Be warm and compassionate toward your imaginary listener as you lend an air of trust, assurance, and customer satisfaction. Use the levels to create three distinctly different reads. Basic interpretation will remain the same, but the manner in which you relate to the product will change. Record your work and listen for these differences in attitude. Experiment, playing the consumer voice close to the mic to lend an intimate, "just between us" feel to the words. As the employee, envision yourself on location. Imagine relating to the customer, leaning over the counter to point out the important areas of the store or demonstrate how a product works, for example. Remember, you genuinely care about your customer. When relating to customers from an owner perspective, wear an imaginary business suit. Put your customers' minds at ease. Assure them that you have taken care of everything.

Spokesperson spots are one notch up the voice-acting scale from announcer spots. Don't get locked into metered, announcer-y reads. Stretch out words. Linger on key words. Hesitate briefly at appropriate places to lend reflective moments. Show your vocal and acting agility.

Peruvian Blend
TV/27 seconds

This is a food product. Use your five senses to make it tantalizingly rich and delicious. See the cup of coffee. Feel how the cup warms your hands. Open up your olfactory glands to the captivating smell. Imagine how it tastes. Hear the coffee perking. Imagine that you are dressed in flowing white fabric. Your skin is pristine. You have perfectly coiffured hair (even though you just woke up and stumbled out of bed for that first cup of heaven). You're out on your balcony overlooking the ocean. From consumer-to-consumer, relate the glorious benefits of Peruvian Blend.

There's something captivating about the smell of rich, hot coffee brewing. And there's something extra special when that coffee is Peruvian Blend. As Peruvian

Blend perks, its aroma is simply . . . distracting. Peruvian Blend. Coffee that tastes as rich as it smells.

Before you say a word of copy, take a deep breath in through your nose as if you are smelling the coffee, and let it out in a pleasing sigh. Starting the commercial this way invites the audience to relax and experience the aroma with you. Don't leave a space between the sigh and the first word. The gap sounds fake and contrived. Instead, sigh and begin speaking on the sigh as it starts to trail off. Emphasize the key words: captivating; smell; and rich, hot coffee. Associate the smell with a wonderful memory. If done effectively, that nostalgic recollection should make the listener suddenly crave coffee.

The second sentence should build on the first. If the energy drops, your listener will subconsciously feel the product is subpar. Peruvian Blend has to sound "extra special." Make the listener believe that this blend of coffee is your own special secret, and your personal choice for special occasions.

Again, taste the product and take your time as you say the brand name in the third sentence. Think of the word "distracting." It is an odd word choice and can easily be mistaken as a negative, but here it should bring a satisfied smile to your face. The coffee poses a delightfully decadent dilemma: should you go to work or stay home and drink another cup?

Reflect on the final mention of the product. Say "Peruvian Blend" slowly. At the moment you say it, decide to scrap going to work and call in sick. While delivering the slogan, tell the audience that the coffee is too sinfully delicious to leave behind. They should try it and find out why. If you breathe in while saying "coffee that tastes" and breathe out on "as rich as it smells," you give the illusion of sipping coffee and getting instant gratification.

Be careful not to push or punch the words in this commercial. Let them flow effortlessly. This is a seductively relaxing moment. Play it close to the microphone for a more intimate sound.

A final note: one of the ironic things about coffee commercials is that they almost never sell that craved "caffeine jolt." (Isn't that the real reason why people inject coffee into their bloodstream first thing in the morning?) Rarely do you see a person getting "wired" in a coffee commercial. They'd probably jump off that balcony into the ocean and drown in all those layers of white chemise. (Maybe that's why taste and tranquillity are the underlying messages in coffee ads.)

Club Sonora

Radio/30 seconds

This spot calls for light-hearted seduction. Relaxed, low voices are preferred. It should be very alluring and descriptive.

If you could design your own resort, you'd probably want a beautiful desert, situated by a cool bay. You'd have an Olympic-size pool for swimming and a shallow pool for volleyball. You'd have waterskiing and windsurfing, at no extra charge. Tennis courts with tanned instructors. Great food and dancing. Entertainment and cozy companionship. Guess what? You're in luck! Club Sonora was designed for you. As close to perfection as a resort can be. Club Sonora, Coconut Bay.

Titillate the person you would most like to accompany you on this luxurious vacation. Use the "Christmas present" theory to add a tantalizing twinkle to your voice. In other words, recreate that mischievous part of yourself that enjoys teasing a person for whom you've bought a gift. Tell the person that you bought him a wonderful present, but don't tell him what it is. Make him fish for the answer. Use this sly emotional condition to set the tone.

Really connect with a strong personalization. Then, act as if you are reading that person's mind. Draw an irresistibly beautiful picture of luxurious pleasure made especially for the two of you. Note the differences in activities. Lend vocal variety to make large items sound large, and small items enchanting. For example, let "entertainment" sound exciting and "cozy companionship" sound intimate and inviting.

The spot has a major transition at "Guess what? You're in luck!" It informs and assures listeners that the fantasy is reality. After all, the hero client designed it just for them. They have only to show up and enjoy it. On the final two lines, summon the listeners to join you on the sun-drenched beach.

Movie Express
Radio/30 seconds
Read this spot two different ways. First, read it as an employee of the company who takes pride in personally delivering the movies. Then, read it as the owner who understands that people's schedules can get busy. For these made-up movies, pretend the first is a rough-and-tumble action picture, the second is a light romantic comedy, and the third is a seedy B-movie skin flick.

> Movie Express makes renting movies easy. We deliver movies right to your door. Just call and reserve your movie one day in advance, and Movie Express will deliver it at no extra charge. Choose from our latest selection of movie releases and special features like *Heck Fire and Damnation*, *Golly Gee Goes to Boston*, and *Beefy Bodies*. Call today and let Movie Express bring your movie home to you!

Product: Movie Express. Consecutive key words and phrases: renting movies, deliver movies, call, reserve your movie, one day in advance, deliver, no extra charge, choose, latest selection of movie releases, special features, call today. If you are the employee, perhaps you are standing outside a loyal customer's home with a five-dollar tip in your hand. You could be slightly out of breath, having delivered dozens of movies that evening. Maybe you're walking back into the store to pick up more movies. Your subtext then could be, "I really enjoy talking to you but I've got to get back to work. There are so many movies to deliver! If you call the store now, I'll drop by your place this evening, too." As the employer, perhaps you just hung up the phone, pleased at having taken another movie delivery order. The employer could also be leaning over the counter, explaining the service to a new customer.

The list of movies is used to illustrate the store's diverse selection. It is the interest garnered from the many video choices, rather than the marketing of the specific movies that are of key importance to the client. The slogan is read, "Let Movie Express / bring your movie home / to you!" Remember to use the slashes to either take a millisecond break, or to change vocal direction either up or down on the next section.

Lofton's

TV/25 seconds

Since this 25-second ad promotes an upscale store, it should be read slowly and elegantly. The accompanying visual highlights an array of tastefully arranged furniture. A still photo of the store's location and telephone numbers is posted during the final five seconds. The voice should be soft, relaxed, and natural. Use the script markings to set up the problem and offer the solution.

> Times are changing / and so is your home. / That's why Lofton's offers the finest in contemporary home furnishings. / Whether your need is a dining room set, living room furniture, bedroom grouping, household accessories, or patio decor, / Lofton's has all the right selections. / Update your home / in style, with furnishings / from Lofton's.

Product: Lofton's. Key words: finest, contemporary home furnishings, all, update, style. This commercial is a wake-up call to image-conscious shoppers. It draws attention to the consumer's dated or worn-out furniture and urges listeners to update their home's decor. As a spokesperson, you need to comfort your "friend," and suggest that it might be time to discard those red, white, and blue beanbag chairs from the '70s and replace them with Lofton's tasteful home furnishings.

Throughout the spot, keep an inner dialogue going. It could say something like, "We'll be there for you, even if you have no flair for furniture shopping. You can trust us to help you select something elegant, tasteful, and comfortable. This will make both of us feel good."

Country Oak

TV/30 seconds

This commercial should sound warm and inviting as it paints a beautiful picture of summer in the listener's mind. The TV shows clips of kids splashing around in a pool and a casual outdoor barbecue party. Halfway through the spot, there's a close-up of the barbecue grill with sizzling burgers and hot dogs. One of the guests bites a hot dog and smiles. The camera pans down to the bag of Country Oak. The rest of the guests grab plates as the chef doles out the food. Everyone smiles and munches away as they agree that the barbecue tastes delicious.

> It's summer again, when all the summer rituals return. Swimming. Playing ball in the park. Friends gathering together in someone's backyard. . . . And of course, cookouts. It's a weekend ritual. Hot dogs and hamburgers served right off the backyard grill. As always, Country Oak "Mesquite style" Charcoal is there. You can't beat the smokey mesquite flavor of Country Oak. Anything else just wouldn't be summer.

This is a nostalgic spot. On-camera, the picture tells a beautiful story of friendship and fun. The voice should match it by conveying warmth and kinship. Let your mind dance with wonderful memories as you list the outdoor activities. Your voice should drop into it's most pleasant, relaxed tone at the mention of the hero product. This suggests that the product is comforting; the chef knows that the food and the party will be an overwhelming success because Country Oak is on the grill. The "smokey mesquite flavor" should sound delectable. Finally, the closing remark should complete the nostalgic cycle by matching the pleasure established at the beginning of the spot.

Spectacles
Radio/15 seconds
Radio time, generally aired in 30- and 60-second time slots, is occasionally divided into two equal parts. The sponsor or store distributor tacks their second spot onto the end of the related commercial to create a "piggyback" spot. This example represents the first half of a 30-second piggyback commercial.

It is important that the spokesperson act as an employee who takes great pride in the job. His voice should have a warm, caring, approachable smile that sets the customer at ease, and should sound intelligent and knowledgeable. Pay attention to the phrasing.

> At Spectacles, / we do more than correct your vision. / We help you select the right frame to add style and elegance to your appearance. / We have hundreds of designer frames to choose from. / Spectacles even makes soft contact lenses / in just one hour.

Product: Spectacles. Key words: correct, style, elegance, designer frames. This commercial takes full advantage of the spokesperson's pronoun, "we." To add that personal caring touch, try placing your hand over your heart. This centering gesture should help you connect to the subtext, "We wouldn't mislead you. We're wonderful people." The hands can also be used to gesture toward the glasses display case. Shrugging your shoulders on the final phrase adds ease and simplicity to shopping.

Google Eyes
Radio/15 seconds
This is the second half of the Spectacles 30-second piggyback spot. Throughout the advertising run, Spectacles rotates the latter half of the commercial airtime with different glasses and contact lens manufacturers. Based on sales, each sponsor is allotted a specific amount of money that dictates the number of times each manufacturer's spots is aired.

The item-price connection is of utmost importance. In the opening, be sure to billboard the product and sale. Explain how the shopper receives the special deal, and play up the benefits. If the consumer buys the product, they get something special in return. Connect this sales concept by showing action in the voice. Insinuate product quality, as well as pride and reliability in the store. Add a nudging reassurance to the slogan so that the listener feels confident in the product and motivated to shop.

> Right now, / Google Eyes / offers two glasses for the price of one. / Stop by any Spectacles location and buy one pair of designer Google Eyes frames / and get a second pair absolutely free! That means you get two distinctly different Google Eyes looks / for one low price. / Google Eyes / at Spectacles. A clear choice.

Key words and phrases: price of one, designer, absolutely, distinctly, low, a clear choice. Slogan: a clear choice. A free product is being given away. Urgency is used to bolster sales with the opening words. Make sure the listener understands that the client and manufacturer are working in tandem by offering two quality products for the price of one. Add an "Oouuu aaahhh, this is spectacular!" feel to the words. Impress the listener with how wonderful this time-limited offer is, and how much the large population of sight-impaired people has to gain.

Viberstate Health Insurance
TV/30 seconds
Viberstate offers a solution to the 50-plus target audience. The intention is to console and appease. It is imperative that you tell the audience you care about their well-being. Preferably, the spokesperson should sound 50 years old or older.

> It is a fact. People over 65, and even some over 50, often find it hard to get health insurance. Viberstate Health Insurance understands this concern. We believe everyone should have good health coverage, regardless of their age or health care history. In fact, Viberstate does not require any pre-insurance physicals. No one is ever turned down. Call 1-800-4-VIBERS today. It will put your mind at ease.

Grab the listener's attention by stating the cold, hard fact. This sets up a fear that will be remedied by the hero client. Let caring and understanding come through your voice in the body of the spot. This occurs from the words "Viberstate Health Insurance" through to "turned down." The final two sentences are a call to action. Use your hand to beckon toward yourself on the word "call." Clearly delineate the three sections of the phone number 1-800, 4, and VIBERS. The final slogan should put the listener's mind at ease.

Sometimes commercials intended to be homey and personable are written a bit too formally. In this spot there are several words that could be changed to conjunctions, and you should mark them on your script: "it is" to "it's," "they have" to "they've," "does not" to "doesn't," and "it will" to "it'll." Now reread the commercial.

Recliner Heaven
TV/30 seconds
This spot calls for the ubiquitous voice from above. As the spokesperson, you look down from your all-knowing position and comment on the poor slob's reclinerless life. Note that there is a lot of copy to fit into 30 seconds. You'll have to rush through the set-up, being careful not to lose any of the fun. Allow enough time for the sell, which occurs two-thirds of the way through the script. Build the momentum from beginning to end. Create an arc of excitement. Begin with relaxed anticipation of wonderful, carefree, TV viewing. Increase the anticipation with each line. Let the crescendo peak at the first mention of the product, store, and clearance sale. Then maintain the intensity until the final mention of the store and the slogan. As with some previous practice spots, there is no such thing as "too big." Give it your all!

> You've been waiting for the big game all week. Your wife's out of town visiting that person you call a mother-in-law. So, you turn on the giant-screen TV, adjust the VCR with two-week/seven-event programmability that your mother-in-law actually taught you to operate, pop a year's supply of popcorn into the microwave, and twist open two cases of beer. There's only one thing missing—a recliner from Recliner Heaven's Year-End Clearance Sale! For a limited time only, you can

choose from hundreds of styles of recliners at Recliner Heaven and really enjoy the big game. Recliner Heaven. Because life should be comfortable.

If relaxation is the goal, this commercial demonstrates the effort and planning required to savor that precious moment. One obstacle, the spouse, is temporarily eliminated from the couch potato's life. Fun is poked at the stereotypical mother-in-law, but be careful that the words "mother-in-law" don't become too negative. This may be too real for some audience members and instantly turn them off to the rest of the spot. Handle her references in a light, playful—although subtle—manner. Build audience rapport and sympathy by using the smug subtext, "You know how she can be!"

Color the list in a way that draws a vivid picture in the listener's mind's eye. Use it to build momentum leading to the missing item: the recliner. After all, you are not selling TVs, VCRs, popcorn, microwaves, or beer! Stair step the list. Have it build in pitch and intensity with each item. Drop the pitch and wag an all-knowing finger at the slob on the phrase, "There's only one thing missing." Open the floodgates and blurt out the answer, "A recliner from Recliner Heaven's Year-End Clearance Sale!" It should sound as if a big, million-watt neon sign was just plugged in and is blinding people within a 100-mile radius.

Emphasize that the sale is only for a limited time. Emphasize the wide selection. "Really enjoy the big game" should be used as the transition into the resolve. Imply that the only way a person can relax and truly enjoy the big game is with a special Recliner Heaven recliner, and, since you are selling relaxation, close out the spot with self-assured wisdom and appreciative advice. The reclinerless slob should know by now that the hero product is, without a doubt, the best investment a person can make. After all, hard-working people deserve to be comfortable!

Body Wise
Radio/60 seconds
Ideally, the host, Simi Wise, should have an effervescent, charming, witty personality. The host should also be warm and able to relate to the audience and should make the shopping experience simple and easy. This spot launches the show's publicity campaign.

Are you shopping-impaired? Do your eyes glaze over every time you enter a department store? Do your palms sweat at the thought of buying lingerie in public? Do you dread waiting in line to buy plastic wrap? Relax, now there's Body Wise— the new way to shop. All you have to do is turn on the TV, watch Body Wise, and select the items you wish to buy. It's safe, easy, and fun! I'm your host, Simi Wise. Twenty-four hours a day, seven days a week I help Body Wise viewers like you conquer their fear of buying clothing and intimate apparel, and their boredom with choosing gardening tools, roofing tiles, home fix-it supplies, and bathroom and kitchen appliances. You never have to leave the comfort of your home! Plus, Body Wise offers smart consumer shopping tips and shop-o-holic counseling advice. Don't perspire and go into fits of convulsions when you shop in public. Shop at home! I do! That's why I started Body Wise. It's as easy as turning on the TV and picking up the phone. It's quick. It's smart. It's wise. It's Body Wise . . . where shopping is always easy.

Showing a full, real, fun personality is the key to this job. Create a history for Simi Wise. If necessary, refer back to "Making It M.I N.E." Really connect with the listeners and their predicament. There should be a lot of vocal variety. Keep the copy light and airy so that watching the show and ordering over the phone sounds effortless. Smile! Remember that the show was created to make shoppers' lives easy. Develop a twinkle in your eye. There are places where you might even give the audience a knowing wink. Above all, remember to play! Laugh if you feel compelled to do so. Laughing adds friendliness and levity. Just remember to never, never laugh on the client's name! This will negate your sincerity and be interpreted as poking fun at the product, as well as at the viewer. (Obviously, a major "no-no.") If it comes from a truthful place, laugh on the sentence, "It's fun!" or on the one immediately following it. (Notice that no crucial copy information is included there.) If you don't feel like chuckling, don't force it. Laughs should sound natural and be an integral part of the host's personality. Laugh while saying the words, as it sounds very fake and stilted to laugh, take a pause, and begin speaking again.

Build the set-up in the stair step fashion. Let one problem quickly and more intensely top the previous one. Take a slight break, or beat, at the end of the set-up. Exhale and sigh, letting the shoulders drop on the word "relax." This begins the soothing resolution of the commercial's body section. Use a laugh to segue into a gentle smile as you personally introduce yourself to the audience. Effortlessly describe the show and what it entails. Begin the resolve at, "Don't perspire." Get warm and fuzzy with the audience when you reveal more about yourself and how you started the show. Make turning on the TV and picking up the telephone sound different from one another. Vocally imply the different physical actions. If it helps, use your hands to make the actual actions. Also, make sure the short, staccato sentences toward the end of the spot lead progressively up to the final mention of the show's name. Relate the closing line with a we're-in-this-together smile. Give this spot your all. Booking a job like this could completely change your checkbook balance!

Chapter 9

Real Person

The end of the 1980s marked a major change in advertising history. Gone were the days of deep-voiced announcers with great "pipes" talking about feminine hygiene products, baby toys, and deodorant. It was obvious to the radio and television listener that spokespeople were paid to say wonderful things about department stores or bathroom cleaners. Consumers yearned to hear voices they could relate to, voices more like their own. Advertising agencies heard this plea and adjusted their writing to include quirky, unique, and believable seemingly nonprofessional voices. Surely, such untrained voices must know what it's like to shop sales! Advertising had entered *The Real Person Zone.*

REAL-PERSON SPOTS

The popularity of real person spots has revealed a world of new voice-over talent. It has also meant a radical adjustment for veteran voice actors. Why is this? First and foremost, "real people" do not sell! Announcers and spokespeople sell. Real people let their love of the product or pride in ownership naturally motivate the listener to buy.

Let's say you just bought a new suit. The store was having an incredible sale. You saved over $100 on a designer label! Are you going to tell someone about your great buy? Of course you are! It's human nature to brag about ourselves when we've done something smart.

As a real person you can never rely on "sorta" liking the product you've been hired to sell. You must believe wholeheartedly that the product you just bought will dramatically change your life! This is where the need and intention work mentioned earlier comes in. I need to impress my boss so I can get a raise. I intend to meet that need by buying the best suit possible, at a price I can afford. New suit = professional appearance = raise. The end result is pride in ownership. A real person relays a truthful situation in which his pride sells the product.

So, when you receive a script, how do you make it truthful? Use a substitution. In your mind, substitute a person, place, or thing for the product or situation. For example, a woman in one of my classes had difficulty breathing life into a script about a kitchen appliance. I had her substitute a mental picture of Mel Gibson every time she mentioned the kitchen appliance, and the copy came alive! Students in the class dashed out the door, cash in hand, ready to buy the appliance. I also gave a similar script to a man. When he substituted Cindy Crawford for the product, he successfully garnered a similar response.

Feelings, emotions, needs, and intentions give real-person scripts depth and character. Adding the five *W*'s (who, what, why, where, when) and M.I.N.E. (Motivations, Intentions, Needs, Emotions) completes the scene. The number one trap of real-person scripts is to get lost in the situation set-ups. Don't slow down the character development section and speed through the product information. Remember who's paying you to endorse their product.

You will notice in this section that all the commercials are marked as radio scripts. Real person spots lend themselves more readily to this medium. When a real person is used on television, he is usually presented on-camera rather than as a voice-over.

Flowers
Radio/12 seconds
This is one of four vignettes, making up a 60-second radio commercial. Each nostalgic story expresses the emotional uplift when a person receives flowers. Connect with a real moment in your own life that parallels this event. It will keep the commercial charged with rich emotion.

> It was my birthday and I didn't think anyone would remember. Then I got flowers from my college roommate. Can you imagine! Flowers! Makes growing older that much easier.

Here we see a person feeling lonely and mildly depressed about getting older. This first line is an attention-grabbing set-up that appeals to our sensitivities about aging. It also establishes an audience of listeners, especially those 29 years and older. Therefore, the most likely voice for this job is one that sounds over 30. The client may even decide to record several versions of this spot for the various age categories.

Now, let's move on to the transition sentence. What happened? The person got flowers from a special friend. Just thinking about that possibility should bring a smile to your face. If not, choose a substitution. Think of a special person you would love to see. Once you've pictured that person, think about him or her for a few seconds and read the third line. You may laugh at the memory of a funny moment together, or shed a tear of joy. As these emotions wash over you, remember to smile and stretch out the word "flowers." You must never forget who is paying for these words.

Finally, the resolution. What emotion is generated when flowers arrive? Is it nostalgia, hopefulness, or love? Any one of these feelings will suffice. If it is nostalgia, subconsciously we are motivated, by the fond memories, to buy flowers. The consequence of not buying flowers is guilt. This is very shrewd advertising, hitting where it hurts. The human emotions of a real person connect the actor and the listener. How wonderful that the person we hear on the radio shares a similar life experience. The listener feels that the actor is speaking directly and specifically to him. End result: flower sales increase and the client is happy.

Zippy Running Shoes
Radio/25 seconds
This radio commercial depends heavily on character development in order to be successful. Quickly decide if you are a professional athlete, a running enthusiast, or an overweight exerciser. The sound effects will depend on what read you choose.

> Like many people, I run to keep fit. But my feet sure take a pounding! I shopped around and decided my feet deserve the best. That's why I wear Zippy running shoes. They're computer designed to reduce the impact on your feet. Now I don't

know much about computer design, but I do know this . . . since I started wearing Zippies, my feet feel so much better, I could run a marathon!

Let's say you decide to play a professional athlete. Choose a specific sport like football, baseball, tennis, or track in which to excel. Once you know *who* you are and *why* you run, select *what* you are doing, and *where* and *when* you are doing it. Are you in the locker room taking off your sneakers after an exhausting game or are you at home and about to go on your morning run? Your focus on the activity hides the sell. Your condition—exhaustion after a workout or enthusiasm at the prospect of having a lean, trim body—sets the tone. Finally, decide who would be the best person for you to talk to about running shoes. Record your various interpretations, changing the personalizations (the person you're pretending to talk to) with each read.

Here's a fun twist. Try running in place. Keep running until you are slightly out of breath. You should develop a slight breathing pattern; breathe in three times then breathe out on the fourth beat. Continue running and read the copy. If you bounce around too much and cannot read the script, keep the balls of your feet on the floor. Set a steady low-impact running pace. Let your arms swing freely. Run slightly off mic on the last half of the final sentence. This adds realism and dimension. Gravel boxes are provided in some studios expressly for this purpose. You run in the gravel box while panting out your lines. The audio engineer mixes in a few sound effects of outdoor noises and the setting is complete. You are now an actual athlete running down a gravel road discussing the merits of wearing Zippies. (Added bonus: the studio workout is at no additional charge!)

Jiffy Lite Dinners

Radio/30 seconds

Enjoy life. Don't get trapped in a busy lifestyle. After all, this product is here to save the day! Imagine that you are the actor in an on-camera, television version of this commercial. What are you doing while speaking: Putting away groceries? Setting the table? Tearing the wrapping off the microwave dinners? Relaxing? Give the character some reality by adding mental or physical movement. Also, consider your "pre-scene" history. Obviously it has been a busy day working and carting the kids around to their various activities, and this physical and emotional condition should be reflected in your voice.

> I knew when I had three kids I was gonna be busy, but not this busy! With Ronnie on the baseball team, Susan taking ballet class, and Erin in the school band, there's never a dull moment. Between working and running Mom's [Dad's] shuttle service, I'm often left with little time to cook. Thank goodness for Jiffy Lite Dinners. I just pop 'em in the microwave and in less than 10 minutes, it's dinnertime. Jiffy Lite Dinners. They're the easiest part of my day.

Those of us with children can relate to this taxing scenario. Childless people may have to use their imagination, but can probably empathize. Above all, remember to keep a bright outlook on life. Do not let all the kid's activities send you whirling into a deep state of depression. Advertising portrays an ideal, albeit unrealistic, world. No matter how hectic your life becomes, there's always a product out there in television- and radioland that can rescue you. Jiffy Lite Dinners add an extra 10 minutes to your busy life. These precious moments while the food is being "nuked" should be spent with your feet propped up, reading the newspaper After all, you deserve it!

This is a script that cries out for the actor to enjoy the negatives. Make fun of your predicament. Keep it lighthearted. Remember, you love your kids; you don't discourage their activities. It's a fact of life that you have to work to put food on the table; you've accepted your responsibilities but relish a little personal time to catch up and relax. If you get burdened down in the negatives, the listener will be turned off and might even switch stations in search for something less depressing.

Stair step the list of the children's activities, reading it quickly while building upward. This gives you room to sigh and vocally descend on the transitional phrase "there's never a dull moment." Let us know how you feel about work and the shuttle service. Set up your dilemma of not having enough time to cook. Let the solution, Jiffy Lite Dinners, spell relief to the hurried parent. The preparation and cooking time should sound fun and effortless. Commend yourself for having made such a fine dinner decision when you deliver the final product name. This introspective approach is a very effective tool; it takes the listener inward on their own journey of discovery to see if the product will work for them, too. The last line offers a comforting and reassuring message.

As you read this spot, note the tempo changes. Typically, the set-ups are more fun to explore than the actual product information. The trap is to spend more time telling a story and less moving the product. Since Jiffy Lite Dinners = time, speed up the first half of the copy that parallels the hectic side of life, and slow down and relax when pitching the product that will add time to the listener's day.

Proposition Q
Radio/25 seconds
The final five seconds of this spot are reserved for the individual, corporation, or organization sponsoring the commercial. Act smug and self-assured because your position is far superior to that of the Proposition Q endorsers. Make the listeners feel that they would be complete idiots to vote "yes." Create a pre-scene scenario that stimulates and feeds your belief system. ("Real life" political ads often have this inherently built in.)

> The proponents of Proposition Q would have you believe that spending more money will solve our city's problems. Are we supposed to swallow that? Of course it's not true. Taxpayers like you and I need better city management, not higher taxes. Don't let 'em fool you. Vote NO on November third. It's a vote for better management, not bigger spending. Vote NO on Proposition Q.

Political ads are a complete art form unto themselves. Cash in hand, political groups buy up large blocks of radio and television time. The campaign usually starts out friendly and personable. Then, as the weeks tick by, larger and larger skeletons are pried out of their proverbial closets and dragged through the mud. An all-out war is waged in the weeks just prior to the election.

As an actor, it is your option to get involved in these messy, emotionally charged political commercial campaigns or not. Unlike life, where few people form personal opinions based on whether or not you use the new, improved laundry detergent, political endorsements reflect your personal stand on issues. If you can say the words in a political ad without compromising your beliefs (and without fireworks going off in your stomach and steam coming out of your ears), by all means record the spot and take the money. If not, remember that it is okay to turn down the job. Personal integrity is gratefully acknowledged by all parties concerned. If you do decide to voice the job, make arrangements to be paid in advance; the till is often scraped clean toward the end of the campaign and after the election.

With these thoughts in mind, take a look at Proposition Q. Do you think this commercial fits into the beginning, middle, or end of the political campaign? Since you are hired to oppose the proposition, report false claims, and motivate the listener to take action, chances are it is the final stages of the campaign. Take a strong stand on the issue, as if you have a personal stake in the matter. Stir emotional controversy in your favor.

In the first sentence, remember to clearly establish the name of the proposition and what its advocates would "have you believe." Throw up your hands in disbelief as you read the second line. Relate the third line directly to the listener as if you mutually agree on the issue. Take care not to be condescending. Diffferentiate between what you support and what the politicians stand for. Don't get tripped up by the word "no." In this commercial, the "no" is *positive* and the proposition is *negative.* Slow down on "better city management" and speed up on "higher taxes." In other words, linger on the thoughts you want the listener to remember and speed through the parts you want the listener to forget. Pacing is extremely important for stressing key points and holding the listener's attention.

Anti-Smoking PSA
Radio/15 seconds
Not long ago, radio and television stations were saturated with cigarette advertisements. Of course, on-air smoking endorsements are now taboo. Even so, the campaign against cigarettes is on the rise. Politically, it is your choice whether or not to voice this commercial. For dramatic impact, cut directly to the emotional quick as you relate your son's touching story of foreseeable doom. Let the reality of the situation live inside you.

> We send mixed signals to our kids. My husband [wife] says, "Yes." I say, "No." One day Billy said, "Dad [Mom], do you wanna die?" My husband [wife] said, "Of course not!" So Billy asked, "Then why do you smoke?"

PSA stands for Public Service Announcement. Radio and television stations are required to set aside a certain amount of airtime to make the public aware of local, national, and global issues. Unlike commercials designed to entertain and motivate the listener to buy a product, PSAs are structured to shock, alter, and raise social consciousness. The message is much more serious than whether or not a person's socks are their whitest white. Many of the issues are life threatening. They affect family members and friends.

As an actor, you may be asked to voice a PSA for little or no money. Some organizations make special arrangements with SAG and AFTRA allowing union talent to be hired at no charge or below scale. This is evaluated on a case-by-case basis. Advertising agencies and recording studios have even been known to donate their time and equipment to needy causes.

PSAs are a welcome change for many voice actors. Regardless of their economic reward, they present opportunities to explore deeper emotions than those required in most commercials. In this anti-smoking spot, the son's clarity and directness are overwhelming. The message is to not use cigarettes because smoking can harm you and lead to premature death. This is illustrated by the son's concern with losing a parent. Begin reading the top of the spot in a matter-of-fact tone. This approach allows for transitions to develop gradually into deeper, more meaningful issues. The last line will have more punch if it comes as a surprise. By beginning lighter and progressing into a darker, more serious area, the final message garners more impact.

City Fare
Radio/30 seconds

Follow the progression of the story. As your awareness of the car expenses increases, so do your frustrations. There should be shock and surprise when the fifty-five-hundred-dollar amount is revealed. Don't have all the answers on the tip of your tongue; as much as we all might like to be brilliant and intuitive on command, that is not always how life works. Allow the brain to work out a solution. Wait for the sound of your calculator catching up. Input the information and react to the results. Don't play the safe, middle ground. Go for broke!

> Let's see. Eighty dollars a month for parking. Two dollars a day for gas. The insurance is $1,000 a year. Can't forget the tune-ups and repairs. And there's the car payment—$185 a month. And the annual registration fee—$110. Near as I can figure, that's about . . . fifty-five hundred dollars a year! That does it! I'm trading in that money guzzler for a City Fare bus ticket. With what I spend on my car in one year, I could buy City Fare bus tickets for about . . . 25 years.

In acting, as in life, you always want to be a "winner." It's never fun to admit defeat. As obstacles present themselves, we are forced to readjust our thinking. This spot for City Fare exemplifies this fact. The person assumes the car is an economically sound means of transportation until the car payments and fees are added up. It becomes glaringly apparent that the car is costing the driver a fortune. The only logical solution is to sell the car and ride the bus, allowing the driver a chance to win the game!

Take the listener on a triumphant journey with your voice. Begin by intending to prove that the car is a money saver. Unless you are a genius, you have to search your notes and financial files or rack your brain for the exact dollar amounts. Allow your true feelings (anger, frustration, shock) to build with each additional item. Let the lightbulb go on above your head when you decide to trade in the car for the bus ticket. It should be an "ahh ha!!" experience. The listener should almost hear the gears in your brain creaking as the winning solution is discovered on the last line. Note that the true weight of the revelation is exposed on the latter half of the closing line. If you are a winner—not a whiner (one of the most unpleasant auditory emotions that should be avoided 99.9 percent of the time)—you will naturally smile at the prospect of getting 25-years-worth of mass transit service for the price of one year of car ownership.

Train Central

Radio/30 seconds

Here's another progressional spot. Imagine the following sound effects to be added later: birds tweeting on a beautiful spring morning; traffic whizzing by; a car honking and a motorist yelling, "Move over, buddy!"; tires squealing before crashing loudly; a five-car pileup complete with horns honking and people yelling; utter freeway chaos and eventual gridlock. Silence is restored on the line, "Who'm I kidding?" The commercial ends with the gentle, rhythmic tranquillity of a train gliding along the tracks. Take time to milk the words and roll them around in your mouth.

> Ahhh, there's nothing like a leisurely commute. The freeway traffic, the friendly motorists, the accidents, five days a week, at the peak of rush hour! Who'm I kidding? Starting tomorrow, I'm taking Train Central. It will be good for my blood pressure, not to mention my gas tank.

This spot is very similar to the previous commercial for City Fare. It starts with an innocent set-up and builds progressively to high-level anxiety. The realization of defeat forces the commuter to choose an alternative mode of transportation. Once a decision is made to take Train Central, normalcy is restored. The commuter breathes a sigh of relief. Again, there is a happy ending.

Creamy Delite

Radio/30 seconds

This calls for a very likable snob who relates unabashedly to the audience. The premise here is that people should throw away those "franchise flavors" and savor a gourmet Creamy Delite Bar. Only those who have tasted the hero product understand what you are talking about. Those who haven't tried it, will have to experience it for themselves and find out what all the fuss is about.

> I've got a problem. I think I'm becoming an ice-cream snob. But I ask you, who cares about those franchise flavors—like granola peanut supreme and Hungarian chocolate—when you can buy a Creamy Delite Bar. You don't just eat a Creamy Delite. You savor it. But if you haven't experienced Creamy Delite you wouldn't understand. So what are you waiting for? Pick up a Creamy Delite Bar and become an ice-cream connoisseur, like me!

There is a give-and-take, negative-versus-positive quality to this commercial. This presents an excellent opportunity to use the microphone to enhance the problem's intensity. The usual five-inch distance from the mic creates a more normal, matter-of-fact tone, but, by moving closer to the mic on the lines that admit love, desire, and guilt over Creamy Delite, a bond is created between the voice actor and listener. In these precious seconds, a secret is revealed and a special moment is shared. This is the "give." The "take" occurs in the explanations. The second sentence quickly "takes away" the guilt by making excuses for the actions and thereby covering up the problem. There is a continuous tug-of-war between being a snob and explaining why this attitude is justified. After all, who likes franchise ice-cream flavors?

The general goal of the spot is to reveal the hardships and benefits of becoming an ice-cream snob. This need is revealed through the love of the product. Creamy Delite tastes so good, you have to love it. You'll have no choice but to accept your fate —to be a connoisseur who's simply not satisfied eating any other brand. The secret is exposed and the dilemma is presented to those brave souls who may otherwise fear becoming snobs. This is a small price to pay for something that tastes so good.

As you can see from these real-person commercials, thorough analysis of the script is necessary. The subtext needs to be explored, allowing the actor to find ways of driving the needs and intentions forward. Simple technical analysis used in announcer spots is not enough. The sell must be hidden. Real people, with all their craziness and idiosyncrasies, unconsciously sell products naturally and succinctly through their emotional attachments. We are all salespeople at some point in our lives. We might as well get paid for it.

Brewsky Spud

Radio/45 seconds

This may be the hardest piece of copy in the whole book. It requires total character emersion. The setting is a sports bar. An important football game is in progress and the hometown favorite is winning. Three or four additional voice actors will provide background cheers and general ambiance. At various points in the copy you have to join in with the fervent voice-over cheering section. These places are marked in capital letters. Note how these cheers echo and punctuate the actor's thoughts.

Never, ever in beer commercials should you appear sloshed or even the slightest bit inebriated! This condones alcoholism and opens the door for major lawsuits against the company. Show how going to a bar and drinking the hero brew invigorates rather than deadens response time. The final 15 seconds are devoted to the announcer "sell" and "wrap-up."

After a long day, I like to stop by my neighborhood sports bar and root for the home team. GO GET 'EM . . . YEAH! Football and Brewsky Spud. They go together. Right gang? (Crowd agrees) Brewsky Spud is home brewed, right here in the US of A. No fancy imports for me! YES!! (Crowd cheers) I understand great granddad Brewsky started making Spud 150 years ago. And Brewsky Spud is still brewed the same way to seal in the flavor. Some big brewing companies say it's old fashioned. Me? I just know it tastes great. TOUCHDOWN!! (Whoops and hollers!) Yep. Brewsky Spud and football. Nothin' could be better. Right gang? (Total agreement from happy bar friends.)

Now is your chance to further understand mic placement and how your proximity and relationship to the microphone creates character depth and field of motion. Imagine that the big screen TV and crowd of viewers are to one side of you. Choose the right or left side, whichever is more comfortable and natural. Turn your face slightly to that side every time you cheer or talk directly to the crowd. (In actuality, the actors may be positioned directly behind you or in a separate isolation booth.) One of your goals as a voice actor is to keep the sound level consistent and not drive the engineer crazy with major sound variations. This way you won't blow out the mic with your cheers.

Give your character's story a beginning, middle, and end. Use one of your own work situations to instantly conjure up an exhausted feeling. Your recent work-related experience begins the spot and allows you to show a definite "arc" in the character. The intentions change. There's a tired feeling in the beginning when you need to unwind. Then, in the middle, with the swell of excitement, you want to enjoy the social atmosphere and the tasty, tantalizing beer. Overall, you have a need for enjoyment. The Brewsky is held up for closer inspection. Pretending to lift a frothy, cold mug to eye level helps create this feeling. Impressed by the beer's credentials, the character agrees that the hero product and the featured sport are a perfect marriage. Finally, with the last intention and a sense of relaxation and contentedness, you have convinced yourself and also the listeners that Brewsky is the best.

A bone of contention is that the actor's focus is divided. There is the audience, or personalization, for whom the conversation is directed, the football game, and the crowd of cheering chums. Remember always why you are there: you dropped by the bar to relax, unwind, and drink some suds. Focus on the beer and your need and intentions will not falter and become dissipated and confused.

Splash-O-Rama
Radio/20 seconds
Use the first two-thirds of this commercial to show how Splash-O-Rama breaks the mold and delivers unique, enriching family fun. Pay careful attention to the mundane use of the word "every." Repetitious words lend major clues to how a script should be emotionally charged and verbally delivered. The real person's boredom with other amusement sources is used to convince the audience that the hero client's place is the ultimate party location. In the beginning, boring background music plays. The tune changes when the ultimate source of fun is revealed. Layered in with the music are the sound effects of people laughing uproariously and water splashing and swooshing.

> You know, I thought I'd taken my family to every amusement park on the planet. We'd fed every elephant and ridden every roller coaster. Or so I thought . . . until last weekend. We went to Splash-O-Rama Water Slides in Jefferson! What a great time! It was a perfect way to spend a hot afternoon.

There should be at least three distinct emotions in this commercial. A slow progressional transition from the first to the second is necessary. In the beginning, the actor relates the boringly frustrating situation. There is nary a smile on the face or in the voice. The eyes start to come alive on, "Or so I thought." The face still isn't smiling, but the person is thinking about a fun-filled time. A wide, slow, and comforting grin appears on, "Until last weekend." Elation erupts as the place, location, and degree of fun is exposed. Pleasant nostalgia sets in as the person recalls the perfect splash-filled day. Reflecting on the fun acts as an emotional catalyst. The desired effect is for the listener to also choose this pleasant diversion. Give a happy, relieved sigh of approval as you say the final sentence.

Chapter 10

Characters

Now it is time to transcend the norm, to explore the outer reaches, to boldly go where no voice has gone before. It is time to create character voices! These are the voices of aliens from Mars who discover how to shop for Earthly values. The slices of cheese that live inside your refrigerator, begging for a spot in your lunch box. The giant ants as they march away from a picnic carrying a stolen chicken breast. Character voices go beyond a person's normal intonations. Unused facial and vocal muscles are stretched and contorted to form human-like voices for cats, dogs, and even ceiling fans.

For some individuals, vocal transformations come easily. The brain acts as a sponge, absorbing any speech characteristics it encounters, be it Cousin Janie Lou from New Orleans, Bob from Australia, Suzie with her high quirky voice, Erin Hiccup with the speech impediment, or countless others. Creating new speech is like programming a high-tech computer. The eyes make a mental picture of the person. Vocal images are scanned in through the ear. The brain memorizes and categorizes the people according to their mannerisms and speech patterns. Finally, the mouth spits out the verbal image.

If you are lucky enough to possess the skill to perfectly mimic a famous person, be aware of the potential for lawsuits. Many celebrities, or their estates if they are no longer alive, control the rights to visual and audio replications. Currently, you will only hear an impersonation in radio and television spots when the commercial is prefaced by, "The voices of Person X and Person Y are played by comedian/impressionist John Doe." With airtime as valuable as it is, this conceptual approach is becoming less and less common. Instead, big-budget clients utilize new video technologies, which enable them to alter movie clips featuring celebrity legends, and superimpose the product into the picture. Money is still shelled out, but the benefit of the picture is considered well worth the expense.

Interactive games often require dead ringer soundalikes. Since this is a relatively new medium, the need for excellent impersonators has increased. Until recently, actors didn't have any contract clauses covering interactive games or residual compensation from the games and their soundalikes. After all, it wasn't until the early 1990s that "talking" video and computer games became a widespread reality. Studios that control movie rights are sure to cash in on this technological bonanza; as a cost saving tactic, they hire cheaper, unknown actors to play the famous person's roll. Contractually, arrangements are made to cover all the bases. Millions of dollars are saved, and the public is still satisfied with the end results.

Not all voice actors possess an innate ability to replicate and create alternate speech. The vast majority, however, are capable of some vocal agility but are simply unaware of their own talents. Like any muscle not used on a regular basis, vocal muscles atrophy. Not exercising the voice prevents the actor from expanding into cartoons, interactive games, and cleverly constructed commercial character parts. Developing an ear for dialects, accents, and unusual speech takes time and practice. You must work hard to develop both an ear and a mouth for such work.

YOUR CHARACTER VOICES

This chapter is designed to help you uncover and explore the many fun, new voices that live inside you, waiting to be discovered. Begin by removing any mental obstacles that prevent you from exploring your full vocal range. Forget the teacher who scolded, "Be quiet. Stop talking like that!" Forgive the parent who said, "Will you please behave normally for a change!" Stop suppressing that wacky side of yourself. You need the freedom to experiment.

Take a moment to reflect on how the voice changes naturally to suit specific situations. As a person stoops over a crib to play with an infant, the lips automatically pucker and the pitch rises to a cute and playful tone. When trying to impress your boss, you stand more erect, your chest juts out, and your voice becomes deeper. In social gatherings, the person adept at mimicking famous one-liners from movies is cheered. As you go through the day, you unconsciously and seamlessly "change hats." Now, you must recognize these vocal variations, and learn to consciously recreate them on demand.

Age range is one area to explore. Recently I held an audition for an interactive computer game requiring a woman to portray a six-year-old girl. Many of the women questioned why an actual six-year-old was not used. Simply, the script was too large, and the budget not extensive enough, to accommodate a beginning reader and all the diction problems that often accompany youths. What an adult can accomplish in two hours, may take a child two to three times longer. As my audition progressed, it was clear that many women could create a young sound, but what was missing in the majority of auditioners was a youthful mentality. The voice was there, but the freedom and flippancy of a six-year-old was missing. Consequently, a lot of the women sounded like women trying to sound younger, rather than like real children.

When you create a voice, you must adopt the character's entire demeanor. Children have a light, naive quality that needs to be displayed. The attitude of a teenager is a blend of adult and child. Sometimes they are very wise, while other times they are completely off the mark. Age dictates whether we talk up to an adult, down to a child, or on a peer level.

Practice aging as you read this example. Begin as an infant, verbalizing unspoken thoughts. Grow to a five-year-old, 10-year-old, early teenager, 19-year-old, 25-year-old, thirtysomething, 50-year-old, 65-year-old, and finally an octogenarian. Reflect on your own personal feelings at the ages where applicable. Observe others in age brackets either forgotten or yet to be experienced, and refrain from caricatures. Create real, complete, breathing people with faults, feelings, and opinions. Stand, move, and think like that person.

> Who are all these strange-looking creatures holding me? That person in the funny hat says he's my father. What does that mean? WHAAA! I'm hungry. WHAAAA! Doesn't any body hear me? WHAAA! Give me something to drink!

Being five is not easy. I keep stubbing my big toe on the bottom of the swimming pool. Mom says if I swim right and don't doggie paddle, things like this won't happen. I don't get it! My toe hurts when I swim, not when I stand.

What's happening to my body? It's changing and I hate it! It is so embarrassing. Sometimes I wish my big brother would move to Australia on the other side of the world where he belongs. He likes to turn out the lights in the bathroom when I'm taking a shower. He is such a nerd.

Do you think that girl who sits next to me in math is cute? Yesterday she asked to borrow my pencil. I'll never sharpen it again 'cause now it has her teeth marks on it! She probably thinks I'm a dweeb because I've got these stupid braces.

College is cool. You get to live away from home and stuff. There are a lot of great babes here, too. Heavy dating scene, if you know what I mean. Costs a lot of dough. Mom and Dad are always complaining that money doesn't grow on trees. What do they think credit cards are for? Duh. Get a life.

I like to hang out in coffee shops and drink cappuccino with my friends. Hey, I'm not a slacker, though. I have a part-time job! What more do people want? My friends and I share an apartment. That's responsible. What can I say, I'm part of Generation X. The name says it all.

Honey, can you pick up the dry cleaning on the way home from work? I'm taking Johnnie and Sally to soccer practice as soon as I leave the office. By the way, the car is running funny. You better take it to the shop. I have a big meeting on Thursday. What should I pick up for dinner?

Can you believe it? Our daughter's getting married. The guy seems nice enough. He's got a management position at XYZ Corporation. We're very proud. Why do weddings cost a fortune? Eloping has its merits, after all.

Now that I'm collecting Social "in"-Security, I get to travel . . . see the world. Those grandkids of mine are precious, but they sure can tire you out. In my day, mothers stayed home with the little tykes. I guess that's why cruises are so popular. People like us need a break. I guess you could say, we deserve it.

Do you want to see pictures of my great grandchildren? I've got 10. That's Bobby. Or is it Ted? The old memory's not what it used to be. Darn cute children. Watch too much television, though. They should get out more. In my day I used to shovel snow for entertainment.

Knowing whether you are large or small can also make a difference. If a script calls for you to be a tiny toaster talking to a huge refrigerator, adjust your voice to the situation. It should sound small in contrast to the deep, resonant tones of the giant cooler. Next, factor in age. Is it a spanking new toaster or an old, cranky appliance. Do the coils heat up when you get mad? Where are they located? Are they on your back, or do they blaze through your eyes? You must make a physical choice, commit to it, and *trust* yourself to follow through with the actions.

Once you know what you look like, you must also adjust your body accordingly. The body memorizes how you sound and circumvents the brain. Versatile cartoon actors, who play multiple characters in one script, are often challenged to carry on conversations with themselves. Microphone placement and body position become key elements in their rapid character changes. The brain doesn't have the luxury of stopping and assessing, "What does this character sound like?" The changes must be made instantaneously. Developing a strong body position and assigning a specific mic placement for each character eliminates the awkward "think" time between voices. Fixed in the body, the characters flow from one to the next without a hitch. The deep-voiced villain with the menacing laugh is played right on top of the microphone, hovering controllingly over his victims. The hero stands approximately six inches away from the mic with chest thrust forward invincibly, protecting the people of the community. The villain's sidekick approaches the mic from a slight angle, cowering for protection. As the characters change, the voice actor's head bobs in and out of microphone positions.

Before you attempt simultaneous multi-character accuracy, try this experiment. Pretend you are a toaster. Get a strong mental image of yourself. Determine your age, body position, and proximity to the microphone. Assign a body focus. That means, focus your attention on a specific part of your anatomy. It might be the brain if you are playing an intelligent character, the heart if portraying a wholesome, loving character, or crunched toes if you have trekked many miles on foot. For instance, you can make your eyes large and innocent when you first read the spot. The next time through, try jutting your jaw out and scratching your whiskers. Create your own choices. The important thing here is to totally commit yourself and not hold back.

> I know I'm a little toaster, but I'm steamed. Just because you're a big refrigerator doesn't mean you can boss me around. Sure you've got an automatic ice maker and a fancy water dispenser, and everyone opens and closes your door all day long. But they still come to me every morning! I always toast their bread nice and golden brown. You can't do that. So leave me alone, and I'll promise not to pop off anymore.

Developing characters requires some homework. This is your opportunity to guiltlessly watch hours of old movies and children's cartoons. Glean as much information from them as possible. Listen to their speech patterns. Practice their breathing patterns. Try to locate their body focus and energy source. Create a complete mental and physical image of the characters. Then, start mimicking the voices that attract your attention or fall into your specific vocal range. Assign each character a name. Use the name to help you remember the body focus, mic placement, and vocal quality. It could be pigeon-toed Louise, the ditz; long-legged Jim, the athlete; or Rooster McGee, the barnyard know-it-all. Continue to build your character repertoire. This allows you to have a stock set of voices. From there, you can play mix-and-match, selecting elements from one character and blending them with another to create a completely new and integrated third identity. The possible combinations are endless.

Audio-cassette training tapes are a source many people use to learn accents and dialects. Many theatrical bookstores carry French, Italian, British, Russian, German, Spanish, Chinese, Japanese, and countless other selections. These are not tapes that teach how to speak the language fluently, but rather how to adopt their specific speech characteristics into your own spoken language. For instance, the romantic French language has a tendency to roll the r's. German is more guttural, like someone clearing his throat. There is an assortment of regional accents, each associated with specific parts of England, and this is also true of the United States.

Everyone learns to master dialects, accents, and character voices in a different way. You need to find out which way works best for you. Do you absorb other people's speech through personal contact? Is it easier for you to replicate voices you hear off the radio and television? Can you mimic exactly a famous actor or character? Are you able to create new voices by inventing your own physicalizations? If none of these outlets work, and you have trouble breaking through your real voice to create new sounds, consider improvisation and voice-over classes geared specifically to shatter this barrier.

The best way to learn is by doing, so once again it's time to put concepts into practice. Get a strong idea of who you are before you begin. Use the copy to make these choices. Trust your instincts. Remember that character voices, just for the sake of showing off and with no bearing on the script, will seem inappropriate or, worse, ludicrously out of place. Personalities must enhance the script, not detract from it. Either play the character *to type* or contrast the script by playing *against type,* but make sure the character has a reason for being there and a foundation for sounding that particular way.

Sneeze Dust

TV/30 seconds

In this commercial, we see a very tidy, proper woman wearing white gloves, matronly dress, and pillbox hat. She runs a gloved finger over the dining table and looks up in disgust at her son who supposedly dusted the room. She then motions to the cupboard, removes the hero product, and applies it to the furniture. She stands back and admires her handiwork. Just then, the doorbell rings. The Sunday afternoon bridge group arrives, each woman wearing a pair of white gloves. Before they sit down to play, they all rub a discerning finger across the furniture. Satisfied with the results, they sit down, remove their gloves, and begin a cutthroat game.

"Hail to the Queen" plays in the background. It is suggested that the narrator read the spot three different ways. Once with a proper British accent, then in a high (but not squeaky), cockney accent, and the, finally with a down-home, country flair.

> In Mrs. Clean's house, dust is a four-letter word. That's why she always uses Sneeze Dust. After all, whether she entertains friends, family, or the Queen of England, she wants everything to be just so. Her rare antiques recapture their original luster every time she uses Sneeze Dust. Put an end to that four-letter word in your home with Sneeze Dust. It always passes the "white glove" test.

This spot only contains a one-sentence set-up, so you must take full advantage of the owner's name. Raise your eyebrows when you say "clean" and see if a "You know how precise she can be!" subtext filters through. Make "dust" sound nasty and totally despicable. After all, it is a "four-letter word." The sheer mention of dust is utterly revolting.

In the second sentence, the solution to the problem begins the body of the commercial. It responds to the dust problem and rationalizes why the hero product is used. As usual, pride shines through when Sneeze Dust is mentioned. Enjoy the possibility of entertaining the Queen of England. Put quotes around "just so." Use this as a reminder to make the room sound perfect with nary a thread out of place. Admire Mrs. Clean's rare antiques. Notice how the hero product helps them "recapture their original luster." Take note that she uses Sneeze Dust "every time."

The resolve begins when the attention is drawn away from Mrs. Clean's home and into the consumer's house. "Put an end" should sound definite and absolute. Find it hard to even say "four-letter word." Feel free to emphasize "your." It follows the switch from the on-camera lady to the listener. Feel satisfied and self-assured when you give the final product mention. Put your viewers' minds to rest when you say the final sentence. This product will impress even the harshest critics.

Funride Cruise Lines

Radio/30 seconds

This script yearns for your stereotypical one-eyed pirate with the weathered whisky-and-cigarette voice. The perspective is that of someone who doesn't understand the fuss about cruise ships and their luxury. After all his hardened travels, he harbors a bit of jealousy. It is the negative sales approach. A despicable character, whom you wouldn't want around, talks disdainfully about something you would just as well not have that person share with you. This, in turn, makes the product sound pretty darn good. Feel free to add or delete minor words if it helps you capture the character. The only information you cannot change is the copy points.

> Ahoy, matey. Seems there are some new cruise ships invading me waters! But they don't have the character and history of my vessel. Sure they've got luxury staterooms, 'round-the-clock entertainment, never-endin' meal service, and three ports o' call. But who needs that when you've got cannons, rum kegs, and gangplanks. Funride Cruise Lines. They give so much for so little. Arrh, it'll never last.

Grab the listener's attention with a bold and playful greeting. Squint your eyes skeptically as you talk about the new cruise ships and how they have ventured into your waters. Stand strong and proud as you describe how good your vessel looks. Talk suspiciously about all their fancy-schmancy assets (otherwise known as copy points). Stretch out the descriptive words. Angrily toss away the phrase, "But who needs that. . . ." Then switch to proud boasting when describing your cannons, rum kegs, and gangplanks. Remember to pick up the pace here so the listener is left with the hero client information rather than an itemized list of what's on board the pirate's ship. Contemplate the ship's luxuriousness when you slowly and reflectively mention Funride Cruise Lines. Notice that the word "so" repeats. Use this parallel to set up "give *so* much / for *so* little." Laugh at the ludicrousness of a fancy cruise ship. Place the disgruntled "arhh" growl in the back of the throat, and let it slip out the side of the mouth. Keep that same gravelly sound throughout the closing phrase.

Sparkle OH!

TV/30 seconds

You are the voice of a talking oven. The oven door is animated. It moves as it speaks to the audience and conveys its smelly, messy state of affairs. There is smoke coming out of the door and charred food on the inner walls. Suddenly, the hero product flies through space and sprays itself inside the oven. The door slams and the oven dials itself to 450 degrees. A digital clock flips to one hour later and the oven door bursts open revealing the sparkling clean insides. The can of Sparkle OH! flies through space again and lands on the open door.

A couple of suggested reading interpretations utilize animated boredom and age differentials. For the first reading, sustain your energy but let the voice go flat and almost emotionless. Then, perk up a little and smile when the oven becomes clean. Another reading can have a "Merlin-esque" approach. At first, the oven is old and cranky but magically becomes young and rejuvenated after the cleaning. Throughout all reads, the voice should sound believable.

> Hello. It's me, your oven. Whew! It sure gets dirty in here! There's the cheese soufflé that spilled over last week, the meat loaf surprise that splattered grease all over me, and little Sarah's cooking experiment that smells like burned rubber. Please do us both a favor and get Sparkle OH! All you do is spray Sparkle OH! on my inside walls, close my door, turn me to 450, and let me bake. An hour later, I'm sparkling clean. Sparkle OH! It makes your oven spotless.

During the set-up, the oven should sound hot, filthy, and miserable. When you appeal for cleaning help, try not to whine. Let the advice be conveyed confidently. Since this is a television commercial, you don't have to punch the product name as definitively. Of course, the name still needs to stand out, but let the visuals do the heavy-duty endorsement. The instructional list should sound simple and easy. Sigh or appear relaxed and pleased when the oven door opens to reveal the refreshingly new look. Show that Sparkle OH! is your friend on the final product mention and closing slogan.

Fieldsit Pillow
Radio/25 seconds
This spot calls for a soft, confident, meditative guru with an Indian accent. Traditional music from northern India plays in the background. Connect the character's need, to sit comfortably for long periods of time, with the product name, Field*sit*. The hyphenated words are placed there to guide the intended accent. Overall, this spot should convey mystic understanding.

> In my business, I do a lot of thinking, a great deal of meditating, and most of all . . . sitting. That is why I use the pillow that nine out of ten gurus recommend, Fieldsit. Fieldsit Pillows are made with only natural fibers. And they maintain their firmness even after hours of sit-ting and me-di-ta-ting. For extended hours of sitting—or sleeping—pick up a Fieldsit Pillow today.

Native speakers are often called on to voice commercials because of their unique and natural dialect. This is usually the first casting choice. Some cities have more ethnic diversity than others, but even if there are many people from the specified region, there is a possibility that the majority of these individuals will not know how to make voice-over copy come alive. This, in turn, opens the door to voice actors with the ability to do believable dialects. If you, as a non-native, perform a dialect, be wary of mocking or insulting a nationality or race. Your performance should be executed very carefully and with respect to the people.

As you read, adopt the religious teacher and spiritual guide qualities of the guru. Your body must be very still and "centered." Breathe out, relaxing the breath. Plant your feet firmly on the ground. Imagine roots growing out of your feet and anchoring you to the soil. You are one with nature. There shouldn't be an iota of tension or nervousness. You must be all-knowing and all-understanding. If it helps, sit on the floor with your legs crossed, or at least envision yourself in that position, as you read the script. Speak slowly, without rushing. This imbues the guru with more power. Never, never sell! Emphasize your familiarity with the hero product and what it offers you to make your students stronger—or at least more comfortable.

Warm and Cozy

TV/30 seconds

Well-bundled observers crowd around a groundhog as it sticks its head out of a hole. There is a groan from the crowd as the groundhog sees its shadow. Reacting to the noise, the groundhog looks up to observe the individuals. The camera pans across their beautiful outfits. The groundhog backs down into its hole. The selected character voice should be your personal interpretation of what you think a groundhog would sound if able to speak. Keep in mind that it is very cold and overcast outside. Also, remember that groundhogs are usually afraid of their shadow.

> Oh, no! It looks like we're in for a long winter. And I had my spring plans made already. Oh well, back to my cold, underground dwelling. Just listen to these humans complain! They may look funny, but at least they know how to stay warm. I wish I could bundle up with a warm coat, a thick sweater, an extra pair of woolly socks, and a comfy muffler. Heck, all I have is fur. They're so lucky to have Warm and Cozy. If I wasn't so afraid of my shadow, I'd shop there myself.

This commercial is a great place to practice using size, age, emotional condition, and outside environment as parameters for creating a character voice. Initially the groundhog is surprised by his shadow. This turns to disappointment when he must then reconcile himself to hibernating for six more weeks. As if that's not bad enough, the groundhog hears the humans groaning and mumbling. Looking up, he finds the human creatures to be odd looking but amazingly warm. The groundhog covets their warm clothes, as he describes each garment—all major copy points. Dejected, the animal accepts his fur, but thinks longingly of the hero store. Reality hits. Alas, the groundhog can never shop there. Only humans have this option.

Tingle

Radio/30 seconds

Okay all you would-be opera singers, here's your chance to cut loose and belt one out. Pompousness is the key! Add a foreign accent if you wish. You can also use the manager's quote to provide an additional character voice.

> When I sing, it is standing-room-only, but it wasn't always that way. Before, when I sang, the front rows were empty by intermission. My manager said, "Either stop eating chili pepper flambé or start gargling with Tingle mouthwash." Well, I was not about to give up my chili pepper flambé. So, now I "tingle" before every performance. Tingle mouthwash gives me a fresh, clean feeling . . . and a full house.

The major places to break into vibrato are on "sing" and "sang," and on "tingle" in the second-to-last sentence. Let the pride and self-confidence show through in the first sentence. Follow this with contrasting disappointment in the second sentence. Place the third sentence deeper in your musical register to give it a darker, more ominous tone. If you are up to the challenge of adding the opera singer's interpretation of the manager, throw in a contrasting voice. Puff up your chest with disgust as you dismiss the idea of forfeiting your favorite dish. Sing the praises of the hero product with operatic pride. Emphasize the word "every." Illustrate how fresh your mouth feels. Use the microphone and move in closer to it as you let the audience in on your secret about the now "full house."

Talkin' Teddy
TV/30 seconds
This is the voice of the latest fad toy to hit the market. Not only does the person who lands this national commercial get paid thousands of dollars in residuals, he also gets paid a separate fee to be the animal's voice inside the product. Hooray for advertising and marketing! It is very important that the voice be lovable, cuddly, and have a great-sounding laugh. Of course, this is a high energy read.

> Hello, boys and girls! I'm new Talkin' Teddy. Spanner Corporation made me just for you. How about that? Listen to this. I laugh (giggle). I cry (boo hoo). I wear a diaper (uh, oh). But most of all I hug people (I love you). I wish you'd take me home with you. Talkin' Teddy and you can be great friends.

You have to put your whole body into this one in order to top the cuteness quotient. A lot of money is riding on the introduction of this product. Make sure you emphasize that it is new. Take your time to produce good sound effects. Act as if you are cuddling a small child when you say, "I love you." Express your deep desire to have a home.

Sundried Prunes
Radio/30 seconds
Soft classical music is playing in the background. An upper-class British accent is most appropriate for this character. After all, you are the butler, or head of the domestic staff help. Everything you do is very precise and proper.

> When I prepare meals for the Uprights, I have to be most careful. Their tastes are quite sophisticated, but they have a bit of a sweet tooth. So when the Uprights ring the dinner bell, I always include some pitted prunes from Sundried. These aren't ordinary prunes. They're sweet and juicy, and I don't have to fuss with pits. Sundried does it for me. (SFX: *dinner bell*) It's time for Sundried pitted prunes.

Words to emphasize are (in order of appearance): meals, Uprights, most, tastes, sophisticated, sweet tooth, Uprights, always, pitted prunes, Sundried, ordinary, prunes, sweet, juicy, I, fuss, pits, Sundried, for, time, Sundried, pitted prunes. Draw a line under the copy points, two lines under the name of the product, and bracket words that need character shading. For instance, "ring" doesn't directly sell the product but it does enhance the character. Therefore, you could roll the r. Also, you should have an opinion about everything. Show pride in your food preparation. Reveal your knowledge of their sophisticated taste and slight disdain or pleasure that they have a weakness for sweets. Take great satisfaction in supplying the healthy solution. Scoff at the competition and relish the taste of the hero product. Take jolly delight at not having to waste time digging out prune pits. Your hero product does the work, and you get all the credit.

Tubster
TV/30 seconds
All you racing enthusiasts, now's your time to ham it up as you call the race. The setting is a child's bedroom. There is an extensive racetrack set up on the floor. Three children are intent on the race. Each has a hand on their favorite car. They pull the wheels back and forth before the race starts, activating the car's automatic forward motion. The camera zeros in on the cars. The possibility of winning the race fills the kids with excitement and pleasure. The voice-over are the words of a child's imagination and the thrill of the race should build throughout the spot. Background ambiance features crowd cheers and car engines. The studio engineer will add echo to the voice so it sounds like an announcer's voice over of a PA system. The echo may distort the sound, so you should enunciate clearly and stretch out the first three sentences.

> Ladies and gentlemen. Start your engines. The Tubster car races are about to begin. (SFX: *gun shot*) And they're off. Tubster Turbo is on the outside. The Tubster Express is leading the pack on the straight-away. Coming up from behind is Tubster Alley, the newest car from Tubster. They're neck-and-neck going into the loop-de-loop. Tubster Turbo and Tubster Express are falling back. And it's Tubster Alley, the winner! Tubster cars. Fast, safe, fun.

This is a high energy spot that positions the toy cars as fast, safe, imaginative, and exciting fun for boys and girls. The three sections are quite distinct. The set-up is almost musical. It is slow, methodical, and filled with anticipation. Since it requires a bold, broad voice, you may want to stand a bit further back from the mic than normal. Continue the long drawn-out speech pattern through the word "and" in the fourth sentence. This provides contrast with "they're off," which is short and staccato.

The body of the spot can be played closer to the microphone. Since you are the announcer of the race, you have a natural reason for punching the car names—to inform the spectators. Increase excitement and tension with each sentence. You may want to stair-step the first three action sentences upward, then drop your voice down and repeat the process; this avoids topping out your voice. Even though your vocal pitch drops midway, the intensity and excitement continues to build.

Close the spot out with a strong product endorsement. Drop the voice down as low as you can in your vocal register to give the hero toy a weighty, rugged sound. Make the final three words sound like their meaning. It is not necessary to take a break between each word, but you should smile knowingly.

News Express
Radio/30 seconds
Use this commercial to again challenge your range of accents. You can substitute some *v*'s for *w*'s and play a German. An outlandish choice is to play an alien from another planet.

When I first came to this country, my English wasn't very good. I didn't have money to spend on English lessons. But every day I bought the News Express. I read it cover-to-cover. Soon I could understand all the articles, features, sports, even the funny pages. Why, I even found my job through the News Express Classifieds. My English is much better now. Bet you wouldn't know I was from _____ [city/country].

In a multicultural society, the hero newspaper is the solution to the language and job barrier and, when coupled with the character's sheer tenacity, helped him to overcome all odds. Financial and language woes are established in the set-up. Buying the newspaper and reading it diligently offers the character a solution. Pride is evident during the listing of newspaper sections, especially the comics. Finally, the spot is resolved through the language and financial conquests. The closing resolve is a challenge for the listener and further proves the usefulness of the product.

Chapter 11

MULTIPLES

Multiples, pairs, two-parters, duets, and dialogues are the numerous monikers given scripts requiring the interaction of two or more voices. The order of events is listen-react-speak. Much as in everyday life, the dialogue bounces back and forth between actors like a ball on a ping-pong table.

Listening and *reacting* to the other actor's words are the key ingredients to successful dialogue spots. Deciding how to play the role and locking yourself into it, with a total disregard for the other actor's delivery, destroys the natural flow of the human relationship. However clever, the result is always contrived and this limits the actor's "emotional life." For instance, if you predetermine that your character should play in an irritated manner, but the other actor delivers lines in a way that makes you feel silly and giddy, you need to relinquish your mental hold over the character and stay with the truth of the moment. That's when fresh, believable sparkles of life are created that illuminate the written page, making the dialogue sound real.

GUIDELINES FOR MULTIPLES

Acting is not an *idea*. It is an *action* in a specific moment. The trusted brain must learn to step aside and allow the spontaneous child inside to come out and play. The heart and soul of a person has to take over. As the other person's lines bounce toward you, you must learn to feel the emotional effect, react truthfully to the situation, and deliver your lines in an appropriate manner.

Timing is another key element in multiple spots. As one actor finishes a line, the other should immediately chime in. There should be no lag time or dead air grinding the spot to a sudden and unnecessary halt. Instead, the dialogue should sound engaging, like a conversation where you can't wait for the other person to finish their thought so that you can add your own tidbit. For this to happen, the actor must prepare to speak before the actual bit of dialogue begins. The actor needs to be loose and flexible, arms animated, breath stabilized, mouth open so that "unsoundly" lip smacking sounds are eliminated, feet grounded, knees slightly bent to allow physical mobility, ears listening, and heart and mind ready to accept information from the other actor. As the first actor finishes the final word in a sentence or phrase, the second actor immediately responds by "stepping on" the tail end of that word. The only time stepping on, or overlapping, the tail end of another actor's line is inappropriate is when the sentence closes with the client name or a major copy point. Then, a slight space of air should be allowed so that the key information can sink into the listener's mind.

Sometimes an actor with only one line of dialogue, sandwiched in between a conversation involving two or more other actors, forgets about his own contribution to the scene. The error occurs when the actor, in awe of his peers' performance, removes his eyes from the copy to watch. Dead air results. Instead of words, embarrassment fills the space. So remember, even if you have only one line of dialogue in the middle of 60-seconds worth of copy, you still must stay "in the scene," follow the script, and not become a spectator. Ignoring this advice guarantees that you will stumble and botch your one-liner. The resulting dead air that snaps you back into reality is the sound of voice-over death. Fortunately, this misfortune is not terminal unless repeated on a consistent basis. One experience usually breaks a voice actor of this habit.

Other bad habits to avoid in the booth are breathing heavily, turning pages, or moving around unnecessarily while another actor is talking. Even if you are not speaking, you still must show respect and courtesy for the microphone and your fellow actors. Besides being distracting, these actions can ruin a take. The mic also picks up clothes rustling and lip smacks that occur just prior to talking, so if you must breathe or sigh heavily or scratch an itch, you should either refrain from these actions until the recording has stopped or quietly lean away from the microphone to minimize the noise. Lip smacks can also be averted by breathing through your mouth; don't close the lips all the way between sentences. To avoid paper noises, refrain from touching the script and music stand during the recording. Forgetting one of these rules will probably result in a reprimand from the engineer, director, or fellow actor.

Microphone placement for multiples varies from one recording studio and session to another. Sometimes each actor has her own microphone; other times they must share one. It depends on the idiosyncrasies of the room, sound requirements of the session, and visual contact needed between director and actors. Often, two mics face one another, allowing the actors to direct their actions toward one another. Some studios prefer to face the actors forward, toward the console room. Positioned shoulder-to-shoulder, the actors fight the urge to turn off mic when talking to one another. While sharing one mic creates a closeness and intimacy in the recording, it also requires the actors to physically maneuver in and out of position to allow room for each other in front of the microphone. Actors touch and brush shoulders with one another in this close set-up. (Keep your breath mints handy for these situations.) The larger the group, the more creative the choreography.

Visibility also becomes a challenge when a pop filter, microphone, or fellow actor blocks your view of a shared script. The script may call for one main narrator and several supporting voices with only one word or phrase to say. The main actor is afforded his own microphone. The remaining actors position themselves in chronological order around a secondary mic. As each supporting actor completes the assigned reading, he creeps quietly out of the way and the next actor slips into mic position. Large groups can also be recorded in a circular pattern with a mic and stand provided for each actor.

Resist the temptation to direct your fellow actor unless specifically requested by your session mate. It is the director's job to direct, not yours. Unsolicited direction can yield animosity, and create an emotional wall between the actors that may be detected in the recording. Instead, concentrate your energies and attention on yourself. More than likely, if you explore your character more deeply, your acting partners will perform better, too.

For ultimate rehearsal benefit, the scripts in this chapter require additional voice actors. If you know someone who performs voice-overs or who is currently learning the trade, invite him over for a practice session. If not, just practice with a friend. Rehearse the spots, record them, and listen to your progress. Critique your work. Pretend you are the director, client, or audience. The read must motivate the audience, and focus on the product and key points without sounding announcer-ish and stilted. Pay special attention to the recorded dialogues: you should sound as if you are speaking *to* one another, not merely talking *past* or *at* one another. Once you are satisfied with your recording, try switching parts. This is a great technique that exercises an actor's flexibility and creativity.

Pick-up Line

Radio/60 seconds

Meet Shirley, the "princess," and Ralph, the "nerd." Ralph is on a phone patch, a technical device that runs through the engineer's control board and alters the voice to sound like it is actually coming through a telephone line. In some recording studios, "Ralph" is placed in an isolation booth so his filtered voice doesn't bleed into "Shirley's" mic. The two actors then wear headphones so they can hear one another as they carry on their dialogue.

Create an activity for Shirley as she prepares for her big date. She could be painting her fingernails, combing her hair, or ironing her dress. The hidden intention in Ralph's call is to gloat. Be careful not to give away his big secret until the closing lines. Even though he is not suave and debonair during the beginning of the commercial, he should be played fairly cool and genuinely interested in Shirley's well-being. In selecting the appropriate voices for these characters, be careful that they don't grate on the listener's nerves. Both characters should be likable.

(SFX: *phone ring and pick-up*)
Shirley: Hello?
Ralph: Hi, Shirley. It's Ralph.
Shirley: (Disappointed) Oh hi, Ralph. What's up?
Ralph: I've been trying to get a hold of you for days, but either your line's busy or you're not in.
Shirley: I can't help it if I'm in great demand.
Ralph: Shirley, you need a Pick-up Line. That way you won't miss important calls like mine.
Shirley: Can Pick-up Line screen out unimportant calls?
Ralph: You bet! With Pick-up Line, you can even retrieve messages when you're away from your phone.
Shirley: Well, Ralph. It's been dandy talking to you, but I've gotta run. I've got a big date tonight.
Ralph: Oh, stupid me! I almost forgot.
Shirley: Forgot what?
Ralph: I won 10 million dollars in the lottery and I called to propose marriage.
Shirley: I accept!!
Ralph: Sorry. That was last week when I called to propose, but I couldn't reach you so I married Lucy instead.

Shirley: Lucy!! Who's Lucy?
Ralph: She's a great gal. Reminds me of you, Shirley. Except for one thing!
Shirley: What's that?
Ralph: She's got a Pick-up Line.

Conflict forms the basis for most two-parters. In this instance, Shirley shuns Ralph's advances until she discovers Ralph's newfound wealth. For a brief moment, the relationship conflict is resolved, but the tables quickly turn and Ralph controls the conversation when he reveals that he married another woman. If only Shirley owned the hero product! Life would be much richer for her.

Part of the fun of playing characters such as these is to highlight their emotional transformations. Shirley opens the spot anticipating speaking to one of her handsome beaux only to be disappointed by the sound of Ralph's voice. She becomes annoyed and frustrated as Ralph refuses to get off the phone, but at no point should Shirley's attitude turn hostile or mean. Negativity immediately turns off listeners, so find the humanity in the character. One way of doing this is by playing the part with the phony smile of someone caught in an awkward situation. Most people can relate to the feeling of being trapped by a person they'd rather not talk to as they search desperately for an excuse to weasel themselves free. Shirley makes a sudden 180-degree turn when she discovers Ralph has money. A million things must run through her mind as she realizes she could have shared Ralph's riches if only she owned the hero product.

Even though it appears in the beginning that Ralph is a loser, he is the winner by the end of the spot! He gets even with Shirley and teaches her a lesson. In his pleasant, nerdy way, he flirts with the obviously uninterested Shirley. He patiently shares his wisdom about answering machines and the product reliability. When Shirley starts to hang up on him, Ralph is forced to divulge the purpose of his call. He sets her up with his money and proposal. Then, in almost the same breath, he rescinds the offer and announces the name of his new wife. Ralph should relish this moment. Revenge is sweet!

Shopping Hub
Radio/60 seconds
This is a co-op spot. All the mall outlets mentioned in this commercial share the advertising expense. The sponsors names have been italicized as a reminder for you to make them stand out from the rest of the copy. Start the ad with an explosion of excitement. Terry can be either male or female. Increase the excitement with John's predicament.

(SFX: *mall ambiance*)
Terry: John, I'm glad I found you.
John: What's up?
Terry: I just saw Marsha coming out of *Booklover's Bookstore*.
John: You mean she's here, in the Shopping Hub?
Terry: Yep.
John: Quick, let's grab some sushi at *Rawfish Restaurant* while we collect our thoughts.

Terry: Not a good idea.

John: Why not?

Terry: She was heading that way!

John: Well the Shopping Hub is a big mall. Where else we can go?

Terry: *Hot Doggers, Fishfry's, New Jersey Pizzeria, Jane Dough's Deli, Ground Chuck. . . .* Choose something 'cause all this talk of food is making me hungry.

John: Wait. Before we eat, I have to stop in at *Sky Fly Travel* to book those plane tickets.

Terry: Where to? Brazil?

John: No, Marsha's parents' house.

ANNOUNCER: Hide out today at the Shopping Hub at Fifth and Cash Streets. With over 110 shops, from delicious restaurants, to travel centers, to clothing stores and small boutiques, Shopping Hub's got it all. Shopping Hub. It's the place to escape.

John: Marsha, what a surprise!

Marsha: So, did you get the plane tickets?

John: Why don't we discuss that over ice cream at *The Fat Cow?*

Energy and tension are the main ingredients in this spot. Unlike the previous example, there is no conflict between the two central characters. The presence of Marsha, the third character, provides the conflict.

Here timing can either make or break the spot. In the beginning, Terry speaks at a quicker pace than John who tries to comprehend his friend's excitement. John's pace picks up when he hears about Marsha. The three lines "Not a good idea," "Why not?" and "She was heading that way!" should overlap. No pertinent copy points are mentioned. John should take time to explain the enormousness of the mall, and speed up the following sentence, which also has no copy points.

Now comes the tricky part. Terry should enthusiastically list each co-op advertiser. Add a touch of reality by seeming to search your brain for the names of the various establishments. Avoid saying each client's name as if on a mundane list. John can help make this awkward section work by injecting short, *positive* (never negative), one-syllable ad-libs between each name. The list should entice people to visit the mall, not bore them.

Determined to buy the tickets, John decides to visit the travel agency. Even though his destination is bleak (Marsha's parents' house), the hero mall and travel agency are positive points. Don't allow either of them to sound bad. The announcer stops the action and allows time to pass. The entire listening audience is invited to experience the wonders of the Shopping Hub.

Whether or not John actually gives in to Marsha's ticket request is left unresolved. If the ad is well received, a sequel may ensue.

Illusions

Radio/60 seconds

Both characters should be played with equal emphasis; one should not overpower the other. The interview takes place in front of a live audience, and the "reporter" should change his proximity to the microphone depending upon who he addresses.

Reporter: I'm here with the world-famous magician, the Amazing Profundo!

Profundo: Greetings! (SFX: *cheers from audience*)

Reporter: Mr. Profundo, you are known worldwide for your amazing magic.

Profundo: That is correct.

Reporter: Would you be kind enough to tell us about your illusions?

Profundo: Ah! Magicians never reveal their secrets.

Reporter: What if I gave you this crisp hundred dollar bill?

Profundo: Well, why didn't you say so! (SFX: *crisp bill popping*) Listen carefully. (Move closer to the mic to add confidentiality and mystique) My Illusions have the most superb happy hour in all the world.

Reporter: Your *illusions* have a happy hour, Mr. Profundo?

Profundo: And, my Illusions even provide free hors d'oeuvres?

Reporter: Free hors d'oeuvres? That's incredible!

Profundo: And dancing, too! Nightly, until 2 A.M.

Reporter: But Mr. Profundo, I don't understand.

Profundo: (Resume original mic positioning) There's no magic to it. (SFX: *gasp from audience*) Illusions is the hot new nightclub, downtown on Granite Street. The barbecued chicken wings are outstanding! Watch me pull one out of my hat. (SFX: *a poof and crowd applauds*)

Reporter: Well, the vision is clear. For a little magic in your nightlife, visit Illusions.

Profundo: It's amazing! (SFX: *crowd cheer*) And tasty, too. Here (SFX: *poof*), try one.

The reporter should consider this interview a major career coup. Impressing the audience by uncovering the magician's secrets is the reporter's primary intention. The approach is strong and direct, albeit a bit confusing as the interview progresses. There should be a clear definition and change of focus between the audience and Profundo, with the reporter's opening and closing lines directed toward the audience. It might help to envision a television journalist who must turn and speak to a camera when introducing and concluding important interviews or news bulletins. To achieve this switch in focus, slightly alter your body position. For example, you could stand tall and speak directly into the microphone when talking to the audience and twist your body slightly to one side (without moving off mic) when addressing Profundo.

Profundo is the consummate performer who knows how to work a crowd. He should be played larger-than-life. Add an accent, roll the *r*'s, imagine him in gold lamé and a turban. Profundo also has a split focus: between his adoring fans and the interviewer. When saying "That is correct," you might bow your head or lower your eyes in mock-humble acknowledgment of your international fame. Be quick to defend your profession, but easily lured by money. Pay attention to mic positioning: remember that secretive intimacy is a great vehicle for conveying major copy points, but too much becomes boring and stale. End with a cheerful "It's amazing!" The final two throw-away lines add a button to the spot.

Jam Spread

TV/30 seconds

Rather than a "talking head" commercial, this is a "talking hand" spot. The camera focuses on two sets of hands, one male and one female. Hand models are used to tell the story expressively. The voices seem to belong to the hands but are really two separate voice actors. There should be a softness, intimacy, and levity about the voices, as they convey a relaxed, loving relationship.

Visually, the spot opens with his hands putting Jam Spread on a slice of bread. He is slightly startled when his wife's hands appear. She picks up the jar. He taps her hand lightly with the side of the butter knife when saying, "Hey, put that down." He then tries to hide the jar behind a bread basket. Caught in the act, he hands the jar back to his wife, who opens the lid to reveal a near-empty jam jar. He retrieves it, places it between them with the label facing directly into the camera, and tosses the butter knife into the nearly empty jar. She places her hand on his when saying, "His name wouldn't happen to be John, would it?" and points out the jam smudge on his sleeve.

There should be no tension and apprehension in the voices, only playful teasing. Use a substitution to help develop a believable rapport.

Woman: What are you doing?
Man: Making a snack.
Woman: What's this?
Man: Hey, put that down.
Woman: Jam Spread. I've never heard of it.
Man: Discovered it when I went shopping last week.
Woman: And now you're hiding it from me.
Man: I'm not hiding it. See, here it is.
Woman: Someone's eaten all of it. It's almost empty.
Man: It must be the Jam Spread pirate.
Woman: His name wouldn't happen to be John, would it?
Man: Whatever gave you that idea?
Woman: You've got Jam Spread on your sleeve.

There is no need to rush this commercial. Relax and don't push it. The woman delights in her discovery and uses her charm and wit to subtly pry loose John's secret. John defends himself in a bashful and irresistible manner. Both actors should smile. Let the words do the work. Listen and respond truthfully.

Save-a-Dime
Radio/60 seconds
Some retail spots use alternating male and female announcers to add auditory interest to otherwise straight, flat information. The two voices do not have a relationship with one another, they are merely information expediters. Use this opportunity to develop your retail announcer skills in tandem with another actor. The voices must work well together to create a cohesive sound. They should speak at the same speed, with the meter between them remaining constant. Each actor should be pleasant, likable, and believable.

(SFX: *music jingle*)
She: It's back-to-school time. And that means time to stock up on savings for the entire family at Save-a-Dime.
He: Right now, Save-a-Dime is featuring boys' jeans, sizes 4 to 14, for only $11.95.
She: Girls' fashion pantsets, sizes 4 to 6x, are only $9.69.
He: Rugged boys' jackets now at the unbelievably low price of $24.99!

She: Colorful Save-a-Dime-brand girls' knit tops and pantsets, sizes 4 to 14, starting at only $8.95.

He: Teenagers will be thrilled with the latest style denim jackets for under $30.

She: And Save-a-Dime has fashions for the adults of the family, too. Men's and women's cotton briefs and socks are on sale starting at $1.97.

He: Plus, Save-a-Dime offers outerwear for any occasion. So, check out the jeans, dress shirts, sweaters, dresses, casual wear, jackets, coats, shoes, and more at special Save-a-Dime discounts.

She: When it comes to saving money for the entire family, Save-a-Dime's got the answer.

He: Start the season right with a stop at Save-a-Dime

She: It's not just a store, it's a way of living.

There is a very specific retail style that exudes confidence, friendliness, and pride. To achieve this, especially when you are working with another actor, it is important to "take your space" in the room. Make sure your breath is stabilized and your body relaxed, with your feet firmly planted on the floor, mouth muscles adequately warmed up, and body energy secured in the chest and stomach areas. (Words can sound too punchy if the energy is focused in the mouth and throat.) The confidence that you know what you are doing needs to settle deeper in the body. Retail item/price dialogue is "unnatural speak" for most people, so use your hands to help you get through it clearly. If you consistently falter on a specific phrase, it may be a clue that you are not phrasing the sentence properly. Above all, smile. Be pleased that you can offer people great savings and fashionable duds.

"Back to-school" is the name of the sale. "Stock up on savings for the entire family at Save-a-Dime" is a phrase telling listeners *what* they should do and *why*, *who* will benefit, and *where* to go. "Right now" points out *when* the sale is taking place. The sales list follows. Pay attention to the commas; they are reminders to alter the voice slightly from products, to sizes, to prices. All three bits of information are important and should not run together on the same vocal pitch. Avoid saying the word "dollars" except on $1.97, where it emphasizes the low cost, and on $30, when a flat rate is mentioned.

Tempting's Morsels

Radio/30 seconds

This particular commercial uses two voices to illustrate the latest marketing craze called "co-branding." This is where two separate companies join together to form a new product that carries both company names. The double brand recognition is expected to double consumer confidence and ultimately boost sales. Voice One represents the Tempting Corporation and Voice Two, the Morsel Group.

Even though this is a radio commercial, it often helps to stretch the imagination and visualize what the ad would look like with an elaborate television production budget. If this was a TV commercial, computer animation would be used. Animated cookies and chocolates morsels would roll off conveyor belts and slide happily into brightly colored packages. Perhaps the chocolates would even dance into the cookies. New packaging that prominently featured both company names would march off together, arm-in-arm. This might not be a real visual, but this scenario is much more interesting than factory workers with hair nets and CEOs sitting behind messy desks.

Voice One: Once upon a time, there was a cookie company named Tempting . . .

Voice Two: And a chocolate company named Morsels.

One: The cookies Tempting made were very, well . . . tempting.

Two: And the chocolates Morsels made were irresistible.

One: Then one day the president of the Tempting Corporation talked to the owner of the Morsels Group.

Two: And together they decided to create a new kind of cookie. A cookie that everyone would love.

One: And that cookie is Tempting's Morsels.

Two: It's got the crunchy goodness of Morsels chocolate.

One: And the chewy goodness of a Tempting sugar cookie.

One & Two: We love 'em. Try a Tempting's Morsels cookie and you'll be hooked, too.

Written like a fairy tale, this spot has a clear set-up, body, and resolve. When reading the spot, add to the mood, and alter the voice, by imagining a specific style of music. Using this technique, read the commercial three different ways. The musical bed might be a light, fluffy fairy-tale nursery sound; rock-n-roll music; or elegant classical melodies floating in the distance.

Condor Café

Radio/30 seconds

This is a poorly written commercial. It takes a lot of creativity to make it come alive. For it to work, you must create a strong bond between the two people, despite their lengthy separation. One way to do this is by using physical movement. Begin the spot with character One slightly off mic. As One walks-and-talks to the microphone on the first line, the audience should hear the approach. Character Two could use the same technique at the spot's conclusion. The beginning and ending mic movements help portray a slice of life. Read this spot with internalized energy and excitement but also with truth, otherwise the reading will sound stiff and awkward. Bear in mind, the restaurant (product) symbolizes the cornerstone for their reawakened friendship.

Voice One: Hey! How are you?

Voice Two: I can't believe it's you! It's been years.

One: Where are you going?

Two: I have a lunch meeting at the Condor Café.

One: The Condor?! I eat breakfast there almost every day.

Two: You're kidding? The Condor Café is open for breakfast?

One: Sure! They make great omelettes, pancakes, and French toast. I especially like their fresh fruit platter and imported coffee.

Two: All this at the Condor Café?

One: Yep! I'm having breakfast at the Condor tomorrow. Care to join me?

Two: How about 7:30?

One: Perfect. Now, you better get to that lunch meeting.

Two: The Condor Café awaits!

One question to ask the director, if given a script like this, is whether or not you can change some of the noncopy-point dialogue to sound more natural. This is a touchy subject so you must be ever-so-careful when making this request. Many directors double as copywriters and are pleased with their writing skills. Comments to the contrary will not endear you to them. If not allowed latitude in this area, you can rely on laughs, gasps, sighs, and short exclamations of surprise or approval to pull the spot out of the scripted zone and into a more likable, believable arena.

Clearly defining the characters will immensely help this commercial. What do they do for a living? Where is the action taking place? Why haven't they seen one another in years? How do they feel about that? Are they surprised, guilty, ecstatic? Is Voice Two late for the lunch meeting and rushing to get there or ambling along with plenty of time to spare? What is the "pre-scene" for each character? The choices that you make will either create a successful commercial or a dud. For instance, which is more interesting: walking briskly to make a meeting that you are late for because your doctor just called and confirmed that you are pregnant, or humming a tune contentedly while aimlessly window-shopping to kill time? For this ad to work, you must show the entire spectrum of your funny, charming personality. Actors who inject life into commercials such as this are hired on a repeat basis. Directors know, beyond a shadow of a doubt, that no matter what dreck they put in front of good voice actors the spot will work!

Luggage Rack

Radio/30 seconds

Even though this dialogue involves an argument, it is important to always keep it light. Focusing on the serious reality of the separation will cause listeners to tune out. Rather than falling into that dark, dismal trap, be charming and lovable. Find the humor in the moment. For example, the man can laugh as if it's all a misunderstanding, and the woman could then mock his dismay as she lightheartedly clarifies the situation. The closing "oh" could either express disappointment, exposing a sensitive man, or happiness, adding a twist to the story. Try reading it both ways.

Man: Excuse me. What are you doing with my suitcase?

Woman: Your suitcase! I bought this at the Luggage Rack.

Man: You did not!

Woman: Yes I did!

Man: Remember, you were moving into my apartment and you needed a set of luggage?

Woman: Yeah.

Man: Well, I dropped by the Luggage Rack because you told me it was the number one discounter of quality luggage

Woman: Right. And you bought *me* this soft leather suitcase with *my* money. Now I'm using it to move out.

Man: But what will I do without a suitcase from the Luggage Rack?

Woman: The same thing you'll do without me. Find a replacement.

Man: Oh.

The ebb and flow of this ad can be dissected into three main sections. Section one: the beginning through the woman's line, "Yes, I did." Section two: "Remember" through the sentence, "Now I'm using it to move out." Section three: "But what will I do" to the end. When one tactic fails and the threat of losing arises, another intention must be implemented. This not only breaks up the monotony of the scene, but makes the dialogue more interesting and less catty.

Cameo
Radio/60 seconds
The woman is very upbeat. Enamored with her car, she has been driving it on the freeway nonstop since 9:00 P.M. when she closed the sale with the dealership. The boyfriend is rudely awaken by her abrupt early-morning call. We hear the conversation from the man's perspective. The woman is on a phone filter, and faint highway noises can be heard under her dialogue. Romantic sparks start to fly when the man realizes that his girlfriend now drives a fancy sports car. All progresses well until he mistakenly blows it and, in his sleepiness, calls her the wrong name.

> (SFX: *telephone ring*)
> **Man:** Hello.
> **Woman:** Hi, sweety. What are you doing?
> **MAN:** (Yawning) It's 2:30 in the morning. What do you think I was doing?
> **Woman:** I couldn't wait 'til tomorrow to call you. I've got to take you for a drive in my new Cameo.
> **MAN:** That's great. I didn't know you were getting a Cameo. Hey, that's one hot sports car. I don't think the world is ready for you.
> **Woman:** You'll be my first passenger.
> **Man:** Okay. How about picking me up at 8? You can drive me to work.
> **Woman:** It's a deal.
> **Man:** So I'll see you in the morning, Maggie.
> **Woman:** Maggie! This is Carolyn!
> **Man:** Does this mean I don't get a ride to work in your new Cameo?
> (SFX: *phone click and dial tone*)
> ANNOUNCER: The new Miska Cameo coupe. More than just good looks, it's got fully independent race-tuned suspension, a four-valve-per-cylinder fuel-injected engine, four-wheel anti-lock disc brakes, and aerodynamic styling that far surpasses all other sports coupes. Starting at under $25,000. The Cameo. It's a real looker. Dealer pricing may vary.

Sports cars are often referred to as sexy. The flirty dialogue is designed to play-up the Cameo's sex appeal by revving the listener's engine. The woman's voice should be enticing and seductive. And the man's, although initially groggy, should become alluring and stimulating. It should be apparent that the man is not interested in talking to the woman until she divulges the nature of the call. Automatically, he succumbs to the seduction of her purchase. He becomes titillated by the notion of sharing a beautiful car with a woman. Of course, all his hopes are dashed when he makes his major name faux pas, and he is dazed, confused, and dejected. The woman begins her role with early-morning flirtation, progressing quickly to seduction. When the rendezvous is set, the man betrays her trust. Shocked, hurt, disappointed, and angry, the woman beats a hasty retreat and hangs up.

To set the tone of this commercial, the man needs to establish the time of day. How do you sound and feel when you are abruptly roused from a deep sleep? Your hair is probably tousled, eyes heavily weighted, and heart racing a little from the sudden disturbance of the phone ring, the voice scratchy, and the mind groggy. It's easy to see why the guy blows it! To play the role, recall that feeling and implement it in the man's first few lines. Don't use your full voice to say the opening word; struggle to get the two syllables out of your mouth. It may help the authenticity to add physical movement like stretching the arms out in either direction or above the head, rolling the neck or shoulders, or scratching yourself. It is not necessary to yawn immediately. Create a realistic yawn in the middle of those two lines by breathing in through the nose and letting out an "ahh" or "mmm" as you start to speak. *Do not* stop talking to yawn! It creates a beat, shatters the illusion, and uses up precious airtime.

The next few lines take the man from peaceful sleepiness to sudden alertness. Wake up and slow down on the key words, especially "Cameo" and "one hot sports car." The flirtation begins with, "I don't know if the world is ready for you." Let the provocativeness continue through the mention of the wrong woman's name. Finally, the man should innocently question whether or not he still has a ride in the morning. Give him a sympathetic glimmer of hope.

Even though it is 2:30 in the morning, the woman is still pumped about her new car. Her upbeat enthusiasm and coquettish behavior is in sharp contrast to the man's groggy demeanor. She inquires about his activities, using this to segue into the main purpose of the call—to brag about her new purchase. The overwhelming delight of ownership should be conveyed in the words "new Cameo." As his enthusiasm increases, so should her charm. They consummate the driving arrangement on the climactic, "It's a deal." Unfortunately, the man ruins the relationship. Displaying sincere hurt and wounded pride on the name correction, rather than shouting, gains the woman sympathy.

Vocally, the announcer tag should reflect the image of the car's sleek, sporty, good looks, and the racy scene dialogue previously explored. Psychologically, it should say, "If you want to be the hottest thing on the block, buy this car!" Treat the opening line like an attention grabber, preparing the listener for the key descriptions and copy points to follow. Stress that the car not only turns heads, but is also exceptionally well-made. Then tell the listener that this sexy car has a bonus—it's economical. Visualize a flaming red sports coupe as you say the brand name one last time. Make your audience agree that, "It's a real looker." End with those closing remarks as you speed through the disclaimer.

Simply Delicious
TV/30 seconds

One word in a nationally televised commercial can earn a voice actor thousands of dollars. This spot illustrates this by utilizing a few wonderfully descriptive words to punctuate the sensational menu choices at this restaurant chain. Voices are chosen according to their descriptive abilities, vocal tone and pitch, ethnic and regional accents, and overall variety. Imagine tasting your favorite dish as you say your word. The visual description precedes the voice-over.

Visual: *close-up of a steaming plate of cheesy lasagna being served to a smiling, wide-eyed customer*	**Audio:** Mouth-watering.
Visual: *customer eating barbecue ribs, thick with sauce, and licking her fingers*	**Audio:** Delectable.
Visual: *fried chicken nuggets in the shapes of well-known cartoon characters being eaten by an adorable two-year-old wearing a bib*	**Audio:** Delightful.
Visual: *a tray of decadent desserts*	**Audio:** Irresistible.
Visual: *close-up of chefs in their white hats smiling proudly followed by the logo surrounded by some menu items*	**Audio:** Simply delicious.

The picture does most of the talking in this 30-second commercial. The voice merely enhances the pictures on the screen. In listening to your recording, do you feel that you do the food descriptions justice? Are you salivating? If not, try reading the spot again. This is a great exercise to help you understand the full sensation and subtle nuances of words. If properly executed, you may have to put a padlock on your refrigerator door! Hunger pangs are inevitable.

Chapter 12

Industrial Narrations

According to SAG and AFTRA, there are basically two types of industrial narrations: Category I, in-house informationals for industrial and educational use where no admission is charged to enter the facility, and Category II, point-of-purchase programming that is designed for the general "buying" public. The categories do not necessarily denote stylistic differences, but rather, the changes in the actor's rate of pay. Category II, due to its wider audience base, stipulates the actor be paid at a slightly higher rate.

CATEGORY I

Corporations use Category I, in-house industrials as a time-saving device to train and educate employees. This could be a video on new assembly line procedures, a motivational sales cassette for the company sales staff, a new employee informational guide tape, or a public awareness program used in schools to promote safety, sex education, global awareness, or the effects of violence and drugs. Classrooms, libraries, and museums use audio tapes as an effective means of conducting self-guided tours, teaching foreign language skills, and numerous other instructional purposes. Many company meetings incorporate video presentations to stimulate employee enthusiasm, demonstrate how a product works, illustrate what the competition is doing, or pitch products to prospective sponsors.

CATEGORY II

Programs that sell products to retail consumers fall under Category II. They are often found in the point-of-purchase areas of department and grocery stores and in heavily trafficked public places where there are captive audiences. Airports, bus and train stations, amphitheaters, stadiums, and shopping malls often run videos to pitch products and services to people. For example, a video monitor set up in the vegetable section of a grocery store may showcase a salad being prepared. The voice-over describes the salad-making process while the monitor features a close-up of hands cleaning, cutting, and preparing the vegetables. Finally, a specific salad dressing is tossed into the mixture with the suggestion that customers purchase these products today and prepare this simple feast at home for themselves and their families.

Car dealerships often use a continuous loop videotape presentation (a self-rewinding tape that plays over and over again) to pitch the many features and benefits of their various models. While the viewer is lured into viewing the presentation for its safety or engineering information, the video ultimately becomes a sales pitch.

OTHER TYPES OF INDUSTRIAL NARRATIONS

Regular work is something every voice actor strives for, and narrative television programs do offer that stability to a select few. Popular nature and wildlife programs use voice-overs to explain the vast array of environmental wonders. Once a week, a familiar, hushed voice speaks "behind the scenes" about the direction in which fish swim, grizzly bear mating habits, and the intricate social hierarchy of bees. Travel programs, focusing on historical locations, buildings, and people, expand the horizons of armchair travelers. If narrating special features interests you, check your local network and cable companies to see if any of these programs currently exist or if they are under development. Inquire as to the best procedure to get an audition. Most likely, you will either need to be an expert in the particular area or need to mail in a demo tape of a documentary-style narration before being granted an audition.

Infomercials, a recent phenomenon in the 1990s, often use voice-over narration to enhance the sale and description of products on television (and occasionally on the radio). In actuality, infomercials are long commercials that initially appear to be regular programming but later divulge their true intent—to sell. Sports and exercise equipment, health and beauty aids, clothing and jewelry, cooking supplies and utensils, books and videos, and travel packages only scratch the surface of the products currently being marketed in this manner. The uniqueness, quality, or perhaps the low price of the product hooks the viewer and the toll-free number displayed throughout the program adds simplicity to the sale, reeling in the consumer. As the voice-over states, "Operators are standing by to take your order."

The telephone is another source of work for the voice actor. Pick up the phone to make a long-distance call and a recorded voice thanks you for choosing their long-distance carrier. Reach a disconnected number and you are told that it is no longer in service or has been changed. Telephone companies, voice mail systems, and business telephone networks all rely on voice actors to create prerecorded messages. They instruct, inform, and relieve "on-hold" boredom. A voice prompts callers to press buttons on their touch-tone phones, while employees are given phone mailboxes within a voice mail system that can either be dialed directly or reached through a series of voice-guided button presses. Another area where voice actors provide recorded information are 900 numbers, which charge a customer a designated amount of money per minute. Topics range from horoscopes, television program synopses, and motivational tips, to sexual erotica, sports updates, and more.

RECORDING NARRATIONS

Narrations cover a wide spectrum. The best way to initially prepare for this line of work is to read long passages of text out loud. It should become part of your weekly regimen. Try adding a light flair to the newspaper's entertainment section, a disquieting feel to the disturbing front page news articles, a corporate edge to the business section, and drama to exciting sporting events. If you find you need an excuse to read aloud, try reading to your children or grandchildren, or volunteer as a reader at schools, libraries, juvenile halls, retirement homes, or radio stations catering to the blind. These are "win-win" situations for all, which provide listening enjoyment as well as a chance for you to explore new voices and feel at ease with the eye-brain-mouth connection required for reading aloud. It is only through extended reading of 30 minutes or longer that you can discover your vocal idiosyncrasies and weaknesses and work to correct them. For instance, does your mouth dry up? Does your saliva crackle when you talk? Do words start blurring together or get transposed? Do you have difficulty with long words that aren't in your daily vocabulary?

The eyes, mind, and mouth must coordinate in order to develop the self-trust needed to read long passages. Often to save time in recording sessions, narration scripts are given to actors "cold," without the luxury of prior viewing. Scripts can run from 40 to 50, or even 60, pages long! The actor must learn to make instinctual performance choices and trust that the words form properly and effectively in the mouth given the time restraint. When possible, many directors will give you a copy of the script a day or two before the recording. This is to a director's advantage as the actor then has time to become familiar with the material and can deliver a smoother, less time-consuming read. But as luck would have it, the vast majority of industrial scripts are rewritten the night before and cleared by the client only minutes prior to the session. In fact, even if an early installment is given to the actor, chances are it will be replaced with a revised edition on the actual recording date. Any notes made on the margins of the old script are gone and left for your memory to recall.

Unlike commercial recording sessions where actors usually stand, long narration sessions are set up for comfort, and the actor has the luxury of sitting on a chair or stool. For many, sitting is equated with massive energy loss through the derriere. Learning to keep the energy up while in a seated position is an art unto itself. Reclining comfortably back in the chair removes an actor from the immediacy of the scene, so reserve that position for resting between takes. Avoid energy drain by sitting on the edge of the chair or stool and leaning forward into the microphone. Once the levels are set, memorize this body position. After long sessions of breathing recycled air (air conditioning systems are often turned off to minimize noise), it may be necessary to take a break to clear the head, get some fresh air, and stretch the legs. Upon returning, it is important to assume the same seating position relative to the mic so that the recording levels match. If the director and engineer are tired and not totally alert, several pages of script can be read before anyone notices that the levels are lower or higher because the actor inadvertently changed positions. It is your part of the team effort to match the voice quality, volume levels, and energy.

Assuming there will be breaks in the recording session, it is best to ask the director before you begin taping how to proceed after each stop. Should you wait for the engineer to slate a new take, no matter how minor, or is it acceptable for you say "pick up" and continue reading from where you left off? Clearing this beforehand simplifies the engineer and producer's editing procedures once you have finished recording.

A few minutes are spent at the beginning of each session for the actor and director to agree on an appropriate word pace and delivery style. Generally, the tempo of industrial narrations is much slower and more deliberate than the pace of commercial recordings. Information must be easily comprehended by the listener. It must be descriptive and clear. Reading too fast or too slow won't hold the listener's attention. The words need to roll around descriptively in the mouth and not be monotone. After the tempo is established, the actor is then expected to make strong choices that suit the milieu, or market, so that long passages are recorded without repeated stops for directorial advice. Mistakes are bound to happen. If they occur, shake them off and don't mentally chastise yourself. You're a human being, not a machine. Simply correct them and move on. The engineer will edit out the glitch later. It is better to make strong choices and risk an occasional error than to deliver an errorless but boring and nondescript read.

When reading multipage scripts, you should arrange the pages numerically on the music stand. Some professional narrators have the keen ability to slowly and quietly remove a completed script from the stand while continuing to talk into the microphone, put it aside, and place a new script on the stand. For beginners and intermediates, this practice is not recommended during a recording session. It is an acquired skill that may take years of on-the-job training to acquire. Paper rustling sounds in the middle of a recording can ruin a take. Therefore, it's safer to place two pages of script side-by-side on the stand. If you feel comfortable, squeeze three pages onto the stand (the end scripts may hang off a bit). When arranging the pages, be sure that your eyes can follow the scripts without your mouth turning off mic. If your head faces to the left when reading the first page, then turns to the center when reading the middle page, and shifts to the right when reading the third page, the differences in mic proximity will alter the sound, rendering it inconsistent and unusable. Use your eyes to proceed from one script to the next. As you finish reading one set of pages, stop for a minute to set up the next. The paper rustling noises during this pause can be removed during editing, but paper crinkles underneath the voice cannot be removed. Therefore, do not turn pages in the middle of a read!

When reading longer scripts, the voice tends to fall into a rhythmic groove or tempo pattern—as if a metronome was turned on inside the body. The eyes see the words clearly, the brain deciphers the message effectively, and the mouth forms the message confidently. This groove can occur within a few seconds of recording or may take 10 minutes or more to achieve. When the reading style alters slightly from beginning to end, many directors opt to re-record the first few paragraphs or pages of script so the opening section matches the style of the more relaxed middle and end.

SAMPLE NARRATIONS

Keeping all these tips in mind, it is time to test your endurance. You might want to keep some water handy when practicing these narratives, since they are a bit lengthier than commercial copy. Some are complete while others are passages lifted from script beginnings, middles, or ends. However, none are more than a few pages. For extended reading, use textbooks, novels, nonfiction books, and the daily newspaper. Practice identifying the distinguishing style of delivery required for each narration. Does it need an intimate one-on-one, real-person sound? Is it strong and punchy copy, indicative of a proud announcer? Or, does it depict a warm, friendly spokesperson? Commit your mind, body, and voice to your vocal acting choices as learned in previous chapters.

Make a mental note of the scripts you feel most comfortable reading and the areas requiring more work. Remember to relax, breathe deeply, slow down (time is not as major a factor in industrials as it is in commercials), add vocal variety, and keep the tempo and energy consistent from beginning to end. Convey that you really and truly comprehend what you are talking about and that you are enthralled by the product. Never imply that the information is boring or "over your head." If you don't seem to understand what you are talking about, the listener won't have a clue either. Decide on your level of expertise—employee, owner, or avid fan—and commit to the choice.

Quality Hospital

This is the opening section of an in-house patient informational video that runs continuously on a monitor located in the doctor's waiting room. Due to the delicate nature of the material, the read requires a caring and compassionate voice. It is meant to raise patient awareness, not create fear and panic.

It wasn't supposed to happen to her. Sue always gave herself a monthly breast exam. She took care of herself, exercised regularly, and didn't smoke. But this time, something felt different. She immediately called her doctor and made an appointment.

At Quality Hospital, we know that one out of three women risk developing a breast lump and one in 10 have a chance of developing breast cancer. Yet with early detection, treatment is often successful. Our safe, painless, and effective low-dose radiation mammography can detect breast cancer in its early stages, long before a lump is even felt.

We recommend that women have their first mammogram at age 35. Women ages 40 to 49 should have a mammogram once every two years. Women 50 years and over should have a mammogram every year.

You could be at higher risk if you have a family history of breast cancer, you are over 50 years old, your first menstrual period was before the age of 12, you've never had children or had your first after age 30, or you are overweight or have a diet high in fats.

There are two distinctly different points of view used in this industrial. The first paragraph is a look inside Sue's mind. As the video shows Sue reliving her experience, the tempo reflects the slow and contemplative mood. In a tasteful, understated, and compassionate way, her discovery is meant to shock and alarm women into taking action. The remainder of the copy focuses on Quality Hospital, its services, and the purpose for making the video—to inform patients of potential high-risk categories.

As with a real-person commercial, substitutions can be used to breathe life into the story. The voice should be very rich with your memories. The first sentence should project an air of impending problems, but still carry a hopeful, everything-is-normal tone. The reality of the situation is acknowledged in the second line. Sue's good health habits should be listed positively. Serious undertones return on the next, transition line. Take time to explore Sue's situation and don't rush through the words. Concerned, but not panic-stricken, Sue takes action.

This is a situation with which the doctors and nurses at Quality Hospital are very familiar. It is because of their experience that they are able to share compassion and concern with their patients. Although the statistics listed in the presentation sound grim, the information is actually intended to inspire hope. For the mood shift from concern to a positive solution, there must be a strong, uplifting transition. Don't rely solely on your voice, but use your body to help instill subtle intention changes by tilting your head, shifting weight from one foot to the other, or leaning in closer to the microphone.

The information progressively grows stronger and more succinct as the script continues. The third paragraph is the call to action, instructing women on how to best proceed. While the fourth paragraph provides an "awareness" list. It is meant to be read deliberately because text for each item will appear on the screen, accompanying the voice. To achieve this, give the opening set-up sentence a musical lift that draws attention to the answers that follow. Each item should sound like a complete sentence, standing on its own. Do not lilt the voice upward and connect the phrases—this lessens the impact. Instead, pause a second between each phrase. Give each phrase equal emphasis. Also, since this is only the beginning of a much longer piece of copy, don't let the voice fade away, or imply vocally that this is the end of the presentation, when the script excerpt concludes. Keep your voice and breath steady as if there is more information to follow.

Workerbee Company

Audio cassettes are less-expensive instructional tools than the more commonly used video tapes. The information in this cassette is designed for new company employees. Like most corporate tutorials, the underlying message is company pride. As you read, use your voice to warmly greet the listeners, as if shaking their hands.

> Welcome to Workerbee Company and to the excitement and challenges of a growing business in this expanding and competitive industry. We feel confident that you will enjoy working with the high-caliber people who make up Workerbee Company.
>
> As a new employee, your job is important to us. We at Workerbee are interested in you and in building your career. Your success is an important factor in the success of the company. This tape is designed to offer you accurate information about company policies and procedures, benefit packages, performance reviews, training, and education opportunities. If you have any questions after listening to this tape, please discuss them with your supervisor or someone in the Personnel Department. They will be happy to assist you.
>
> Performance reviews are conducted on a biannual basis. At those times, your supervisor will give an oral and written review of your work. Superior performances are awarded one-hundred-dollar bonuses, while good performances merit a twenty-five-dollar honorarium, and fair to poor reviews receive a warning. Three warnings provide grounds for dismissal from the company.

The first paragraph exemplifies a typical corporate opening. The welcome should be inviting, confident of the listener's success, and full of pride for the organization. Leaning closer to the mic and mentally or physically extending a firm handshake can bridge the gap between the actor and the new employee audience with a warm and caring "hello." The voice should possess strength but also sound soft, relaxed, and nurturing. A gentle smile extends a feeling of caring for and appreciation of the company. Any personal negative feelings about an organization should never filter through the voice into the narration and adversely influence the listener.

In the second paragraph, a sense of team spirit should be conveyed. The use of the pronoun "we" implies that the company and the listener must work together cohesively. If you, the new employee, are successful, we, the other employees, will be successful, too, so pay careful attention to the facts in this cassette.

The final transition begins in the third paragraph. The copy has moved from open armed welcome, to call to unified action, and now to the "guts" of the tape. Obviously, not all the information in this section is positive. Negative issues must be handled delicately. State the policy without adding an emotional bias.

Corporate narrations such as this can be very dry. They should be performed clearly so information can be easily digested. As usual, hand movements are helpful in lists, where each item should stand on its own, not be linked to the following data, and not imply that there is more boring information to follow. Selecting your personal need for having the listener hear the information, and making appropriate intention changes, can make dry information sound interesting.

Nature Series

This is a sample segment from a television documentary focusing on the endangered Florida cougar. The style should be like storytelling—adventuresome, enlivening, and entertaining. Use a hushed, behind-the-scenes voice indicative of someone who might be only a few yards away from a wild animal and doesn't want to startle the animal or draw attention to herself. Stand close to the mic, and do not push or force the words. Simply share this magnificent story with your viewers.

> The deer approaches the opening, unaware of the cougar's presence. Slowly and quietly, Shuka creeps toward his prey. Hearing a twig crack, the deer turns and faces impending danger. There is no time to run before the six-foot-long, 200-pound male cougar pounces on its back and bites its neck. The deer, a favorite food of the cougar, has met its match. He has fallen victim to the balance of nature.
>
> Meanwhile, Carla is at the den watching her kittens. Smaller than males, females have similar reddish brown fur on the upper part of the body and white hair on the underbelly. There are three eight-day-old spotted cubs. Litters range from one to five cubs every other year. In a few months, Carla will teach them how to hunt.
>
> Shuka returns carrying part of his kill. Carla seems pleased with his hunt. As she stands up to eat, the kittens scramble around looking for milk. They mew for their mother, who seems disinterested at the moment.
>
> Off in the distance another cougar howls. It eerily resembles a domestic cat, only it is much louder. It soon turns into a loud screeching noise. This is the cougar mating call. Cougars do not have specific mating seasons like other animals. They can breed at any time of the year, and cubs reach sexual maturity between ages two and three. So, while this family grows and matures, another life cycle begins. We will return three months from now, and see if another litter has arrived.

Nothing has to be sold or punctuated in this documentary. It is an exercise in developing mesmerizing storytelling abilities. In reading this story, a true love of nature should be apparent. There is danger, excitement, and pathos in the first paragraph. The second paragraph focuses on the cute and cuddly aspects of the wild animal. In the third, there is a feeling of family unity and everyday existence. While, the last paragraph illustrates the continuation of the life cycle.

Experiment with pitch placement, proximity to the mic, speed changes, imagery, and voice fluctuation to add special interest and uniqueness to the read. Imagine the action occurring on the screen as you read the script.

Company Voice Mail

Automated voice mail systems are becoming increasingly popular as a means of handling in-coming business calls. The recording often provides the listener with numerous options, depending on the nature of the call and the response that is needed. The information must be friendly, useful, and concise. Each instruction must be able to stand on its own, should it be interspersed throughout other areas of the network.

> Welcome to the Company Voice Mail system. If you know the extension of the person you are calling, please enter it now. Otherwise, please stay on the line and an operator will assist you. If you are calling to place an order, press one. If you need to be connected with the shipping department, press two. To speak with a sales consultant, press three. For payment, press four. For shipping and receiving, press five. If you do not know the correct extension or are calling from a rotary phone, please press zero or stay on the line and an operator will be with you shortly.

Add vocal inflection in the following sentences as if the numbers and names are being recorded at the same time. For instance, "you" and "extension" may be pitched slightly higher on the musical scale, allowing the numbers (recorded later) to fit more naturally into the same melodic territory as the two words previously mentioned. Then in the next sentence, assume that the employee's name will be recorded at a higher level than the rest of the sentence. "Is unavailable" should slope progressively downward on the musical scale.

> You have reached extension number _____.
> _____ is unavailable to answer your call right now. Please leave a message after the tone or press zero to be connected with the operator.
> If you would like to speak to someone in our sales department, please press three.
> Please stay on the line. A representative will be with you shortly.

In a level, almost monotone voice, say each number. This allows the computer to automatically arrange the numbers to fit the extension requested. Too much vocal variety creates uneven combinations as the words branch together to form complete sentences.

> one
> two
> three
> four
> five
> six
> seven
> eight
> nine
> zero

Many companies allow their employees to record their own name into the system. For practice purposes, record the list of names printed below. Make sure the names are pitched properly to fit smoothly into the melody of the line "is not available to answer your call right now." Be careful that the names do not start to drop in pitch as you become tired or bored with the repetitiveness.

Elaine Clark
Morris Code
Polly Cooper
Michelle Jones
Robert Lee
Marcia Mays
Freeman Planet
Chuck Roast
Kent Stately

Once again, the names recorded earlier need to fit into the blank provided. The second blank is for gender reference. The closing blank is for the excuse.

Thank you for holding. _____ will be with you as soon
as_____ gets _____.

he
she
off the line
back from break

The numbers recorded earlier can be used to complete some of the following information. "O'clock" and "thirty" should match or complement the tonal pitch of the previously recorded numbers.

I'm sorry but the office is closed. Please call back at _____ _____ Pacific Standard Time.

o'clock
thirty

As you can see, a lot of thought needs to be put into this type of recording. The information should not jar the ear or sound overtly robotic. The voice should have a subtle melody that easily adapts to the word insertions. Vocal pitch levels, tone, dynamics, pacing, and volume should remain consistent throughout the recording. Voice mail systems, computer software programs, and interactive games are all based on this same random selection technique.

Syber Deluxe 3000

This is an example of a television infomercial. The program begins with a health and fitness expert who appears on-camera, extolling the many benefits of proper diet and exercise. In the middle of the program, the camera cuts away to an "at home" demonstration. The voice-over script below explains how the "real person" on the screen uses the product. There is pulsating, motivating music playing in the background that keeps the beat of the person's exercise routine. The sell closes the segment.

In reading the spot, try to incorporate a haze in the voice that matches the filtered photography used by the endorser to create a TV-program (rather than an advertisement) atmosphere. Allow the voice to drop down deep in the throat, then add a little bit of breathiness. The script should be read slowly to accommodate the normal speed of the action in the visual.

> The Syber Deluxe 3000 is unlike any other exercise machine you've ever seen. It is compact, lightweight, easy to use, and stores neatly under the bed or in the closet. And, with only 15 minutes of exercise per day, your body will look leaner, firmer, and more healthy.
>
> To begin using the Syber Deluxe 3000, simply step on the easy release bar and snap it into position. Your exercise program is ready to go. It's that simple! The heavy-duty rubber band system easily adjusts to your fitness level. Simply remove the peg from the patented notched-weight system and insert it into the exercise bar. Now, the Syber Deluxe 3000 is ready to tone, firm, and strengthen your chest, arms, abs, buns, and legs. And after only 15 minutes a day for eight weeks, you'll see unbelievable results.
>
> Shouldn't you get off the treadmill? Order the Syber Deluxe 3000—guaranteed to give you a sleeker, more beautiful body. And if you order now, Syber Deluxe 3000 will even include a free 45-minute exercise video.
>
> Don't delay. Call 1-800-S-Y-B-3000 today to receive your Syber Deluxe 3000 and exercise video at the low introductory cost of only $194.99! It will be billed to your credit card in three easy installments of only $65 a month, plus tax, shipping, and handling. The Syber Deluxe 3000. At last, an exercise machine that really works.

The infomercial begins with a "soft sell" approach and progresses to a slightly more aggressive "order now" mode. Vocal undertones convey confidence in the product and its results, ease in set-up and usage, and a relatively low price. The script also preys on the consumer's self image to help ensure the sale. If your health and appearance mean anything to you, you owe it to yourself to buy this product. Additionally, the company has your best interest in mind because they charitably divide the payments into three monthly installments. Therefore, money should not be a deterrent. To further illustrate this financial ease, the announcer doesn't mention the word "dollar" in the larger monetary amount. The machine only costs "one ninety-four ninety-nine."

Happy Homes Realty
The example below does not hawk product like a cheap salesperson. This is a small portion of a 40-page script describing the difficulty people have in relocating to another area. The recording will be dubbed on cassette and given out to Happy Homes relocation clients. It should seem to represent a real person's hopes and fears about the relocation process. Never should the listener feel the speaker is an actor; he is a person going through the same anxieties as the listener. This technique is used to illustrate the company's compassion and understanding and to gain the client's trust. Later on, an announcer will comfort, admire, and support the speaker for his or her bravery and offer advice to the listener on how Happy Homes can help ease the burden of the relocation process.

> **Sally:** When John Frank called me into his office, I had no idea he would offer me a management job. My projects have gotten good reviews lately, but I never dreamed I'd be offered a promotion this early in my career. It's something I've

dreamed about but didn't expect to happen for at least three more years. But here it was—a chance to prove myself. I just wish it wasn't in Boise.

What will Arnie think? Will he be willing to give up his job? How about the children? Emily is on the cheerleading squad this year and Aaron just made varsity. They'll hate leaving their friends. I'll miss my friends and relatives, too. After all, I've lived here all my life. It will devastate my parents. They're getting older and need me around. But this job is just too good to pass up. There'll be a lot more money, so we could afford to fly back once or twice a year. And, I've been complaining to Arnie that we need a larger home. Two more rooms, which Arnie and I could use as offices, would be just perfect.

Announcer: Moving is never easy. It means leaving familiar surroundings and the ones you love. It means packing up your belongings and moving them to another town, another state, sometimes even another country. The relocation experts at Happy Homes Realty understand this concern and are there to ensure that the transition goes smoothly for both you and your family.

It's a well known fact that the moving process is stressful. Whether your job has a tendency to periodically relocate you or you are moving for the first time, each member of the family has their own set of problems and concerns that needs to be addressed openly and honestly. The key to a successful move is *communication*. That means talking to each member of the family about the move and listening to their thoughts and respecting their feelings.

Arnie: When Sally told me about her promotion, I was stunned. On the one hand, I was thrilled for her. I understand how important her job is to her. On the other hand, I'm not sure if I'm ready to move. I'm in the middle of designing a new product at work, and it wouldn't be fair to the company to leave at this stage of the project. I know I should support her in this, she certainly was a tremendous help for me when I changed jobs a few years ago, but this is going to have a tremendous impact on the family. Will I be able to find a comparable job in the Boise area? What kinds of schools are available for the children? What are all the effects of moving while the kids are in high school? How will our lifestyles change?

Industrial scripts such as this can be recorded in various ways, depending on the producer's budget. If talent payments are not an issue, all three actors would be called in simultaneously to read the script in chronological order. Although this is the most logical way to record the information, sometimes the announcer is called in separately, and is later edited into the appropriate sections. The husband/wife team would work together during the remaining session time so that they could hear each other's dialogue and respond accordingly. A third recording choice is to tape each actor separately, one at a time. If four hours of recording time are scheduled, the booking might look something like this: Announcer from 1:00 to 2:00 P.M., Sally from 2:00 to 3:30 P.M., and Arnie from 3:30 to 5:00 P.M. Although recording each actor separately may save the producer money on the talent end, much more time and effort is required to patch the segments together in post production.

In analyzing the script, Sally's dialogue should be flooded with contradictory emotions. She is both elated by the promotion and concerned about her family's reaction.

Her thought process resembles a roller coaster, dipping down into the negative aspects of the move and cresting at the possibility of a larger home and more money. Arnie's character is on a smaller emotional wave. He respects his wife's happiness and business success but is unsure of how to deal with his current job situation. The nonpartial announcer ties the sections together by offering understanding and advice.

Both Sally and Arnie have lists of questions in their copy. Each question should stand on its own, so allow three or four beats between them. This provides the listener with time to reflect on her own situation. Real, heartfelt acting is needed to fill the words with sadness, exhilaration, and anxiety. These emotions are needed to trigger the listener into revealing her own emotional turmoil and acknowledging her need for the services of Happy Homes Realty.

Pride Corporation
Many corporate industrials are produced specifically to instill pride in their employees and increase in-house productivity. Minor problems within the organization are downplayed because, after all, the company is great! In reading this corporate propaganda, use your deepest, friendliest, most self-assured voice. There should be no hesitancy that could be mistaken for weakness or ineptitude.

Visual: *company logo*	**Audio:** Pride Corporation believes in value, in the day-to-day business needs of the operation, and in a system that benefits the bottom line. This is why we have integrated an easy-to-use Automated Business System at every employee's work station.
Visual: *product close-up*	**Audio:** It is the personal business solution to new product installation, to training, to service, and to support. In short, Pride Corporation understands the value of its investment.
Visual: *dissolve to employees*	**Audio:** And that investment is you.
Visual: *Jane and Bob at ABS*	**Audio:** ABS will enable you to understand the needs of the customer even before those needs present themselves. Customer downtime, a complaint voiced by many of our customers, is fast becoming a thing of the past.
Visual: *shipping*	**Audio:** That is because we've just shipped new documentation, new user manuals, new workbooks, new quick-reference guides, plus new audio and video training tapes—tapes produced right here at Pride—to all our customers. After all, Pride believes, "Who better to train someone about Pride than an employee of Pride."

Visual: *close-up of materials*	Audio: Throughout the coming weeks we strongly urge you to familiarize yourself with this information. It is sure to provide the business management solutions needed to meet the specialized demands of your specific markets.
Visual: *materials morph into a globe*	Audio: After all, it's through your hard work that Pride has emerged as a multi-million-dollar corporation with over 2,000 employees in seven countries.

Of course, the video presentation goes on to explain some of the highlights from the newly recorded and printed material and how the new ABS (Automated Business System) should be used, but it is left up to the employee to fully understand the details. Copy such as this usually stress words like "value," "benefits," and "solution." Lists are used to emphasize magnitude and scope and shouldn't be glossed over.

Although not a reprimand, the phrase "a complaint voiced by many of our customers" should be treated as an aside or throw-away. The purpose of the presentation is to emphasize solution and forward progress within the corporation. With great pleasure, the shipping information list is presented to a hopefully awe-inspired audience. That is followed by a firm pat on the proverbial back. The call-to-action is in the final section. It carries the undertone, "Our company got to be this large and successful through hard work and dedication. You owe it not only to yourself, but to Pride, to learn this information. Now, go out and work hard!"

Chapter 13

Multimedia and Books-on-Tape

MULTIMEDIA

Multimedia is on the cutting edge of technology. The term "multimedia" was coined in the mid-1980s in Silicon Valley, the high-tech area of northern California, to define the combined use of text, sound, and graphics in the computer. Since then, multimedia has evolved to the point where computers can handle animation, text, photography, moving graphics, full-motion video, and wider sound bandwidths. This blending of sound and moving picture in a computer environment has increased the work for voice-over actors in the interactive educational and entertainment computer software and hardware market. CD-ROM (compact disc-read only memory), CD-I (compact disc-interactive), and ITV (interactive television) are the cornerstones of this emerging technology.

In multimedia, an actor's vocal requirements are endless. They include reading lists of singular words which are then electronically patched together to form complete sentence responses for specific questions; narrating large texts (such as CD-I encyclopedias); creating voices for animated characters in cartridge, computer disc, and CD-ROM games; "edutainment" programs and tutorials that can teach a child to type, a computer novice to use a software program, or an adult to fly a plane through computer simulation.

The home video-game market is an over-five-billion-dollar industry. When it first began, there was very little storage capacity on the 8-bit cartridge for anything more than a few *uhs, ahs,* and *groans.* Then 16-bit machines widened the spectrum of voice use, but capacity was still limited. The CD-ROM, which has hundreds of times the storage capacity of the cartridge, shifted the technology to include more speech. Suddenly, a product could have an audio personality, so it was no longer sufficient for companies to use the "guy down the hall" as the voice.

For entertainment software developers, recording the voice has created an interesting challenge. Rather than a voice being saved on tape, it is digitized (converted into numbers) enabling it to be stored, modified, and played back by the computer. The digital system's sampling rate and the number of bits of resolution affect the final quality of the recording. The sampling rate establishes the audio frequency range over which the system is effective. At any rate, a high-pitched voice is harder to accurately recreate than a low-pitched one. The number of bits of resolution available during each sampling cycle establishes the system's ability to capture differences in volume, so more bits allows for greater distinction between loud and soft passages, while fewer bits requires the actor to work harder to enunciate, create expressive nuances, and keep the highs and lows of the voice in a closer range. Often, the digital voice recording is compressed to conserve data-storage capacity. When this is done, the highs and lows are condensed, noise is increased, and the words become somewhat garbled. Therefore, at certain recording sessions, the actor may have to stay within a carefully monitored pitch range. The CD-ROM, which has the highest capacity, can reproduce the voice beautifully. Less sophisticated technology, like the devices in children's talking books and dolls, muffles the speech, making it less recognizable. For more information, you can subscribe to magazines such as *Inter@ctive Age, New Media, Electronic Games, Wired*, or *CD-Rom Today*. There are also directories, such as *ADWEEK's Directory of Interactive Marketing* (1-800-468-2395) and the *Hollywood Interactive Entertainment Directory* (1-800-815-0503), that provide company listings.

Multimedia offers terrific opportunities to act and use many character voices. Voice requirements range from the natural speaking voice to wild characters. The following are some samples.

Good Versus Evil

This example of a CD-ROM interactive game narration is a chance to explore the dark and light areas of your voice. The *Evil Sorcerer* and the *Good Queen* are polar entities struggling against one another for control of the Great Island World. Strong, emotional, yet realistic acting is needed to bring the animation to life.

> **Evil Sorcerer:** I, the Evil Sorcerer, am the great lord of wizardry. I ruled the Great Island World, but it was taken away from me 2,000 years ago during the Battle of Darkness and Light. A spell was placed upon me by the Good Queen. I was exiled to a cave beyond the Seas of Zarti and was destined to live eternally as a granite statue unless someone opened the Jar of Turbulence. Mistakenly, the Good Queen's heir opened that jar. The spell is now broken, and it is my time to seek revenge! I must regain my land, rescue it from the Queen's sunlight, and return it to darkness. The people's joyous laughter must be silenced. With the help of my evil servants, this land will once again be mine! Darkness and terror shall reign forever. *(evil laugh)*
> **Good Queen:** For 2,000 years the Great Island World has prospered. I, the Good Queen, brought happiness and sunlight into this once bleak and dismal land. During the Battle of Darkness and Light, I was able to defeat the Evil Sorcerer, turning him into stone and sending him into exile. But evil is returning to this peaceful place. My son, Prince Reuben, has mistakenly opened the Jar of Turbulence breaking my spell, and now the Evil Sorcerer is free once more to wreak havoc on my people. I fear their laughter will turn again to despair. The rich, golden lands are threatened with darkness and destruction. I must gather my allies together to fight this demon wizard. Good will prevail over the evil shadows of annihilation. Light and joy must reign forever in this land!

Men with deep, resonant bass voices are the first casting choices for the Evil Sorcerer. Women with light, mellifluent soprano voices are perfect for the Good Queen role. The vocal separation between the two characters creates a sharp contrast for the listener.

Recognizing characters' contrasting traits is one way to make vocal choices. Enjoy the destructive aspects of the dark voice, or wallow in the perfection of the good role, while fearing the sorcerer's evil. Develop a personal stake in the outcome of the game so your storytelling inspires the players to protect and defend their particular side.

Math Fun

This represents an "edutainment" interactive computer software program. The math problems appear on the screen and the voice commands give the user encouragement. The phrases and single words must be recorded so they can be used interchangeably as responses to all the possible answers, levels of proficiency, and various stages within those levels. For instance, when recording the long list of numbers, it is important that you not get fatigued. All the numbers should be pitched at relatively the same position on the musical scale and spoken with the same enthusiasm. This allows each word to fit neatly into the open-ended sentences without sounding overly electronic or unnatural. One way to achieve this is to pause for a beat (one second) between each number and use the hands or another part of the body to guide you in proper voice placement.

> Welcome to Math Fun. Type in your name, then press "enter."

> This is level _____.
> That is correct! The answer is _____.
> You have _____ mistakes.
> mistake
> one, two, three, four, five, six, seven, eight, nine, ten, eleven, twelve, thirteen, fourteen, fifteen, sixteen, seventeen, eighteen, nineteen, twenty, thirty, forty, fifty, sixty, seventy, eighty, ninety, hundred, thousand, million
> and
> dollar
> dollars
> cent
> cents
> Try again.
> Not bad!
> Excellent!
> Congratulations!
> You're ready for the next level.

When listening to your recording, do the single words fit neatly and consistently into the blanks in each of the sentences? Do the phrases sound encouraging? If not, re-record them in a manner that gives the user verbal encouragement and stimulates him to get excited about learning. Mistake commands should never chastise, but also try to avoid sounding phony or too sweet.

JUSTCOOL: LX2000

This is a highly technical narration for a computer-generated audio/visual trade show demonstration. The booth display features large-screen monitors mounted side-by-side filling an entire wall. The visuals feature video clips highlighting the actual product, while animated simulations show how it works. Trade show demonstrations must compete with the noise and commotion from adjacent competitors' booths. Your reading needs to break through the confusion, grab the listener's attention, and set the technically savvy buyer at ease with expert advice. The name of the company, the innovative qualities of the product, the trade show setting, and the language used in the script are clues to the narrative style. A technical announcer should be confident, hip, and dynamic. Initials and numbers baring no meaning to the layperson challenge the narrator to sound like an industry professional. You should give the impression that you have the credentials to take the product apart and put it back together blindfolded.

Even though this script pitches a nonexistent product, it tests your ability to make sense of something about which you know nothing. Read the script and incorporate proper sentence conjugation skills. *Hint:* Breaking the sentences up so they make sense to the listener implies that you are intelligent and knowledgeable.

> This is what computers looked like 30 years ago. This is what they looked like last year. And this is how JUSTCOOL Technology has revolutionized the industry. The all new LX2000, the computer of the future! Compatible with the ubiquitous GYP Existential Learning Component, the LX2000 will revolutionize the information superhighway with increased speed, reliability, user-friendly ease, and memory. Plus, it can be integrated into your workstation as a stand-alone component or with the PLN, TZX, and EQE megatechnosystems. Adaptability only takes a few minutes! Simply slide the LX2000 converter PYT switch into the designated position, plug it in, and turn it on. For additional hookups and expanded technomondokeyswift accuracy, there are two outlets on the back, one switched, one unswitched, and a three-line surge suppressor. It's a system like no other. It screams with power! Not only that, it also features a BA55G. Yet another electronic breakthrough from JUSTCOOL Technology. Both the LX2000 and the BA55G far surpass the speed and reliability of anything the competition has to offer. Built to last well into the next century, the LX2000 is the only instrument with a lightweight magnesium alloy casing for increased portability, endurance, reliability, and sleekness. It also fits the JUSTCOOL LB10 Generator Two workstation! The LX2000 is the future, and JUSTCOOL Technology is the leader, clearly ensconced on the cutting edge. Don't be left in the Dark Ages. Join this brave, new technological world. Ask your show representative for dealer pricing.

Just like commercials, the script has a definitive beginning, middle and end. The first three sentences set up the introduction of the new product. The body of the script begins at the fourth sentence and continues through the final four phrases, which recap the name of the product, the parent company, and its status in the high-tech world.

A clear attitude of impending change should be apparent in the opening set-up. Mock the antiquity of the first computers, mildly approve last year's models, and glorify the latest development. Smile proudly from the beginning of the third line through the end of the script. Utilize all the muscles surrounding the mouth, just as you would in a retail commercial. The information should be clear and distinct.

Take time to introduce "the all new LX2000." In a matter-of-fact tone, state its relationship to the GYP component. Since you are dealing with professionals who understand the buzzwords, it is not necessary to stress the words "Existential Learning Component." What is important is that the product is "compatible" with a widely used system and will "revolutionize" the superhighway. Take your time when listing the system's benefits so the listener can really focus on them. Note that the word "or" is often emphasized in industrials to distinguish parallels and stress versatility and compatibility. Also, explaining how the system is set up should sound effortless. One way to achieve this result is to read the material slightly faster, as if shrugging the shoulders and implying, "It's nothing."

Long words like "megatechnosystems" are made-up "techno-speak" used to familiarize you with the necessity of phonetics and root word recognition. By looking at the word, you'll see that it actually means large (mega), technical (techno) systems. Having a general understanding of complex word meanings helps those words roll off the tongue more easily. So, rather than panicking and tripping up when words take up half a sentence, break down the word to its root meaning. If the root word definitions elude you, use phonetics to sound out the syllables. Write the phonetic spellings on your script to help you automatically recognize the correct pronunciation and avoid breaking into a cold sweat as the words approach. If necessary, repeat the word several times out loud until it becomes second nature.

The rhythm changes with the reminder that the system is "like no other." Play with the description of the "screaming" power system, but do not venture out of character. This is the one opportunity to have fun with the dialogue, but you must also stay within the parameters of the announcer role. Rather than raising the pitch, drop it and use the base notes generated from the pit of the stomach to describe the power. (A note to remember: power originates in the gut.) Then, top that information with the fact that the LX2000 features a BA55G, confirming the company's foothold in the industry. Conclude the presentation with the reassurance that the company and hero product deliver cutting-edge excellence. If consumers do not wish to be left in the dust, they must invest in the technology of the future.

Software Orientation

The voice requirements for this particular job are soft and personable. The voice actor should sound knowledgeable but not detached or inaccessible. It should seem as though the voice from the computer is talking to a friend or peer. Read it slowly and descriptively, and be careful not to talk down to the user. Make sure that the listener understands the names and functions of each described item or action. Even though the system is complex, it should never sound insurmountable, so imply that the operation is simple and easy to master. Allow a beat or two at each pause. This space between commands gives the software programmer flexibility in dropping each sentence into its proper branch of the system.

Welcome to the Software Orientation program. It is designed to help you understand how to use the system more efficiently. So, for the next few minutes, sit back, relax, and enjoy the ride. I will click the mouse for you.

On the center of the screen is the sketch pad. This is the area where the geometry is created. As you can see, objects are created by choosing a tool from the palette along the left side of the sketch pad. The pointer selects a circle tool, and places it near the center of the sketch pad. Notice how easily this simple geometry is modified by adding a line tangent to the circle at a 45-degree angle to the horizontal.

Observe the selection of the line tool. If the line is selected from the *modify* pull down menu, it can be attached to the circle by clicking the left mouse button in the desired quadrant of the circle and dragging the mouse to achieve the preferred line length.

Now, click the right mouse button twice to perform this exercise yourself. *(pause)* Good. Select the circle tool. *(pause)* Place it in the center of the sketch pad. *(pause)* Excellent. Select the line tool, then pull down the *modify* menu and select *tangent*. *(pause)* Click the mouse button in the lower right quadrant of the circle and drag the line to the desired length. *(pause)* Congratulations! You are ready to begin!

One of the beauties of being a good voice talent is performing so effortlessly and convincingly that listeners truly believe you are an expert on the subject about which you speak. Listen to your recording. Do you sound as though you have an inkling of what you are talking about? Can you follow the action on the screen? If not, how do you expect the listener to understand? Does the final congratulatory accolade sound light and sincere or contrived and pushed? Is there an air of encouragement for the user to begin? If your answers are yes, technical material may be an area you should pursue.

Letter Round-Up

A tough western character is needed in this game. Many games are broken down, such as this, into isolated sentences and paragraphs. Since the relating graphics are often not completed at the time the voice is recorded, the actor must use his imagination to create a pre-scene event and dramatize the sentences accordingly.

I'm the owner of this cattle ranch. I can rope 'em, tie 'em, and brand 'em faster than any other rancher this side of the Mississippi. But I hear a big storm's a'comin', so I need some help gettin' these cattle to market before the first snow. Are you strong and brave? If so, click the start button and type in your name. If you don't sign in, we won't let you near the chuck wagon . . . and you'll be needin' your strength. Herdin' cattle's tough work.

Look out! You're going to fall into the ravine!
That was a close call!
Don't move! There's a rattlesnake!
Oh, no! It's a stampede!
Cattle rustlers are approaching. Find your rifle.
I don't know if I can make it.
You'll have to lead the herd.
Better luck next time, partner.

Choosing the appropriate voice depends highly on the visuals. For instance, there are tremendous graphic differences between claymation and cartoon renderings, dark sinister comic book characters, and realistic photos. Try reading the copy several different ways based on various images. The realistic character could be dirty and gruff, the dastardly image could have a sinister undertone, and the animated cartoon could be more light-hearted and slapstick.

BOOKS-ON-TAPE

The job opportunities for dramatic readings on audio cassette are expanding. Audio bookstores are springing up everywhere. Book and video stores are devoting more and more shelf space to audio books. Audio catalogs, which provide the convenience of buying or renting unabridged books-on-tape and having them delivered right to your door, are offering more listings. Libraries, too, are expanding their audio book, text, and play sections. New books are being recorded every day to meet the growing demand.

Celebrities and authors voice the greatest number of books-on-tape. Understandably, recognizable names increase sales. But an actor or author's fame doesn't guarantee talent in bringing a reading to life. Many stars are visual talents, not vocal talents. Narrating books-on-tape requires exceptional storytelling abilities and an adeptness at emersing listeners in vivid prose imagery. Fortunately, that opens the door for non-name actors with unique book reading skills.

Although not always applicable, readings take on added dimension if the voice talent is able to perform a variety of roles. Using contrasting voices or personality traits gives the listener both aural gratification and the added benefit of easily and rapidly distinguishing one character from the next. Each character in the book should sound true-to-life. Heavy caricatures and over-dramatizations, like making an elderly person sound creaky and crotchety or a man imitating a female by pitching his voice into a high falsetto, should be avoided. For instance, a princess who is enchanted and in love may speak softly and wistfully; a strong king may speak slowly and elongate his vowels, portraying regal elegance; and an evil villain may punctuate the consonants in a clipped speech pattern, revealing the sinister side of his character.

Books-on-tape require vocal stamina. On average, a good reader who makes few mistakes can record approximately 10 pages an hour. So short books can be taped in only a few hours, while longer books may require weeks to complete. Directors who understand the physical demands on the voice rarely schedule recording sessions exceeding four or five hours in length. After long stretches of time, actors tend to leave the sound booth feeling like wet noodles; their jaw muscles aching and their brains fried.

When the voice-over portion of the book is recorded, the director and engineer are left with the clean-up work. It requires hours, days, even weeks to edit the voice recordings plus add music and sound effects. It is during the editing process that the true talent of the voice artist is either cursed or praised. Even though it is the engineer's and director's jobs to ensure consistency, no sign of weariness or change in vocal pitch should be apparent.

Although the majority of books are recorded in the presence of a director and engineer, some readers have the luxury of contracts with publishing houses allowing them to work in the privacy of their home studio. A deadline is agreed upon and the actor is given the flexibility to record the material in two- or three-hour increments, at whatever time is best suited to their schedule. For these fortunate few, it is a storybook life. Also keep in mind that book-on-tape recordings fall under the AFTRA phonographic code. Nonunion voices must negotiate their own contract. It is not absolutely necessary to have talent agency representation in this area to get work, but it helps.

If you are considering this line of voice work, spend some time in the library or audio bookstore researching audio book companies. Produce a two to three minute audio cassette tape featuring your book-reading talents and make duplicate copies of your demo tape to send, along with a cover letter and self-addressed stamped envelope, to the specific person within each company who hires voice talent. Audio book producers listen to cassettes and match voice qualities with book styles. If your tape shows merit, you may be called in for an audition, and if all goes well at the audition, you may be given a contract. Once you get work within a company the chances increase for you to get future projects. If you are rejected, your demo tape may be returned to you with suggestions for ways to improve your reading style. In either case, trying to get work in this area is worth a shot. After all, you can't find out whether you've "got it" unless you try.

Below is one sample script. Use it to explore different vocal choices as well as to add descriptiveness and intensity to the words. Then practice reading entire books aloud.

Wedding Daze

This is my humble attempt at a potboiler romance novel. Try reading it with feeling.

Danny slammed the door behind Susan and stormed into the kitchen.

"I'll kill him!" he fumed as he opened the freezer door.

Pulling out a tray of half-frozen ice cubes, he twisted it until one jumped out and shattered on the floor. The cold liquid center made a puddle on the linoleum. Furiously, he fought with the remaining ice cubes, turning the tray upside down over the sink and banging it with his fist. The cubes spilled out and crashed violently against the sides of the porcelain.

"Are you okay?" Susan yelled from the living room.

Too angry to respond, Danny wrapped a dishtowel around a few broken cubes of ice and returned to the living room. Susan was lying back on the soft, green sofa when he entered, her light cotton dress falling open, exposing the lower part of her thigh. He was startled by her long, thin legs and temporarily lost his concentration.

"He didn't mean it," she asserted as Danny sat down next to her.

Being careful not to hurt her, he gently placed the cold rag on her eye. She winced as the cloth settled on her bruise.

"You should have let me push Brian's car over the cliff," he mused.

"Don't say things like that."

He smiled and kissed her index finger, sending a jolt of electricity through his body. Startled by his forwardness, Susan tried to appear preoccupied. She picked up her purse and began searching for her car keys.

"It's late. I better get home and see if Brian's there." She struggled to remove herself from the soft, enveloping sofa cushions.

"Can't you stay a little longer? You should keep ice on that until the swelling goes down."

"It's fine, really," she whispered, removing the ice pack from her eye and placing it in Danny's hand. Their eyes met for a brief, glorious moment. He yearned to kiss her, but she turned away and dug her hand deeper into her purse to retrieve the elusive car keys. Tenderly, Danny reached over and placed his hand on her chin, turning her face toward his.

"Let me take a look at it once more before you go." He slid closer to her on the sofa and gently touched the puffy, red area under her eye. "I'm afraid you're going to have to wear dark glasses for awhile."

"Thanks for the tip. I'll be sure to remember that."

"I could make it better," he said placing his right hand on her exposed thigh. "Close your eyes. I've got a secret formula. Some things you have to accept."

Looking down at his hand, her breathing deepened. He leaned over and kissed her on the mouth. It's wrong, she told herself, but she couldn't seem to resist. She'd loved Danny since her marriage to Brian began falling apart two years ago, and her moist, sensuous lips responded, sending his heart racing. They fell back on the sofa and were lost in the soft, feathery pillows. For a moment it all seemed so perfect, as if they belonged together. Without thinking, she started to wrap her legs around his, but suddenly she stopped and pushed Danny away.

"I've got to go," she breathed, nervously grabbing her purse and throwing her coat over her arm. "I'll call you tomorrow."

Danny stared at the floor as she opened the door. She yearned to look into his eyes once more, but he didn't look up. Would he ever forgive her? Susan closed the door behind her and was gone.

This may not be the great American novel, but it is a somewhat sensual practice story. The objective in recording books-on-tape is to tell a vivid and enlivening story while making few, if any, mistakes. The story and characters must have an emotional life, a sense of action, and an intriguing quality that keeps the listeners anxiously anticipating more.

Were you able to incorporate different feelings, tempos, or voices into each main character? Was the opening paragraph charged with Danny's anger at Brian and the sexual electricity between him and Susan? Was the sensuous aspect of their relationship readily apparent? Is there a clear give-and-take quality to Danny and Susan's relationship? If not, record the story again, implementing these suggestions.

There are many other types of narratives you may be required to read, each challenging voice flexibility. Children's stories often call for animal sounds and voices, and parental tones, along with a few different children's voices, which should capture the spirit, mentality, and effervescence of youth. Mysteries and science fiction works might demand a more sinister narrator and many strange sidekick personalities. While classic novels may sound best when read by a mature, stately voice. Always tape yourself when practicing so you can play back the recording to gauge your success and improvements.

Chapter 14

The Demo Tape

The demo tape is a voice actor's audio resume. It is used by producers, directors, and talent agents to assess the voice talent. Rather than describing a voice in words, the demo tape gives potential employers the unique opportunity to hear the actor's voice range, technique, acting ability, and level of emotional depth. Casting decisions can then be made based on voice quality, style, versatility, timing skills, believability, diction, and overall "fit." If the voice fits the project and the producer likes what he hears, the actor is cast in the job, or, at the very least, gets an opportunity to audition.

Demo tapes are used to illustrate a distinct style of delivery characteristic of specific areas in the voice business, showcasing talent in a job-appropriate manner. Commercial, industrial, character, cartoon, and jingles are the most common forms of voice-over demo tapes. Commercial demo tapes are suited for advertising agencies and production companies. Industrials are geared primarily toward production companies, and a select number of advertising agencies that cater to the industrial end of the business. Character voices are often used by commercial, cartoon, and interactive software and game producers. Cartoon tapes focus on animated voice dexterity. Jingles tapes display products being endorsed and pitched through song.

FILLING THE NICHES

Because of this diversity within the business, many voice actors possess multiple demo tapes. The larger the market, the more likely the established voice talent will have a variety of niche-appropriate tapes. A commercial demo designed to illustrate subtle voice-over sales skills is inappropriate for a cartoon producer. Jingles tapes featuring singing and advertising promotional abilities are out of place in an industrial production company. Cartoon tapes, though enjoyable, have little or no use at an advertising agency. Even within an advertising agency, the voice-over and jingles departments may be separate from one another. Therefore, tapes must focus on specific areas of the business. Never assume that a blanket tape, which includes a snippet of a jingle, a couple of character voices, some industrial reads, some animated character voices, plus a sampling of real person, announcer, spokesperson, and two-parter commercials, is going to get you work. Producers are busy people. Casting decisions and opinions are often made in 10 or 15 seconds. If the vocal style at the beginning of the tape is inappropriate for the listener's line of work, it's very likely the tape will be ejected from the cassette player and tossed into the trash.

Television promos, high-tech and medical industrials, storytelling, and radio station disc jockey work are additional areas of the business requiring demo tapes. The decision to make separate, specialized tapes is based on one's qualities, abilities, and desire to infiltrate various fields. Even when a voice tape focuses on one section of the business, it should demonstrate a wide range of abilities within that specific category. Medical or technical training and comprehension lends itself easily to techno- or medical-language industrial voice-overs. Words seemingly unpronounceable to the average person, become a gold mine to the voice actor who can decipher and speak the language. Television stations keep tabs on promo announcers who have the unique vocal ranges and styles necessary for promoting everything from heavy news items to afternoon children's programs. A books-on-tape demo is the perfect choice for actors with good reading and imagery skills. "Sound checks" are used by radio station announcers to demonstrate their particular personalities and styles; mailed to prospective radio stations, these are samplings of real or would-be radio programs featuring the announcer along with snippets of musical programming. From this, radio station executives decide if the announcer suits a specific time slot and station format.

For most people entering the voice-over world, one or two demo tapes is all that is necessary and economically feasible. A shelf full of assorted voice-over tapes often takes years to acquire. Perhaps this limitation is to the beginning and intermediate voice-over actor's advantage. There are so many little nuances within each field that performances easily become muddled and not properly honed when the focus is scattered. Instead of jumping into all areas simultaneously, select one or two areas to conquer at a time. Then, once you feel comfortable and established in those arenas, stretch your limits. Use this newfound knowledge and understanding of your vocal range and abilities to create a new tape aimed at a totally new area of the business.

THE BASICS

Although there are no hard and fast rules, a demo tape is approximately two to three minutes in length. Most producers listen to tapes impatiently with their hand anxiously poised on the fast-forward and eject buttons. This is partially due to the office time pressures, but also to the sad fact that more people produce bad tapes than good ones. A good demo offers entertainment value. It never affords the listener an opportunity to turn it off. A new acting approach or vocal variation pops up and surprises the listener every five to 15 seconds. It leaves the listener acknowledging and appreciating the actor's range and abilities, and wanting to hear more. Even if the producer doesn't hear the specific voice needed for a project, it is assumed that the actor can probably do it.

Tapes typically consist of snippets of work cleverly edited together to hold the listener's attention. Juxtaposing spots with slow tempos against faster pieces, and high voices against lower ones, demonstrates greater range than similar segments following one another. Position the best work at the beginning of the tape. If the producer only has 15 seconds to listen to your demo, let it be the best 15 seconds you have to offer. Splicing non sequiturs together is another way to add levity and interest to the demo. For instance, if a piece of copy says, "We're the best at making dog food," follow it up with a cut from a completely different spot that gives an inappropriate answer, like ". . . because Roger has a problem with gas."

Only put your best work on the tape. Never fill time with subpar or nonmarketable recordings. Better for a tape to be a good, strong one minute and 27 seconds, than a slow, excruciatingly long two minutes. On the other hand, don't feel obliged to edit a tape down to two minutes if it contains an exceedingly entertaining four-minutes-worth of work. Producers don't listen to tapes with a stop watch in their hands.

Commercial demos are often constructed on a bell curve. Spots containing your uniquely identifiable "money voice" (the voice that most frequently gets you hired) and personality are placed at the beginning and end of the demo. They act as a reference guide or vocal marker. Within those first few seconds, the listener is able to assess your voice and place it in an appropriate age and personality category. No matter how outrageous and diversified the spots in the middle of the demo get, the listener has mental reference markers, at both the beginning and end, for evaluation and comparison. Each spot builds in intensity or wackiness, peaking about halfway to two-thirds into the tape, when the spots decrease in craziness and level out with the closing money-voice marker.

There are two approaches to producing character and cartoon tapes. The most commonly used style is for the various character or cartoon voices to be ordered randomly in a way that displays the greatest contrast in vocal range and characterizations. For instance, a beautiful fairy princess with a high fluttering voice would be edited in next to an evil warthog with a deep gravelly voice. Like a rainbow of colors, the tape would arc, increasing in intensity, speed, or dementia toward the middle of the tape, and taper off at the end. Every once in awhile the pacing of the tape should slow down just enough for the listener to catch his breath. The end of the tape should be uplifting and fun so that the listener retains a smile or laugh.

The second option for a character or cartoon tape is to create a story. This is called a concept tape. A clever scenario is used to give the characters an excuse for talking. For example, it could involve time travel and diverse extraterrestrials. Another concept would be for the hero character to be trapped in a room with a zillion doors. Behind each door is a new character who interacts with the hero in some way. Should you decide to produce a concept tape, make sure that it is very well thought-out and executed. These types of tapes fall easily into one of two categories: extremely brilliant or incredibly stupid.

Segments from industrial tapes can be slightly longer than commercial, character, or cartoon tapes. Rather than the quick five- to 10-second clips used in the other tapes, industrial tapes can handle 10, 15, or even 20 seconds of the same material. This allows the producer time to evaluate reading skills. Variations in the theme of industrial tapes include soft, behind-the-scenes clips; big, pumped-up-with-corporate-pride copy; technical finesse; and descriptive ease. Proximity to the microphone, speed of delivery, vocal placement, and attitude all demonstrate versatility. Once again, the money voice should lead the tape.

Theoretically, demo tapes are comprised of real work. For the beginning voice actor, this is an obvious impossibility. Even a voice actor who has been in the business for a couple of years may not have enough real work to make a demo that is totally reflective of her personality and vocal range. In this case, the blanks must be filled with "make believe" work. Appropriate material should be written or found specifically for use on the tape. Then the scripts need to be recorded in a professional recording studio. Each recording needs to be mixed with either music or sound effects. Finally, all the pieces are edited together.

COMMERCIAL DEMO TAPE COPY

Demo tape copy can be procured from many places. Advertising agencies have piles of old scripts, so writing or calling several agency producers, directors, writers, or their assistants to request some sample scripts may prove fruitful. If you have a talent agent, ask to use some of the audition scripts. Voice-over class instructors might lend their scripts. If you decide to use magazine copy, rewrite it to be less visual and more conversational. Listen to commercials on the radio or television and borrow their style to create your own commercial.

Creating your own demo tape is a difficult process, especially when it is the first tape. It is almost impossible to direct yourself in the studio, and blindly relying on the audio engineer to direct a demo tape has drawbacks, as well. It is an artistic gamble because the engineer might not even want to be involved in the directing process. After all, the engineer's primary job is to record the voice, ensure that it sounds clear, add appropriate music and sound effects, and edit the tape to the client's satisfaction. This is already an overwhelming amount of work and responsibility for just one person. Offering strong direction on script interpretation, word emphasis, vocal placement, and emotional adjustments quickly becomes a lesser priority. More often than not, the end result is a demo tape that sounds terrific on an engineering level but is flawed and weak in the acting department. For optimal results, a professional demo tape producer should be consulted. Especially on the first demo tape, a third pair of ears in the studio is essential. Only then can each participant concentrate on his job. The actor can act; the producer can direct the talent, suggest sound effects, and offer editing advice; and the engineer can record the sound, mix in the sound effects, and edit all the material together professionally.

Many voice-over teachers offer demo tape production services. Selection of the appropriate demo tape producer should be based on the success of that person's students, the quality of the demo tapes produced, and mutual rapport. Voice-over students who study with several teachers have a broader spectrum of talent from which to choose a director/producer than students who study with only one. Services should include selection of a wide variety of scripts to highlight the actor's strong points, rehearsal of the scripts prior to the recording session, strong and diverse direction during recording, selection of appropriate background music or sound effects, editing advice, and final edit order. On completion of the tape, the director should provide advice on tape duplication, artwork for the cassette and its box, and marketing suggestions.

A demo tape should reflect an actor's personality as well as vocal range and depth. If existing advertising copy does not achieve this, new scripts must be written. Scripts should be created to reflect a strong affinity toward a product, place, or service. After all, it is much easier to sell something you believe in than something you don't. Begin by making a list of your 10 to 12 most marketable desires: vacation spots you enjoy; restaurants you frequent; various stores where you do your clothing, grocery, prescription drug, office supply, and appliance shopping; health and beauty items you swear by; cars you dream of owning; charities you support; musical or theatrical events you like to attend, and so forth. Then describe why you are attracted to that place or product. You might write, "I love shopping at Green Grocery because the fruits and vegetables are always fresh and delicious. The butchers in the meat

department cut-to-order. And, I never have to wait in long lines when I check out."
After you have written the descriptions, assign an acting style (retail announcer,
hard sell announcer, tag, spokesperson, real person, promo, character, or multiple),
and adjust the scripts accordingly. For style and formatting ideas, refer to chapters 6
through 11. The Green Grocery description easily translates into a real person spot. If
there are already too many scripts in the real person category, switch to another writing
style for diversity. The Green Grocery description could turn into an announcer retail
spot with, "And no Fourth of July picnic would be complete without specialty cut
beef and pork ribs from the butcher shop. Delicious Georgia peaches are only 10 cents
each. Snap green beans, fresh from the fields, are only $1.25 a pound. Russet potatoes
are just $3.15 for a 10-pound bag." It is not necessary to use complete spots with a
beginning, middle, and end. Sometimes only a set-up is necessary, while other snippets
may only include the body or the final resolve. Use beginning, middle, and end segments
to add variety to the tape.

Doing your homework before entering the recording studio saves a lot of time
and money. First, use a stopwatch to time each script. Trim any commercial exceeding
15 seconds, and note music and sound effect requirements on each piece of copy.
Second, rehearse each script. Explore character traits, emotional status, vocal and mic
placement, and tempo. Jot down all your decisions because once you get in the studio
things will move much too fast for you to rely solely on your memory. Third, decide
on a rough edit order. Be flexible enough to understand that this order may change
once you record the work. A spot that you thought would be wonderful as the lead-in
piece may not turn out as well as you anticipated, and the order will need to be
adjusted to accommodate the strongest recording.

In larger markets, top voice talents often edit out the product names on commercial
demo tapes. This is done to reduce the risk of being eliminated from job consideration
due to the fact that there is an old spot on the tape pitching a competitor's product.
Although a slight job risk is involved in using product names, it is believed by many
people in the industry to be a valuable piece of information. Clients want to hear how
you "handle" a product. They don't want to arrive in the studio only to discover that
you don't know how to subtlty create name recognition. That could be disastrous!
So unless you are a seasoned professional with a track record of work, disregard this
tactic. Instead, intersperse at least three or four product names throughout the demo.
The other snippets can feature sections of commercials that are descriptive or
interesting but do not mention the product by name.

THE RECORDING STUDIO

Be sure to get a good night's rest before you go into a studio to record your demo tape.
It will be one of the most exhausting sessions you will ever experience. Your mind and
body must be sharp and alert so that you can quickly and fluidly change characters,
voices, and attitudes every 10 minutes as you jump from one script to the next. If you
are working around meal times, grab a nourishing snack or meal an hour or two
before going into the studio. You want to have plenty of energy during the session and
not encounter fatigue or stomach grumblings. Avoid dairy products, carbonated
drinks, spicy or salty foods, and cigarettes. (Note: Some actors like to smoke prior to
recording to add depth or haze to the voice.) You want your voice to be clear and crisp

and devoid of unnecessary mouth noises and throat irritations. Drinking hot water helps open the throat and clear the palate. Order the scripts incrementally from soft and slow to loud and crazy or vice versa, depending on your personality and energy level. A low energy person would start off with soft and slow scripts and progress upward while a high energy person would do better blowing it out in the beginning and slowing down and relaxing into the softer, gentler copy.

Depending on the studio, recordings will either be *analog* or *digital.* Reel-to-reel recordings are analog. Demo tapes recorded on this equipment are usually laid down on a two-track machine. Four-track, 16-track, and even 24-track are available in most recording studios, although unnecessary and expensive in a demo tape situation because the entire realm of music and sound effects that could be layered on each track of tape would potentially overwhelm the voice. With two-track, one track of tape would handle the voice while the other would be used to layer the musical beds and simple sound effects.

Digital recordings, which have eliminated the need for analog equipment in most studios, are quickly becoming the recording style of choice. These recordings are made one of two ways: directly into the computer or onto a DAT (digital audio tape). It requires a lot of memory to record directly into the computer, so, depending on the system, some studios must record onto a DAT first and then transfer the selected takes back into the computer for editing. Outtakes are preserved on the DAT but do not take up memory on the hard drive and random access memory (RAM), although some more-sophisticated computer systems do have the memory capacity to retain and manipulate the recordings. Recording directly into the computer is quick and efficient. The computer screen keeps track of all the takes and shows a voice graph of the recording. Selected recordings can be removed from the entire list of recordings and placed together visually. Editing on the computer offers a distinct advantage in that no tape is physically sliced. Vocal wave patterns, which appear on the monitor, are manipulated to achieve desired results via computer commands. Once completed, the final recording can be dumped back onto a DAT and given to the client.

Due to the choices of recording styles, it is best to spend a few minutes with the engineer prior to the session to discuss recording procedure. In addition to the manner in which the material is recorded, additional questions to ask would be: Are the edits going to be butt-cut tightly next to one another? (This is when the sound remains level throughout each recording and the commercials abut one another.) Are a couple of the spots going to be cross-faded? (This is the gradual dropping and then increasing of the sound level at the end and beginning of the commercials to fade in and out between them.) Is the final spot going to have a slow, trailing fade-out? Making decisions like this ahead of time reduces the time and money spent on post production. Cross fades, although clever, should be used minimally. The seconds it takes to fade one spot into another can potentially lose a listener's attention. Butt-cuts are much faster and keep the tape "hopping," since no time is lost in the transition. Fading out the final cut on the tape gives the tape a softer, gentler ending. Abruptly ending the tape with a sliced edit can surprise a listener unnecessarily. Only use this technique if this is the desired effect. Ending tag lines, for instance, lend themselves nicely to abrupt endings, as with "Brought to you by the National Pumpkin Growers."

Once the recording is complete and all the edits have been made, the master tape will be in one of two formats: DAT or reel-to-reel. The small DAT cassette offers the highest sound quality and is steadily gaining popularity. Reel-to-reel tape, although an older format, is still an excellent medium. If using reel to reel tape, be aware that there are two different speeds. Tape speed is measured in inches per second, or IPS. Fifteen IPS is recorded at a faster tape rate and is, therefore, higher in quality, cleaner, and easier to edit. Seven-and-a-half IPS is recorded at half the speed of 15 IPS. Since the recording covers less tape, the sound quality is slightly muddier and tends to lose a little bit of the voice's high end. In demo tapes, however, this sound difference is minimal, especially since the duplicate tapes are reproduced on cassettes—a medium with an inherent hiss that hides any minor quality defects.

CASSETTE DUPLICATION

Pricing demo tape duplication rates is a bit like comparing apples and oranges. Is there a remastering fee involved? Are the tapes going to be Dolby or non-Dolby? Is the tape going to be standard bias or the more expensive chrome? Is the cassette shell (encasing the tape) going to be white, black, clear, silver, or gold? What is the total tape length? Will there be paper labels on the cassette or is the information going to be stamped directly onto the shell? How many dubs (duplicate tapes) should be ordered? Knowing how to answer some of these questions can potentially save you money in tape duplication.

Deciding which final master tape format to use, DAT, 15 IPS, or 7 1/2 IPS, depends on how the cassette duplications are going to be generated. Many tape duplication facilities use a bin loop master to create the dubs. The original master tape may have to be remastered so that it can be recorded repeatedly onto a continuous spool of cassette tape. That tape is then mounted on a special bin loop machine that cuts each demo tape to length before sending it to the cassette loader. Then, the tape is inserted into individual cassette cartridges. No excess tape is wasted in the process; the tape is cut to length and there is only a little bit of leader at the beginning and end. Sometimes when dubs are made via a bin loop master, a remastering fee is often charged. If this happens to be the practice at your dubbing facility, select the highest quality tape (DAT or 15 IPS reel-to-reel) for your original master. This minimizes next generation sound quality drop-off when the demo is transferred from one high quality master onto another.

Even though DAT and 15 IPS tapes are the best quality, they may not necessarily be the best format if the dubbing house uses double-speed cassette duplication equipment. Then a 7 1/2 IPS master is needed. Double-speed cassette duplication is higher quality than fast speed dubbing, but the difference is minimal. Real-speed tape duplication, the highest quality duplication available, is not necessary because of the expense and time required to reproduce large quantities. Consequently, high-speed and double-speed cassette dubs are the established norm for demo tape duplication.

Another decision to be made at the dubbing house is whether or not to have the cassettes duplicated with Dolby sound reduction. Dolby softens the highs and lows of the voice and evens out the recording. Unfortunately, this recording process only works on cassette players with Dolby capabilities. Roughly 50 to 75 percent of your listeners will have Dolby playback capabilities, and there is always the possibility that they will forget to press the button that activates the function. The result of a Dolby cassette played on a non-Dolby system is brighter sound quality. Some listeners unknowingly interpret this brightness as excessive popping and sibilance. Therefore, non-Dolby dubs are the safest bet even though cassettes with Dolby sound reduction sound much better. So, take your pick and mark your cassette as Dolby should you choose to use it.

Tape length is the major cost factor in cassette duplication. The longer the tape, the more expensive the rate. Many studios use the abbreviations C-5, C-10, C-20, C-30, and so on, to signify the total playing time (front and back). A C-5, for example, has two and one half minutes of tape on both sides. If the length of the master tape exceeds the specified cut off point, a larger size cassette must be ordered. Many studios only sell tapes in five-minute increments. In this case, a portion of the duplication fee will be spent on blank tape. The more blank tape on the cassette, the greater the risk that the person listening to the tape will have to hunt for the voice-over recording, get frustrated at not finding it, and throw the cassette away. This is why duplication houses with bin loop machines are the best bets for demo tape production; the tape is cut to length, and there is never any dead air.

Often, the demo tape is listened to hurriedly and not rewound for the next listening. Avoid the blank tape syndrome by recording your demo on both sides. There is seldom an additional charge for double sided dubbing, and, this way, no matter which side, your voice will always be heard. Plus, you can save money on multiple demos by recording different information on each side. Many people record the commercial demo on side A and the industrial demo on side B. If you decide to do this, try to keep the tape lengths of the two sides to within approximately 10 seconds of each other.

Once you get the cassette, you should put it in a hard plastic box, often referred to by the brand name, Norelco. Opt for this style rather than the soft plastic box. Boxes come in three basic colors: clear, clear and black, and clear and white. There is generally little or no difference in price between color choices. Shells come in four colors: clear, black, white, and gray. Silver and gold shells are also available in some studios at a slightly higher rate. Another aesthetic choice is whether to use standard bias tape or chrome. Standard bias tape is the customary choice due to the additional cost associated with the sleek looking chrome tape. On a final note, it isn't necessary to shrink-wrap the cassettes; the clear wrapping used by distributors to prevent store customers from playing with the inside cassette is an unnecessary expense and a listening deterrent.

Order quantities dictate the actual cost per cassette as relative to cassette length. Many studios have price breaks at 250, 500, and 1,000. Your quantity depends on your market. If there are 250 audio producers, directors, and casting directors in the market, order 250 tapes for them, add 50 to 100 for your agent, and an additional 100 for your use. With the duplication price break at 500, it may be more cost effective to order 500 tapes than 400 or 450. As a guide, the total cost per cassette with box and mastering fee should fall in the range of one to two dollars per cassette.

ARTWORK

Demo tape packaging must reflect the actor's overall professionalism, confidence, and dedication. It should say, "Open me first. You won't be disappointed!" A tape with the voice actor's name scrawled on a wrinkled piece of paper, loose hair or fuzz protruding from the edges, and dirt smeared across it won't be played, let alone touched. The cassette and J-card must be clean, neat, and professionally printed. Artwork should feature your name in a bold, eye-catching manner. The recipients are experienced product packagers, presenters, and advertisers. To entice them to play your tape, you must cater to their area of expertise. Commercial producers receive stacks of demo tapes every week. Poorly presented demos, no matter how superbly executed the tape, automatically fall to the bottom of the listening stack. Dazzling or clever artwork gets noticed first. Do not scrimp in this area.

Demo tape art ranges from full-color cartoon renderings and multicolor artistic designs, to one-color printing on colored stock and basic black ink on white paper. Hundreds of dollars can be spent on the design and layout alone. Fortunately with the widespread accessibility of computers, graphic art fees can be minimized if not altogether eliminated. In fact, black ink and color laser printers have made it possible to create professional looking artwork at home at very little cost. Presently, a box of 300 labels sells for under $30. But remember, whether you pull in favors from artistic friends, pay a graphic artist to design your box, or create the artwork yourself, make your name the primary focus. Make it bold, easy to read, and memorable. If you have an agent, use the back flap of the J-card to list her telephone number and address. If you don't have agency representation, list your own phone number (but not your address).

Avoid the temptation to use the all-purpose photo headshot on the front cover of the demo tape. It is not necessary and can actually be a detriment. Assumptions are often made about a voice based on the photo. Therefore, only use a headshot if you are firmly entrenched in the business and your familiar face adds credence to your tape or you have a photo that effectively reflects your personality and complete dedication to the voice-over business in a humorous or appealing manner. For instance, Joe Paulino, a talented and well-known voice talent in both San Francisco and Los Angeles, has used his photo successfully on demo tapes. One commercial demo several years ago featured him straightening his tie while buried waist deep in reel-to-reel tape. Another demo tape shows his face partially hidden behind a microphone. Each time, the photos were created with a voice-over theme.

Plan your art design and color choices around your printing budget. The printing of 1,000 one-color J-cards may cost approximately $150. Base your design choices on this amount. Potentially, you can save money by surveying print shops. Inquire as to whether or not they have designated "color" days. Since the printing plates remain the same color, and don't need to be cleaned between print jobs, the color fee may be reduced or even waived. Another cost variable is paper stock. Price varies according to weight, color, texture, and finish. Select a moderately sturdy-weight paper, similar to the stock found in store-bought music cassettes. If professional printing costs are beyond your budget, consider a less expensive alternative. Some office supply catalogs sell J-card inserts designed to be printed on a laser printer. The rate for these homemade semi-professional-looking J-cards is about one quarter to one half the cost of the professionally printed cards. Of course, the trade-off is more time printing them at home, office, or computer store.

On the following pages are some samples of basic J-card layouts. Size dimensions are marked on Figure 14-1 so you can use it as a guide when creating your own artwork. The fold lines indicate where the printer will score the paper so that it bends easily into the cassette box. Note how the name is boldly printed on both the front cover and spine. On the spine, make sure your name begins at the top of the paper and faces left, toward the shorter flap. That way, when the cassette is laid on its side with the front facing up, the spine type is positioned right side up. Also, if the cassette is stacked upright like a book, the name will still be easily readable. Clearly displayed on the cover are the words "commercials" and "industrials" to identify the type of voice-overs contained on the tape. Refrain from printing the words "demo tape" on your J-card. The people receiving the tape know what it is. On the back flap is the actor's phone number (if there is no agency representation), a necessary piece of information if the actor expects to get any bookings off the demo.

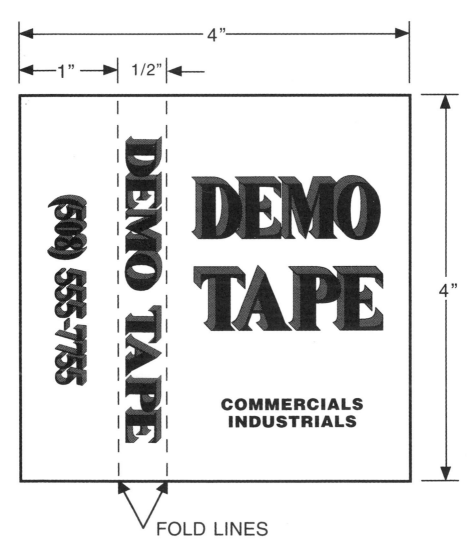

Figure 14-1. J-card with dimensions.

If you decide to angle your name on the front cover, as in Figure 14-2, ensure that it slopes upward. This uplifting slant is a strong, positive, and visually appealing position. Rotating the name downward so it slants toward the bottom right-hand corner denotes weakness and insecurity. It also gives the unwanted impression that the name is sliding off the paper. Located in the far right corner is the actor's union affiliation (SAG and AFTRA). When applicable, this is important information and should stand out clearly. The SAG/AFTRA type size is reduced and the words are level, rather than slanted, adding clarity to the information, but not detracting from the actor's name. On the smaller back cover, is the name of the talent agency and its telephone number. Although this information appears in the same font, you might want to replace it with the actual agency logo and address artwork. Talent agents, because of the representation agreement, prefer that you only list their information, not your own personal contact number.

Figure 14-2. Sample J-card illustrating angled name placement.

People with longer names often rotate them sideways to fill the cover lengthwise, as in Figure 14-3. Although this is not the preferred layout choice as the tape must be turned to be read more clearly, it does simplify a problem. The name remains large, rather than being greatly reduced or angled severely to fit horizontally on the cover. On the back flap, the name is reduced and positioned in the upper corner to allow room for a phone number. The blank space to the right of the name can be used for the agent's stamp, the actor's phone number, or a combination of the two. If you decide to use your own contact number rather than the talent agent's, never list your home address or mail box address. Use precaution and protect your privacy and safety.

Listing credits or recorded elements are J-card printing options. (Some people print that information directly onto the cassette, but then it is impossible to read while the cassette is in the player.) The outside back flap can be used to list the recorded cuts in order of appearance. The inside cover is another place to print this listing. Or, you could use this space to attach your business card. An extended cassette J-card, similar to the folding inserts in store-bought music cassettes, is another area to print information, stories, photos, cartoons, and the like. Whichever you choose, the listener is provided with something to stimulate the eyes while listening to the tape.

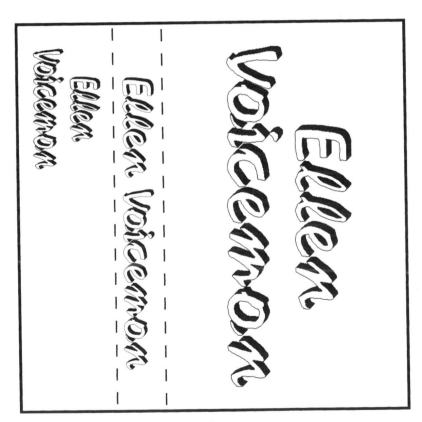

Figure 14-3. Sample J-card with alternate name placement.

The cassette shells should also look professional. Once again, several options are available. Information can either be stamped directly onto the cassette or printed on paper labels. Typically, cassette imprints cost less than paper labels due to the labor and materials savings. There is also less handling involved with imprinting because the shells run through a machine that stamps the printed image directly onto the cassette. The cassettes look professional and additional paper costs are eliminated. The only deterrent to printing directly onto the cassette is an aesthetic one. The color choices and coverage area of imprints may be limited. Therefore, check with the dubbing house and ask to see some samples prior to making a printing decision. Keep in mind that imprinting on clear shells is often hard to read. Dark ink on white or light gray shells, and white or yellow on black cassettes, are the strongest color complements.

The advantage of paper labels over imprints is color bleeding and the number of color choices. Labels can add a fuller, more dramatic splash of color to the shell than a simple name. For example, the background on a paper label can be a solid blue with the name reversed out in white. Aesthetically, this may create a more exact match with the J-card. Cassette labels sold in office supply stores provide an economical option to computer savvy artists. With the greater accessibility of color printers and interesting font styles, home-produced labels can provide a clean, professional look.

Whether you select cassette imprinting or paper label printing, camera ready artwork is necessary. Figure 14-4 shows the dimensions of a cassette label. Be aware that there are minute differences in size from one label manufacturer to the next, but this example is fairly standard. When designing the label, use the larger top section for your name. Additional space is available at the bottom of the label to list the demo type, and any agent, phone numbers, union affiliations, along with the cassette side and contents listings. If the tape features commercials on both sides, consider printing the same information on both sides. Double-sided printing is an additional expense but is much more appealing, although not absolutely necessary.

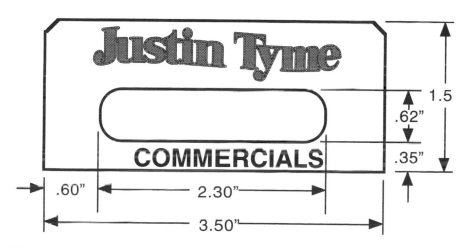

Figure 14-4. Cassette label with dimensions.

Figure 14-5. Sample cassette label.

Figure 14-5 above shows how all four sides of the cassette label can be used to balance out the important information.

If you like stickers, you might be able to get some personalized mini-labels printed for free at the same time the cassette labels are printed. Ask your label printer if the inside ovals on the cassette label paper are in place during printing or if they are already punched out. Many printing shops print with the center ovals intact and, after printing, punch them out and throw them away. Instead of wasting that center label, create artwork and paste it into the center section. It can be your name, a slogan, the year, or whatever useful information fits into the space. Then, have the printer collect the center labels after the label printing is complete and store them in a bag. Voilà! Personalized labels at no extra charge.

THE COST FACTOR

As you can see, there is a lot involved in making a demo tape: the director's fee for finding or creating the appropriate copy, rehearsing the talent, organizing the material prior to recording, as well as actually directing the talent while in the studio, and producing the final results; the recording studio and engineer's fees for their time and supplies; design and production of J-cards and cassettes; and cassette dubs and boxes.

Voice-overs is not an inexpensive field. The cost equates to setting up a small business. A first tape breakdown might look something like this:

director/producer	$150 to $800
recording studio (4 hours) plus use of equipment	$250 to $600
graphic design	up to $200
printing (500 labels and J-cards)	$100 to $500
C-5 cassettes and boxes (500)	$400 to $600
Approximate cost range:	$900 to $2700

Obviously, this is a substantial amount of money to invest. One reason first tapes cost so much is because they are created from ground zero. Corners can be cut, but you should never jeopardize the final outcome. If you want to make a mark in the business, it is crucial that you are represented by a quality, well-produced, and superbly-acted tape.

UPDATING DEMOS

The life span of a demo tape should only be as long as you feel comfortable sending it out. For some, this may be four months. For others, it's years. However old the tape becomes, it should always reflect the entire spectrum of your abilities. If you continue to grow as an artist (as well you should) there will come a time when the old tape does not match your current abilities. Take this as a signal to produce a new demo tape. Also, listen to advertising trends and character voices currently in vogue. Gear your new tape to fit the changing market. Voice work that you were paid to develop, if not already incorporated into your audio presentation, should be included in the new mix.

As you are hired, request a reel-to-reel or DAT copy of your work. When possible, get a cassette recording for your own listening pleasure. Be patient but persistent; it often takes months for the producer to send this material. Asking for a copy before leaving the recording session makes it much more likely that you will receive the copy in a timely manner. Only request work of which you are proud, which features your voice in a manner usable on a demo tape, or which represents a vocal style not reflected on your present tape. Once enough material has been collected, figure out an appropriate order, and book time in a recording studio to edit it together. Create fake copy if the new material doesn't completely reflect your current voice-over understanding and abilities.

Once edited, spend a week or two listening to the new demo and shopping it around to your talent agent and friends in the voice-over business. Solicit their opinions and incorporate any editing changes you deem necessary before making the dubs. Generate new artwork to reflect the new you. You can adhere "New & Improved" labels on old J-cards or print new ones. If you have a highly recognizable label design that works for you, simply change printing colors. Whatever you do, the new tape should be clearly distinguishable from the old. You want the world to hear the new tape and throw away the old.

Chapter 15

Getting an Agent

Having a voice-over agent is not absolutely necessary, but it sure as heck helps! Talent agents represent people with the primary goal of getting them work and negotiating the best possible financial deal. An agent is someone you must be able to talk to, trust, and respect. They act as liaisons between the talent and producers, directors, writers, and casting directors, and they arrange auditions and jobs. Reputable agents do not require a registration fee, but work on a commission basis. If you don't work, they don't make money. Work a lot, and they happily cash your commission checks. So, if an agent asks you to pay a fee up front, keep your wallet in your pocket and walk out the door!

Acquiring a voice-over agent is a good first step in building your voice-over career. Begin your research by looking in the business telephone directory under "talent agent" or calling your local SAG or AFTRA office for the current list of franchised agents. When calling agencies inquire as to whether or not they have a voice-over department. This is a specialized area of the business and not all agencies handle this line of work. If they do, get the contact person's name, as well as the address and zip code, and the proper procedure for submitting a voice-over package. Gather as many names and addresses as possible and submit to them all. Especially in the beginning, when you may not know the size and reputation of each agency, you should keep your options open and allow the agents to decide whether or not you are worthy of their representation. Then if two or more agencies want to sign you exclusively, consider it a nice problem. Interview with each one and make your decision based upon what they have to offer, your rapport with and admiration for the agent, and your gut reaction. Signing with an agent is like entering into a marriage: both parties want it to work out for the best.

THE PROCEDURES

Most agencies require a demo tape, cover letter, résumé, and self-addressed stamped envelope when you solicit representation. Don't expect the tape to be returned; the agent will either call to set up an interview or use the envelope to mail a positive or negative response. Consider it a step in the right direction if agents take the time to critique your tape in their letters of rejection. This signifies some merit in your abilities or they would not waste valuable time writing to you. All is not lost either if the stock letter of rejection arrives in the mail. There are many reasons why an agent doesn't sign an actor, besides the obvious confidence-shattering conclusion that your talents are subpar. Often times, the agency already represents people in your voice category and cannot justify adding a new person. Or, you may have submitted at the wrong time of the year; some agencies purge their current talent roster and sign new talent only once or twice a year.

If two or three weeks pass without a response, it is your responsibility to take action. Many agencies take months before they go through their stack of new demo tape submissions. The only way you can find out if your tape is buried at the bottom of the pile or lost in postal purgatory is by calling. Inquire politely as to whether or not they have received your tape. If they have, ask whether they have had a chance to listen to it or when they expect to review it so that you may call back in a timely manner. Jot all this down. Then, call again after the proposed listening date if you haven't heard anything further. An actor must walk a fine line between annoying agents and politely persuading them to listen to the tape. By all means, do not alienate this person! You want representation.

If you are currently signed with an on-camera agency that has an active voice-over department, getting an agent may be somewhat simpler, because there is the possibility that your present agent will represent you "across the board" in the voice-over department, too. Before you come to any firm conclusion, though, talk candidly with him or her to see how they view you in relation to their current talent roster. Sometimes an agent has a hard time viewing an actor in a different light. If you do not have total confidence in one another in the voice-over department, you may need to seek alternate representation in this area.

One advantage to already having an agent, is knowing the current standing of local talent agencies. Some agencies focus on SAG and AFTRA union work while others handle nonunion clients. There is often a hierarchy within the agency world. As a beginner, it is flattering to be accepted into one of the more highly esteemed union-franchised agencies. It looks great on the résumé. The disadvantage is that newcomers often have to vie aggressively for their agent's attention. Since they are competing head-to-head with the firmly established pros, it is hard to be considered for all the jobs. For this reason, smaller agencies may be the better choice for someone just starting out. Leaner, hungrier agencies are more likely to push their hot new talent. Rather than being a small fish searching for job nibbles in a big pond, the talent is a big fish hooking numerous jobs and auditions in a small pond. It's a trade off—money versus prestige. Only one pays the mortgage!

Once you have an agent, he needs to be well-stocked in demo tapes. Ask him how many tapes he prefers keeping on the shelf at one time. Don't overload him all at once, but just ensure that an adequate number is on hand. Demo tapes are valuable tools. Many jobs are booked directly off them. The agent submits tapes, the client selects a voice, the agent notifies the talent and clarifies the time, place, date, and type of job, and calls the producer back to confirms the booking.

Many voice agents hold auditions in their offices. A group of voice actors are called in at specific times. All the actors are recorded onto a single cassette, which is then shipped directly to the client who listens to it, selects a voice, and calls the appropriate agent back to put the talent "on hold" or to make an "avail" check. An avail check is an inquiry into the actor's schedule and availability. A "hold" is a system whereby the client expects the job to occur at a specific time but still has a few unknowns to clear up before confirming the booking. The talent is requested to keep that time period on hold until further notification. A "booking" is the actual job. All the necessary information is given and the actor is expected to show up on time, if not a few minutes early.

Many talent agencies specializing in voice-overs put together an "agency reel." This is a comprehensive cassette, exhibiting the broad range of voices in the agency's talent pool. Often, the tape is divided into men's voices on one side and women's on the other. Each actor's segment, as specified by the agency, runs from approximately 40 to 60 seconds. Each mini-demo is introduced with the actor's name, and the J-card lists them in order of appearance. The top talents can either be featured at the beginning of the tape or interspersed throughout. In lieu of receiving a slew of individual demo tapes, clients receive one convenient master tape featuring numerous voice talents. Agency reels are expensive to produce and duplicate, so don't be surprised if your agency asks you to pay a small fee for the privilege of being on the reel.

Again, it is your responsibility to ensure that the agent is well stocked with demo tapes. Always check your files. If tapes are running low, bring in a stack the next time you are in the neighborhood. You should also call once or twice a week to check in with the agency. See if there is any work available. Alert the agent and "book out" any time you are going out of town or are unavailable for bookings and auditions. When you return, call and confirm your return so your name doesn't inadvertently remain on the "unavailable" list.

UNDERSTANDING AGENTS

Talent agents have their own unique way of evaluating talent. The following interviews are provided to give you some insights into their world.

New York agent Steve Kaye, Don Buchwald Agency (D.B.A.)

What do you look for in new talents, especially when they come in for an interview?
In our agency, we are in the enviable position of having been around for about 20 years in the voice-over field. So, at this point in our careers, we are fortunate to have people come to us with a track record and a history of work. For the most part, we work with seasoned and active voice-over performers.

Of course the lifeblood of every agency is finding the new breed and the new talent, so we're always listening and looking for new talent, as well. We listen to the radio and television, and we go to the theater and bring in new people in that manner. In an interview, it is less what you ask of a person and more what they sound like. Can they read copy, and can they act? Generally, their demo tape tells us everything we need to know.

How important is versatility?
Versatility in the voice-over area is extremely important. The more versatile you are, the more opportunities you have to audition. Since the whole voice-over "game" is a numbers game, the more you're "out" and "good," the more jobs you're going to win! It's critical to read for as many situations as possible. If you are versatile and can do all different kinds of characters and styles, and be flexible with your voice quality and tone, you're going to work more. So, it becomes very attractive to a talent agency to have someone who's versatile.

New talent accommodates the needs of the advertising industry. At any given moment there's a trend in the advertising game. Sometimes it's younger voices, sometimes it's older, more mature voices. You've got to be staffed in both areas. We have a large stable of people, who have been with us for many years, who are the older, experienced voices and are considered the prototypes of the business. On the other side, we represent a lot of younger people who do a whole different kind of voice and satisfy a whole different "game plan."

How often do your voice actors go out on auditions?
Our market activity and volume of auditions is directly related to the flow of moneys into the advertising agencies. When production is down, auditions dry up and become less frequent. So, there is no real average and it changes week-to-week and month-to-month. During busy times, a good voice-over performer is out five, six, seven times a day, reading for seven different jobs on that given day. Slower times may be reduced to one or two calls a day, or five or six calls a week—as opposed to 20 calls a week.

Do you nurture new talent? If so, how?
We are not an agency that is staffed with the majority of "up and coming talent." There are agencies who specialize in younger voices and younger people, but don't have the stable that we do. We have 50 to 60 percent of the older, more established actors and 40 to 50 percent of the less-experienced people. So, if new talents have a quality that we feel is sellable, we advise that they go to a professional commercial voice-over coach and get some practice and experience. Although they may be wonderful actors, the commercial game is an art form in and of itself. There are wonderful actors who cannot read commercial copy. By virtue of that, they can be stars in their own right, they can win Academy Awards, but they simply don't know how to read 30-seconds-worth of copy in 28.6 seconds. Timing is something talent must learn.

Talent that we feel has potential, we send to a voice coach, have them put together a small two- to three-minute demo tape so that we have a tool to market them with, and send them out on as many auditions as possible in order to get experience.

What do you perceive as the voice actor's primary job?
A voice-over actor's primary job is to follow the direction of the producer and give the read that is needed as quickly as possible. One of the needs in doing commercial copy for voice-overs is getting 28.6 seconds down pat. That's no easy task, when given a sheet of paper to get down to the second! Now, there are some people who have stop watches in their heads and are extremely adept at it. Those people work an awful lot! The quicker you give a producer or director what they want, the less money they spend in the studio. For someone who simply cannot get the timing, it can take two hours to do a 30-second spot! Whereas, someone with more skill gets the job done in half an hour. So, someone who has the ability to follow direction and render it in "on time" becomes extremely valuable to advertising people.

What percentage of men versus women voice actors are signed with your agency?
The percentage—not in our agency but on the street—is that men do perhaps 70 to 75 percent of the work and women do about 25 to 30 percent. That is up from last year. It could be a little better for the women now, but it is still highly disproportionate. As you can well imagine, by virtue of the fact that men work considerably more than women, we could not have as many women on the list as men or we wouldn't be able to service them properly and would have a lot of unhappy clients. So, we must have more men. They work three times as much.

Are there any drawbacks to being an agent and dealing with actors everyday?
As an agent who has been functioning in this field for 25 years, I am aware that we are dealing with people with great needs. You're controlling their livelihood, and, as a result, they become very demanding. You get used to very few accolades and a lot of complaining about earnings and activity. That is probably true with any service business. People don't thank you enough for the job that you've done. Of course, there are many exceptions to the rules. Generally, the people who agents deal with are anxious about their careers. However, the rewards in dealing with vibrant, talented people are tremendous and make working in the talent business an exciting and challenging experience.

Los Angeles agent Steve Tisherman, Tisherman Agency

When you receive someone's demo tape, what do you listen for specifically that makes you want to represent them?
The number one thing I listen for is the way they interpret copy. Voice and voice quality are second and third. I'm listening for honesty, believability, and heart, as piddling as it sounds. There has to be some substance going on in there. In a TV commercial, the product is the star. The voice-over performer is there to surround it and sugarcoat it and enhance the product in the spot, but not to intrude on what we're watching. Many stage actors and actresses don't understand that concept. They are "king" when they're on stage. The key is interpretive quality.

How do you "fill out" the agency with different voices? Are there different ranges?
Absolutely. Voice-over agencies get a call for practically anything at any point in time. We have to have every avenue covered, looking for what is hot and what's being asked for, because there are trends. Some things fade away and come back. We have to be on top of it to handle that type of person and be able to provide that type of person out in the marketplace.

What proportion do you think you have of men versus women voice actors working through your agency?
Oh, I would say 75 percent men, 25 percent women.

Do you have any pet peeves about actors?
The thing is, when someone sends a tape out, they should be sending out their best stuff, but they don't! They make excuses. They say things like, "It's not the best tape, but I'm sending it to you anyway." Well then, if it is not the best tape why don't you put together the best tape and then send it to me! They always have excuses. Actually, they should be sending it out to me saying, "Hey, I've got some damn good stuff here! I think you're the agency for me." But they don't. They say things like, "I've got a better spot coming next week." I don't want to hear that. You only have one shot at representation. I know that's not what they want to hear. The other choice is to submit another tape down the line.

Do you ever interview prospective talent and decide not to sign them with the agency?
Oh, sure. There are elements you hear on a tape, so you go ahead and arrange an interview. I select clients not only on their talent, but on their loyalty, humanity, or other things I find out only through talking with them. That's the only way I can see if we're going to have a problem. I want to try to avoid those situations.

How hard is it to deal with actors from out-of-town? Do you just like working with actors from Los Angeles, or are you willing to work with people who live in other cities?

It is difficult having long-range relationships. Producers want actors in an hour or the next day. Turnaround is very fast. Having people not available, or hard to reach, or out-of-town makes my job more difficult. If I continually say, "My talent is out-of-town, or on a movie, or just unavailable," I eventually start thinking, "I can't use that person. He's unavailable."

The only out-of-town talents I work with have faxes and pagers, and pick up messages quickly. Obviously, if I give that person some copy, they have to do it from where they are. They record a demo, and mail it out along with a note that says something like, "I'm vacationing in San Francisco today," "I'm just up here for the day," or, "I told my agent that I'm up here visiting." I don't like to tell anyone that my talent lives 500 miles away. The problem with working this way is that my talent has to record the copy from where they are without any direction. There's also the added risk of the talent not being able to arrive in Los Angeles in time to make the job. I have to tell the client, "I can't get them that fast." If I can't get my talent to the job, I have to pass. Sometimes I have to be creative—convince the producer to record the voice in San Francisco, or arrange a later time or date to record so that the talent can get down here.

San Francisco agent Joan Spangler, Look Talent

What's the most important element that you want to hear in a demo tape?
The actor has to have an ability to act. It should have heart and truth. I want to buy into whatever is going on. I want to be unaware that I'm hearing a commercial.

Let's say that you have ten demo tapes in front of you from prospective clients that have wonderful, truthful reads but the voices all sound alike. How do you select which talent to represent?
If they all sound alike and have a "selling" quality, I might be interested in meeting with them all. From there I can make a decision. Otherwise, I'm looking for a voice quality.

On demo tapes, do you prefer commercial spots to be ordered a particular way?
No, the only thing that really matters is that I like to have the first spot be just a real person talking about something personal. After that, I really don't care which order the spots are in. I find that most people don't know what their real sound is and hide it fourth or fifth on the tape. I suggest that the actor open the demo with that "real" spot. This way, the listener immediately has a strong image of that person.

How important is it in a secondary voice-over market to have separate demos for commercials, industrials, characters, and cartoons?
Unless a client has incredible strength in many different areas, I don't think it's a good idea to do it. For actors with a lot of versatility, having multiple tapes is useful, especially if it helps avoid confusing people.

As a voice-over agent, what do you consider your hardest job?
The toughest thing that I do is say "no" to someone who's never going to be able to do it. The next hardest thing to do is find the right niche for people who are good, but not multiple-voiced.

Is there a drop-off of voice-over actors losing interest or moving out of the market?
I'd have to say no, not necessarily in the voice business. Theatrical and on-camera talent tend to move on to Los Angeles or New York to do film or Broadway. Voice people seem to stay in the Bay Area. Voice-overs are something they can do locally without having to move around the country. Of course, some people eventually get bored with doing it and stop. For people who I thought were going to be wonderful but for some reason it just doesn't happen, they move on and go back to medical school, or explore other career avenues.

Do you have any pet peeves about actors during the interview process?
Many times it is a matter of good and bad manners. Unfortunately, I think that many people just didn't have good manners taught to them when they were growing up. They don't know how to be business-like in a meeting.

What percentage of talent versus business do you think an actor should have?
I would rather represent someone who has 70 percent business and 30 percent talent, than the other way around. People who understand that it is a business are on time, they promote themselves, and they're always creating new material. It's just a lot easier for me, on the business end, to represent them. Someone with a lot of talent who doesn't return phone calls and doesn't keep the agency stocked in tapes, and doesn't understand how important it is to write thank you letters to producers after the first job, isn't going to get the next job. The actor and the agent need to work together. Obviously, it's always going to be that the actor does the majority of the work because the actor has more time to do it than the agent. The agent should be the touchstone for what it is you're doing. And if you plan to do a promotion, you might want to run it past the agent first. Certainly with any new tape you want the agent to listen to first, make sure that it's in the correct order, and that you're covering what's important in that particular market. You then have to do the work to fix it. Although, I understand that there are agents in Los Angeles who have time to take the actor's finished product, sit down, listen to the tape, reorder it, and rework it. I can't imagine that! Having nothing else to do but create a new tape for the actor and hand it back and ask the actor to make a hundred copies! It doesn't happen like that here. We don't have that kind of focus. We want to hear the tape before it goes to mass production, listen to whether or not it needs any changes, and return it to the actor to correct.

Do you have any tips to offer voice actors?
I've always felt that improvisation is the common denominator in actors who work the most. These people can go into a studio and fill in a word here or there, or an attitude, or anything that creates something new off the page. It makes the writer look good and it makes the producer and director look great! They'll remember that and bring the actor back for other jobs.

San Francisco/Bay Area nonfranchised agent Wendy Yee, Actor's Phantasy

How would you describe yourself as an agent?
I have a reputation for being brutally honest with the actors who enter my office. Fragile egos usually have difficulty with me. An actor must be able to accept constructive criticism and not get flustered by it. Agents are busy people. We don't have time to

coddle talent. We have to feel confident that the talent we are sending out to auditions and jobs are prepared and capable of working under pressure, even in the worst possible situations. If they fall apart in my office, it doesn't instill confidence in my mind or move them to the top of the "must see" list. I don't like to work with talent who just whine and complain about not working. Instead, they should take an honest look at their skill level and see if they can remedy the job situation by trying to *improve* themselves, their *skills,* and not just their marketing materials. Practice, take classes, read books, whatever it takes, but do something!

How do you know when one of your actors improves?
Once a week I open my doors to talent so they can show off their stuff. I give them a voice-over script and allow them a couple of minutes to look it over before presenting the copy. I test them to see how well they take direction. Is this the only way they can read the copy or can they switch gears and immediately implement my direction? If they can't adapt to directorial changes, they haven't shown me anything.

What do you look for in a voice?
Having a great voice isn't everything. It's how the person uses the voice that matters. Can they make the coffee sound delicious, add a smile to the voice, or access emotions and use them readily in the appropriate places?

Do you have any pet peeves regarding talent?
It's irritating when actors are not truthful about their abilities. Honesty is the best policy. If you say you can do something, you sure as heck better be able to do it. Don't lie; be truthful to yourself and your agent about your talent level. I also find it irritating when talent put obscure, unrecognizable or broad, over-the-top accents on their demo tapes as a way of showing "versatility." This is particularly true if the accent isn't a valid regional accent or hasn't been thoroughly studied and made completely believable. Do not say you can do an accent—or worse, put it on your tape—if you have not done your homework! In the corporate business world, where I book a lot of talent, the choices— whether voice-over or on-camera—have to be politically correct. If the job calls for a Hispanic American, they'll hire a Hispanic American. It's that simple, especially in an ethnically diverse place like the Bay Area.

How do you decide which actors to represent?
I decide which new talent to sign according to market trends and vocal quality. Within those parameters, I test the actor to see if he or she can take direction, fit within the confines of the copy, and do what is asked. Versatility and skill level are extremely important. If I ask them to do something different, they better be able to shift gears and do it! I have to have complete confidence in the actor. I need to know that the job will be performed well and that the directors will get exactly the read they need.

CREATING A RÉSUMÉ

The demo tape, in all actuality, is the actor's audio résumé. It offers the listener an opportunity to hear the work rather than simply read about it. Talent agents and casting directors recognize that asset, but often need additional written information for their files. A written résumé contains contact names and phone numbers, union status, job listings, training, and special skills. Attention should be paid to aesthetic details that create a professional appearance. Experiment with typefaces, use of capital letters, indentations, and underlined words. How the information is presented can have just as much impact as what is written.

This first résumé example (Figure 15-1) is that of a beginning voice talent. The name is boldly centered at the top of the page. Underneath is her personal telephone number. Once she gets representation, that number will be replaced by the agency name and number. Below the phone number is an acknowledgment that this résumé is for the sole purpose of soliciting voice-over work. Under the actual work categories, she has divided her three jobs into two categories. No reference is ever made to pay rates or job dates. What is of primary interest to the agent is the *amount* of training. The moderate investment implies that this actor is not totally green and warrants possible merit. Some of her character voices sound intriguing, and her special skills show a dedication to the business. She practices her oral reading once or twice a week and can possibly do good accents with her limited foreign language skills. All in all, the résumé looks professional and well conceived.

Actors in small- to moderately-large-size markets frequently find it difficult to earn a living solely on voice-overs. That honor is reserved for a select few voice-over experts. Therefore, if acting is intended to be a full-time occupation, it may be financially advantageous in the early stages of the career to submit a comprehensive résumé to the agent listing stage and on-camera experience in addition to the voice-over work. This allows the agent the flexibility to get the actor work in other areas of the business, including print, film, television, commercials, industrials, theater, and trade shows. Since appearance is important in these other areas, a black-and-white headshot should also be submitted. Certainly, if an actor is only interested in voice-overs, a headshot is completely unnecessary.

Figure 15-2 presents an established, agency-represented actor in a moderate-size market. Once again, the name stands out clearly in large, bold type. Underneath are his union affiliations. In addition to the television and radio unions, AEA is listed. It stands for Actor's Equity Association, the stage actors' union. Theater and film/television listings name the show, role, and production company or director. Due to possible product conflicts, the actor has not provided a list of commercials. If requested, it would be supplied. In pitching an agent, however, an actor may want to list some of the commercials in this space or attach the list for reviewing purposes. This person is firmly entrenched in the voice-over market and lists only the top credits. If asked, a complete or current list of clients could be provided. The training section shows his diversity within the business. He has taken stage, commercial, and voice-over classes. He also holds a BA in theater. The special skills section expounds on his voice-over prowess, athletic agility, and musical abilities.

Computers, unlike the old typewriter, make it easy for actors to create a distinct visual image with their résumé that subliminally suggests a specific personality and style. Heidi Ho's résumé showed an openness and a willingness to learn. The typeface in Tom Moderate's résumé displayed a strong confidence. Holly Sweetvoice, in this next example, uses a font that suggests femininity, creativity, and lightness. Using the computer enables each actor to easily create a style that can be consistently reproduced on the résumé, demo tape, and cover letter. If the agent disapproves of the look, a simple click on the font icon changes the style.

Heidi Ho

(408) 555-1098
VOICE-OVERS

COMMERCIALS

Fast Serve Pizza   Cable TV

Clean the Earth   PSA

NARRATIONS

Life in the Dorms   Student Film

                                    (BYOB College)

CHARACTER VOICES

Old Lady   10 Year Old   Valley Girl

Small Dog   Spunky Punk   Waif

Texan   Georgia Peach   Dudette

TRAINING

Voice One, San Francisco   *Beginning, Intermediate, Monthly Drop-ins*

Voice Career Or Bust, El Paso   *Character Voices*

SPECIAL SKILLS

Weekly reader for the blind, library storyteller, speak a little French, German, and Russian, fluent in southern accents.

Figure 15-1. Sample résumé for a beginning voice talent.

TOM MODERATE

SAG · AFTRA · AEA

HEIGHT 5'10"   WEIGHT 160   GREAT AGENCY, INC.
HAIR BROWN   EYES GREEN   (213) 555-7623

THEATRE

TUPELO HONEY	*JOHN*	GREAT REP THEATRE
BANG BANG	*HILTON*	OLD CITY THEATRE
BERT CAME HOME	*BERT*	~ ~ ~
SEE YA!	*DANNY*	RIVERBOAT THEATRE

FILM/TELEVISION

TRUCKER MAN	*DETECTIVE*	JOHN DOE, *DIR.*
HELLO, BETTY	*REPORTER*	THEME PRODUCTIONS

COMMERCIALS   LIST AVAILABLE UPON REQUEST

VOICE-OVERS

HUNDREDS OF RADIO COMMERCIALS AND INDUSTRIAL NARRATIONS INCLUDING CRUNCHY CEREAL, DARN GOOD TIRES, PET TREATS, RAINY'S CARWASH, TRUSTWORTHY BANK, SPARKLE SODA, HOWDY CORPORATION, MOON SYSTEMS, PRIVATE SECTOR, ECONOMY CORP., AND THE VOICE OF BILTY IN THE CD-ROM GAME, BILTY BINGO MADNESS.

TRAINING

LUCKY ACTING SCHOOL - ADVANCED SCENE STUDY
LIKE THAT SMILE - COMMERCIAL ON-CAMERA TRAINING SERIES
VOICE TWO - ADVANCED VOICE-OVER DEVELOPMENT
BA THEATRE - GREAT UNIVERSITY

SPECIAL SKILLS

CHARACTER VOICES, IMPRESSIONS, BRITISH, POLISH, AND PARISIAN ACCENTS, WATER SKI, TENNIS, PIANO, GUITAR, BOWLING

Figure 15-2. Sample résumé for an established voice talent (moderate-size market).

HOLLY SWEETVOICE

SAG / AFTRA

VIO Unlimited, Inc.   (212) 555-3100

COMMERCIALS *(Partial list. Complete list available upon request)*

Toiletbowl Shine	National TV
Buy Golly	National TV & Radio
Help the Homeless	National TV Promo
Fluffy Hair Products	National Radio
Lookin' Fine Department Store	Regional Radio
Hip Hop TV	Network Promo
"Hello City"	Cable TV Promo

Local Radio and Television: Deluxe Car Repair, Shoe Shiners, Mighty Pretty Florists, Tall & Slender, The Bottom Half, Gleamers, Hammocks, Etc., Deck & Patio Designs, Organic Foods, Kiddie Toy Stores, and Bank On Us.

ANIMATION *(Current list)*

Little Katie, Mighty Woman & Beemer......	The Adventurettes
Dog Gone & Sweetie Pieplate	Gone's Here
Java Lynne, Mommie, & Witch Margaret .	Gerbil Tails
Vampy, Princess, Queen Bee, & May	Creepy Castles (CD-ROM)

ACCENTS & DIALECTS

Cockney	Upper Class British	Scottish
Austrian	Irish	Fijian
Italian	Portuguese	Spanish
Russian	French	Chicago

SKILLS

A.D.R., Looping, & Walla

Figure 15-3. Sample résumé for an established voice talent (large market).

Elaine Clark

SAG   AFTRA

VOICE-OVERS

COMMERCIALS *(Partial list)*

Chevron	Quaker Chewy Granola Bars
PineSol	California Milk Advisory Board
PG&E	Hidden Valley Ranch
Manwich	Fuller-O'Brien Paint
Union Bank	World Savings
KGO-TV	Camino Healthcare

INDUSTRIAL NARRATIONS *(Partial list)*

Levi's	California State Automobile Association
PG&E	Phillips Home Theatre
Sprint	Lawrence Hall of Science
Bank of America	The North Face
Legal Video Services	Better Homes Realty
Apple Quicktime	Consumer Auto Choice

MULTI-MEDIA *(Partial list)*

NeXT Computer - voice for the tutorial software program
Mario's Time Machine - casting/directing   Software Toolworks
Dark Wizard - casting/directing   SEGA
Mavis Beacon Teaches Typing! (v. 3) - casting/directing Software Toolworks
Spawn - casting/directing   Sony Imagesoft

SPECIAL INTEREST *(Instructor and author of voice-over book and video tapes)*

There's Money Where Your Mouth Is! (book)	Watson-Guptill Publications, NY
There's Money Where Your Mouth Is! (video)	Desktop Video Products, CA
Invest In Your Voice (video)	Desktop Video Products, CA
Marketing Your Voice (video)	Desktop Video Products, CA
Voice-over instructor & director	Voice One, CA

ACCENTS, DIALECTS, & CHARACTERS

Voices represented on the Character Demo: Evil Queen, Dwarf, Cockney Girl, Fairy Princess, New York Goldilocks, Medieval Princess, Big Bad Wolf, Sorceress, Jack's Mother, Jack in the Beanstock, Equestrian, Little Red Riding Hood, "Grandmother" Wolf, Upper Crust British Woman, Puss 'N Boots, Royal Queen, Shoemaker's Wife, Elf, and Royal Assistant.
Additional voices: Southern accents (specialties in Texas, Louisiana,& Georgia), Boston, New York, Romanian, German, French, Australian & New Zealand.

COMMERCIAL, INDUSTRIAL, & CHARACTER DEMOS AVAILABLE UPON REQUEST

Figure 15-4. Author's résumé.

Holly's résumé reflects an established voice artist in a large market. Heading the page, the information is arranged symmetrically, like an hourglass. Her name and agency lines match in length, while the center line acts as a visual separator between the two. Underlining and italic type is used to separate and clarify information. In this case, bold typefaces are avoided, as they would disturb the balance and create undesired heaviness. Under commercials, her more prestigious credits are listed in order of importance and recognizability. Grouped together, is a partial list of local radio and television commercials. The animation category lists the characters on the left and the program or game on the right. A list of perfected accents and dialects is included, along with related skills, establishing her foothold in the industry.

The last voice-over example (Figure 15-4) is mine. It shows a partial listing of commercials, industrial narrations, and multimedia credits. Because of my diverse background in performing, casting, directing, writing, and teaching, the résumé reflects these various points of interest. A space at the right-hand corner above the words "voice-overs" is reserved for my agency's stamp.

WRITING A COVER LETTER

A cover letter should be included in the talent agency submission along with the demo tape and résumé. This is the actor's opportunity to introduce herself; explain why that agency's representation is desired; describe voice range, tone qualities, and versatility; and highlight impressive work experiences. The letter should be neat, well-written, short, to the point, and informative. Be sure to include your daytime telephone number and mailing address. You may have a great submittal, but if the agent cannot contact you, the information will end up in the circular file. If you only provide an evening phone number, it is unrealistic to expect the agent to wait around until after work to call you. As with any other business, regular hours are usually 9:00 A.M. to 5:30 P.M. Also, if you are not around every minute of the day, make sure you have an answering machine, pager, or voice mail system. At work, if you do not have a direct phone line, alert office personnel that you may be receiving an important call and should be notified immediately. Give those people a list of the agents to whom you are submitting applications.

The actor in the following cover letter (Figure 15-5) takes advantage of having previously met the agent. She begins with a reminder of this and truthfully compliments the agent's insight. The second paragraph clarifies the enclosed materials and describes her voice quality. The third paragraph displays business prowess, pointing out that all the necessary information is provided to contact her. Closing the letter is a thankful acknowledgment for the agent's time and a desire to start working as soon as possible.

Once the package is in the mail, allow two weeks before you follow-up with the agent to avoid any unnecessary irritation. Listening to and evaluating a tape takes time. Remain patient. After two weeks with no word, politely call the agent, following the procedures outlined earlier in this chapter. If the tape has not been listened to, hopefully your call will help elevate your submittal to a higher position in the stack. If, by chance, the agent answers the phone, introduce yourself and refresh his memory of your submittal by describing the tape package. Agents are inundated with tapes; don't make them play a guessing game. If you are told that you are not suitable for the agency, you might query the reasons why. Do not interrogate the agent! Merely ask if

Jane Agent
Deluxe Talent Agency
Place on a Street
City, State, Zip

Dear Ms. Agent,

It was a pleasure meeting you at the Voice One voice-over class on July 29th. I was quite impressed with your clear critiques and directoral suggestions.

Enclosed is my voice-over demo tape and resume. As you may recall from last week's class, I have a deep raspy voice. You also informed me that my vocal quality is currently in vogue and very saleable.

For your convenience, I have enclosed a self-addressed stamped envelope. If you prefer contacting me by phone, my daytime telephone number is 555-8154.

Thank you for your consideration. I anxiously await your response.

Best regards,

Hope

Hope N. Pray

Figure 15-5. Sample effective cover letter.

there is something specific they did or did not like about your tape. Thank them for their time and advice. Their insights can only serve to help you improve yourself. If the agent is busy, don't press. You don't want to create a negative opinion about yourself that can forfeit future chances of being signed with that agent.

Getting an agent is not an easy process. Sometimes it takes several submittals before one is landed. Be tough! Actors who give up after the first rejection do not belong in this business. Just like all the other areas of show business, voice-overs requires focus, dedication, and drive. Business sense directs the actor toward work, but good talent holds him in place. If you are rejected by all the possible available agents, you must improve your skills, make a new demo tape, and resubmit; or try to get work on your own off the current demo and use the credits to pry open an agent's door. The second attempt to get an agent should be somewhat easier than the first. Use any newfound knowledge to cater to the agent's preferences and needs. Find out what sells, and then work up a new presentation and *sell* your voice-over talents!

THE INTERVIEW

It happens, you get the interview! You are elated. Suddenly, panic sets in. What do you wear? How do you act? What's going to happen? Relax. Compose yourself. Breathe deeply.

When you get the interview call, get the petty stuff out of the way first. It will help ease your mind. Select a comfortable, upscale-casual outfit to wear. It should be something that makes you feel good about your appearance. Clean, neat pants and shirt are fine. You want to walk into the office with confidence, not sucking in your stomach and wishing you had lost those 10 pounds you promised to lose three months ago. Remember to select something that doesn't make noise; you may be asked to perform in front of a microphone.

Once you get there, the agent will probably want to speak with you for a few minutes. This gives the agent an opportunity to evaluate your personality and style. The most obvious questions will relate to your training and voice-over jobs. Do not be surprised if you are asked where you were born or raised. This is a way to get to know you better and to pinpoint any regional accents. For instance, is there an indistinguishable word pronunciation on the demo tape? It may be due to the fact that you grew up in a southern state, the New York area, Chicago, or Boston. Is it usable in terms of potential work, or will you need to develop a more neutral, regionless speech?

During the interview, it is important to listen and behave in a businesslike manner. Answer questions truthfully and *be yourself*. If you feel inclined to ask questions, do so. The interview should be a mutual experience. Do you like the agent? Will the two of you be able to work together? After all, if you get signed, the agent will take a percentage of your payments.

The demo tape may be discussed. This is often a sign that the agent is interested in you. Otherwise, why would they bother? Breathe a sigh of relief and tell your stomach to quit doing the tango. Listen to any advice and take mental or even written notes. Agents tend to have strong opinions about what they do and do not like based on market trends, personal taste, past experiences, and the success of their top talent's tape. It may be suggested that you cut some things from the tape and rearrange other spots.

Another section of the interview process may involve cold reading. Reading copy with little or no study time is the nature of the business. It is an excellent way to judge aptitude. Give it your best shot. Remain calm and don't push. Listen and incorporate directorial suggestions. If you do not understand the direction, ask. It is better to clarify direction than to totally disregard or misinterpret information. Above all, trust your abilities. This is your time to shine. Stay focused on the copy and its intentions. Do not be distracted by the phones ringing, people popping their heads into the office, or agents who keep talking during your study time with the script. Preparing and reading the copy can be a juggling act. If you balance it properly, at the end of the interview you may have an agent.

The only thing remaining after this preliminary process is the official agency acceptance or rejection. Query the agent if the answer is, "We don't have a place for you in our agency at this moment." Determine any specific reasons why that decision was made. Don't get angry, just keep your cool, thank the agent for his time, and add positive affirmation that the problem will be rectified. If you see that the agent is wavering between signing and not signing you, suggest that you work together on a short three- to six-month trial basis and reevaluate the situation later. It may not work, but it's worth a shot.

Beyond a firm handshake, there is little pomp and circumstance associated with getting signed by an agent. While you are doing internal somersaults, it's business as usual for the agent. After an exchange of encouraging words, you will be relinquished to fill out an array of forms. When you are finished with the paperwork, go out and celebrate! You are on the voice-over fast track.

As an added bonus, it is common courtesy to send the agent a hand- or typewritten note of appreciation (see Figure 15-6). If the agent decided not to sign you, also graciously thank him for his time and advice. The few minutes it takes to write and acknowledge someone's time demonstrates good business sense and leaves the door open for consideration at a later date.

Sending a thank you note to the newly signed agent cements the relationship and adds credence to their decision to sign you. Figure 15-7 is an example from an actor who was recently taken into a talent agency's fold.

AUDITIONS

Auditions can be nerve-racking until the newness of the process wears off. In fact, several years ago, a voice-over student of mine went to his first agency audition and managed to make every mistake possible. He arrived exactly at the specified "call time" and was immediately whisked into the office to begin. Once inside the room, he sat in the agent's chair and relaxed, expecting to be handed the copy and discuss it with the agent. After all, the interview process had been fairly relaxed and the copy had been discussed at length prior to performing. Surprised, the agent repositioned him behind the microphone and asked for a "read through." Of course, he had not picked up or seen the copy. Gaining annoyance, the agent walked out to the lobby, grabbed a script for the rookie, and waited a few minutes while the actor read through it. When it was time to record, the actor reached up to adjust the microphone and broke it! After the agent taped the microphone back together, the audition was recorded and the actor was quickly escorted out the door, never

Dear Ms. Agent,

It was indeed a pleasure meeting you yesterday. I learned so much during the interview and am eager to incorporate the changes into my demo tape. Thank you for taking the time.

As I mentioned yesterday, I am dedicated to voice-overs. My plan is to continue studying acting, improv, and voice-overs. One day soon, I hope to be one of your clients.

Sincerely,

Chad D. Kathy

Figure 15-6. Sample thank-you note.

Dear Mitch,

The meeting with you today was incredible! As discussed, I've already booked time in a recording studio to rearrange some of the segments on the tape. I, too, believe that the demo tape will sound much better with the Soapy Suds commercial at the beginning. I've already called the dubbing house and all 500 tapes should be duplicated by Friday, April 13.

I look forward to working with you. I'll be by in a couple days to show you my latest idea for a promotional mailing.

All the best,

Sean Morgan

Figure 15-7. Sample thank-you note.

to return. The agent promptly gave me a call and firmly suggested that all actors understand audition etiquette.

When called into an agent's office to audition, plan on arriving 10 to 15 minutes earlier than the allotted call time. If a sign-in sheet is provided, register your name, time of arrival, and the call time. Pick up the copy or "sides," and use this preparation time wisely to analyze the script and practice reading the copy aloud. Find a quiet place to practice if it helps ease inhibitions. Recruit a reading partner if the script involves multiple characters. Pay attention to the audition order and listen for your name to be called. Auditions are not the time to be coddled and pampered; do not expect a lot of hand-holding. Stay centered and calm and don't get wrapped up in the frenzy of activity. Ask the best way to move the mic if you need to adjust it. Either the agent will do it or you will be told the best way to move it. While the agent sets recording levels, read through the copy. Mentally and physically absorb and incorporate any directorial suggestions provided by the agent. Then, wait for the signal to begin. When the tape starts rolling, slate your name slowly, clearly, and confidently, in a manner that reflects your personality. Wait a beat and begin reading the copy. When the reading is finished, the tape will be stopped. Wait until then to talk or make any comments. If a second audition is allowed, take a few seconds to adjust to an alternate performance mode. Depending on the agent's preference, you will either slate your name again and say "take two," simply say "take two," or omit the slate completely and deliver the alternate reading. When the audition is complete, thank the agent for her time. If you feel like it, chitchat with her as you leave the room. Keep the conversation and energy positive. Be a winner! Once out the door, do not interfere with the audition process. Leave the agent alone to attend to the next auditioner.

One temptation at auditions is to talk with fellow actors. This is all well and good as long as it does not interfere with your audition preparation. As a general rule, it is best to postpone long discussions until afterward, and keep the focus on the task at hand. If there is someone with whom you wish to have an extended discussion, suggest that you meet after the audition. The friendship can then be nurtured on a noncompetitive level.

The turnaround on voice-overs is quick. Generally, talent is selected within a day or two of the audition. Only the chosen talent is informed of the "win." The passing of time acts as a natural, gentle cushioning to ease the blow of not being selected. If the phone does not ring within three days, assume the job went to another actor. Most agents prefer not being pestered about who actually got the job.

CONTRACTS

Agencies have differing policies. Some allow actors to have freelance arrangements with other agencies, some rely on verbal exclusivity agreements, and others require signed contracts. Nonunion contracts are unique to each agency. SAG and AFTRA, however, have standardized forms. Both the talent and agent sign an agreement to work with one another exclusively. In some instances, if the agent who signed the contract leaves the agency, the contract becomes null and void and open for renewal or renegotiation. Some have a time limit for minimum amount of work the agency is required to provide in order to keep the contract valid. If an actor doesn't earn a designated amount during that period, he has ample cause to dissolve the contract.

Be lenient with this option. It often takes more than three months to get established. If, after a period of time, things do not improve, start interviewing with other agents. Play it safe; arrange other representation before making the switch.

CHANGING AGENTS

Deciding to change agents is a tough, emotional business decision. Strong attachments can be formed between agent and actor that can make it hard to break away. Just remember that voice-overs is a business, not a popularity contest. If the work dries up or slows down, one of two things has occurred: either the actor or the agent is not doing his job. Acting with agency representation is a team effort. The actor must be reliable, perform well at auditions and jobs, and self-promote, while the agent must provide ample opportunities for work. If the agent sends the actor out on auditions, the agent fulfills his part of the bargain. If the actor fails to win the auditions, that loss cannot be blamed on the agent. The burden of responsibility falls upon the actor to improve his skills. Should the auditions and jobs dry up or slow down beyond the normal periodic market lulls, a problem may exist between the actor and agent that needs to be resolved. The actor should interview with other agents to keep the job opportunity door open and arrange a meeting with the current agent. If the problem cannot be resolved satisfactorily, he should leave the agency and sign with one that is "on hold." Take control of your career. Never leave on a bad note though; there may come a time when you need this agent again. Old agencies close, new agencies open, agents change agencies, and actors move up to more high-powered agencies or shift down into smaller agencies to get more personal talent management. It is a cycle in the acting profession. Finding and keeping work is a delicate balance for both actors and agents.

One final note of advice, think through any agency move very carefully. Write a genuine and sincere letter to your agent, resigning your need for their representation. Do not place blame on the agent. Keep the information positive and professional. Writing and mailing the letter of resignation can be a great emotional release. And signing with a new agent will be exhilarating with its promises for a new beginning.

Chapter 16

Marketing Your Talent

Self-promotion and marketing are essential elements in voice-overs. It is critical in building name recognition, getting auditions, and booking jobs. Relying solely on talent agents to do all your marketing is unrealistic. Agents represent many actors and cannot concentrate on just one person. Conversely, an actor's primary focus is on himself, and no one is more qualified on that subject. It makes sense, then, that the actor take control of his or her own marketing. This includes distributing demo tapes, making follow-up calls, and sending out postcards, thank you notes, and other mailings.

You might ask why marketing is necessary. Isn't it enough, after all, for an actor just to have talent? Producers should be lining up, waiting to use me in their next national advertising campaign! I know who I am and what I can do. Shouldn't they be able to recognize my abilities? Ah, if only it was that easy. Actors must present their talent to the world much the way new products are introduced on the market. If an unknown brand of cereal suddenly appears on the grocery shelf, are you compelled to buy it? Probably not. It becomes lost in the sea of well-known brands with established track records. Why should a contented consumer give up a favorite cereal and replace it with an unknown? Only the truly adventuresome, desperate, or bored take such a gamble. An advertising campaign must accompany the introduction of a new product. Consumer interest is peaked by the media who bombards listeners with advertising blitzes promising such things as sensational taste, nutritional benefits, packaging design, and crispiness. Discount coupons encourage first-time buyers to try the product at substantial savings. Coupons are later used to restimulate product awareness and encourage customers to continue buying the product.

Name recognition, value, quality, and trust are the key elements in marketing yourself. Just like the new product in the grocery store, voice-over artists need to alert their client base to their arrival, as well. That means establishing a name in the marketplace, offering good voice-over services for the price, and creating a trusting relationship with the clients so that a strong foothold can be gained in the industry. Postcards, business cards, and letters are the normal marketing approaches. Matchbooks, pencils, pens, and candy are also helpful promotional gimmicks. Since advertisers sell for a living (and may even be immune to the sell), voice actors need to learn what sells, too.

To begin your marketing campaign, think of yourself as a product. What voice-over qualities do you possess that are unique, different, or interesting? There must be something about you that sparks curiosity. Is it your voice quality? Style of delivery? Versatility? Humor? Years of experience? Or, is there something special about your name? When voice actor, Joe Paulino, started his career many years ago he used the slogan, "Not just another rubber voice." It was a clever and successful way for him to alert clients to his versatility and humor. I elevate the common name, Clark, to distinction by mailing out miniature Clark candy bars along with my demo tape. When I make follow-up calls, the producer automatically remembers my name, the demo, and the treat. (Candy, it appears, does not remain exclusively on the hips—but also on the mind.)

Why is name recognition necessary? In order to be frequently requested at auditions and jobs, producers must know that you exist and that you have talent. Writers often tailor scripts to established actors for that very reason; their name is well-known and they have a proven track record. Agents have to push much harder to get the unknown talent heard. By the very nature of obscurity, the actor spends a lot of time at cattle-call auditions where the chances of getting the job decrease proportionately with the amount of people auditioning.

AWARENESS CAMPAIGN

Mailing or hand delivering the demo tape, and supporting it with marketing materials, indicates to writers, producers, directors, and agents that you are available and eager to work. For new actors just starting out or seasoned talents who have emerged artistically with a new and improved tape, the first year of the campaign is the most crucial. An aggressive direct mail and telemarketing plan should be devised. After the expensive demo tape mailing, budget approximately $100 per month (during the first year) to cover printing, postage, and telephone calls. Follow it up very two to three months with new reminders. Between each mailing, call the producers to link a familiar voice with the promotional materials. Develop a relationship with them. It is a lot harder for a producer to turn down someone they know and like than someone for whom they have no affinity. In time, hard work, persistence, and dedication pay off.

Begin the awareness campaign by mailing or hand delivering the demo tape. In the envelope, along with the tape, include a personal letter, handwritten note, or postcard to introduce yourself and impart a bit of personal information about yourself and the contents of your tape. Be creative. This is your opportunity to make a strong first impression. Don't expect to meet the producer if you drop off the tape. Most likely, the tape will be left at the reception desk. If that is the case, call the producer later that day or the following day to see if the tape was received. Chances are, you'll get their voice mail. This is perfect because it offers the producer the good fortune of hearing your voice! If you mail the tape, it is best to put the materials in a bubblewrap envelope to protect the tape from being crushed during mailing. The lightweight plastic also keeps mailing costs down. When mailing tapes, wait one to two weeks before calling to see if the tape has arrived. This allows ample time for the post office to deliver the tape and the recipient to add it to his listening pile.

Figure 16-1 is an example of a promotional postcard that accompanies a tape. It boldly and confidently introduces the actor and suggests that the producer listen to the tape and hire the talent. The demo phone number at the bottom left corner shows that the actor is a clever business person. The producer can then call the voice mail system, answering machine, or computer phone line, to hear the demo tape or other recorded material. Depending on the sophistication of the system, the actor can actually track the in-coming calls. The agent's phone number, listed on the bottom right-hand corner, lends credibility to the actor, by implying that the actor is a good performer, worthy of talent agency representation.

Figure 16-2 is a unique appeal for work. It exposes the actor's vulnerability and honesty in a truthful, yet humorous, manner. Space in the bottom right-hand corner allows room for a handwritten note, adding a personal touch.When creating a memorable mailing you must transcend the norm, go beyond the mundane. After all, you are pitching your *creativity, unique talent,* and *style!* The quality of the promotional material automatically affects the recipient. Many actors hide behind the words. For instance in Figure 16-3, the sender continually apologizes. She's new, she hasn't worked, she doesn't have an agent, and her name has negative connotations. She pleads for her tape to be listened to and unsuccessfully feigns confidence. She even has the audacity to think she's ready for anything with only three years of training and no actual work experience! Perhaps talented, she sets herself up for failure.

Just when you thought you'd heard everything ...
a new talent comes along.

Buster T. Voice

Listen to the demo. Hire the voice.

Demo line: 555-DEMO Fine Agency: 555-6161

Figure 16-1. Sample successful promotional postcard.

CARRIE M. HOME

Hire me,
my kids need braces.

DIRECT LINE: 555-4907
MITCHELL TALENT: 555-9291
ORTHODONTIST: 555-3100

Both girls just got braces ... Ouch!

Figure 16-2. Alternate promotional postcard.

Hi!

    My name is Sue Boring. I am a new voice-over talent. Although I have not worked professionally on any jobs, I have been studying with Elaine Clark at Voice One for three years. I am confident and ready for any situation. Please listen to my demo tape. I don't have an agent at this time but can be reached during the day at 555-4231.

    Thank you.

Sue Boring

Figure 16-3. Sample unsuccessful promotional postcard.

When saddled with a bad name, you have three choices: change your name, live with it, or use your name to your best advantage. (Common names like Smith, Jones, and Clark have similar problems; although not undesirable, they are easily forgotten or confused with other people.) Seize the moment and poke fun at the name or highlight it in some manner so that it is memorable and catches the producer's attention. In Figure 16-4 below, she ignores the negative connotations and stresses her versatility and eagerness to work. She strives for credibility by using the quote from her voice-over instructor. (For working actors, casting directors and producers are the preferred quotable sources. Just beware: if you use a quote, make sure you can live up to the high standards it expresses. Someone's name and reputation are on the line.) Note, too, that the bold type denotes confidence.

Still another approach is to send the producer a formal letter. It requires more time to read than a postcard, but if well-written, can prove successful. This is especially helpful if you have either met the producer or spoken over the phone. Personalize each one, avoiding the generic, all-purpose form letter. Find some common bond between you and the producer and start building the relationship. Keep the information positive and relevant.

In Figure 16-5, Sue Boring establishes a rapport with the producer. First, she greets Rene by her first name. Being a fairly informal business, first names are usually acceptable, especially if the actor has met the producer or spoken with her on the telephone prior to mailing the letter. Next, Sue refreshes Rene's memory about their conversation. She creates a positive recollection about the vacation and puts the producer in a good frame of mind while reading the letter. Thirdly, Sue confidently

SUE BORING

Why settle for one voice,
when Sue Boring has <u>many</u>!

"Whether it's soft and sexy, wild and crazy, young or old, Sue's got it all."
Elaine Clark, Voice One

To find out if Sue's right for your next voice-over job, listen to the demo tape ... or call and book her direct at 555-4231.

Figure 16-4. Sample promotional postcard illustrating creative use of name.

SUE BORING
(213) 555-4231

August 25, 1995

Rene Gade
Bee, Cool, & Hip Advertising
48 Street St.
City, State, Zip

Dear Rene,

I enjoyed talking to you on the phone today. It's sounds like your vacation was a blast. I've always wanted to go to Bora Bora.

While you were soaking up the rays, I put together a new demo tape. It shows a lot of versatility. In fact, Elaine Clark at Voice One said this about my voice-over acting: "Whether it's soft and sexy, wild and crazy, young or old, Sue's got it all."

I look forward to having an opportunity to work with you. Your spots for Soft-O-Butter are marvelous!

Best regards,

Sue Boring

Sue Boring

P.S. Even though my name is "Boring," when I get behind a microphone ... I guarantee you that I am not!

Figure 16-5. Sample promotional letter illustrating creative use of name.

expresses her versatility and includes a quote from a reputable voice-over instructor to gain credibility in the producer's eyes. In the final paragraph, Sue assumes that they will work together and looks forward to their meeting. She also strategically reveals her knowledge of the business by congratulating the producer on an excellent advertising campaign. And finally, in the closing postscript Sue pokes fun at her name, turning the negative connotation into a positive one.

It is not enough to mail out a demo tape and note and expect the phone to start ringing. Always follow up the tape mailing with a telephone call. You have the right to find out if the information reached its intended designation. Well over half of the people who send out demo tapes never pick up the phone to inquire whether or not they were received. A quarter of the people who do make the follow-up calls don't know what to say once they've got the recipient on the line. They expect the producer to remember exactly when they received the tape, answer unasked or assumed questions, and read the caller's mind. That is ludicrous. No one has time for such amateurish games.

The following dialogue illustrates poor telephone technique:

Actor: Hi, I'm calling to see if you got my demo tape.
Producer: Who is this?
Actor: I'm sorry. My name is Dick Cranial.
Producer: Yeah. I think I've got it here somewhere.
Actor: Great! (long pause) Well, I hope you can use me sometime.

Not only does the producer have to fish for the actor's name, but the actor apologizes for not immediately identifying himself. To placate the caller, the producer assumes the tape has been received. Whether or not it was listened to is another question. Unsure of how to respond, the actor waits in the hopes that the producer will carry the conversation. When that doesn't happen, the caller chooses the easy way out and hangs up.

Here's a much more skilled tactic:

Actor: Hi, my name is Susan Silk. I mailed you a voice-over demo tape a few weeks ago. It's bright red with white lettering.
Producer: Oh, yeah. I remember receiving it.
Actor: Super! Have you had an opportunity to listen to it?
Producer: Not this week, I've been swamped.
Actor: I know how that is. How about if I call you back next week. Maybe things will have slowed down a little.
Producer: You better wait 'til after Friday.
Actor: No problem. If any voice-over jobs come up between now and then, please give me a jingle. I'm quite versatile. In fact, I have a radio spot running right now for Speedy Shop.
Producer: I'll be sure to keep an ear out for it.
Actor: Thanks for your time.

In this example, the actor took control of the conversation and related to the producer. The producer opened up and responded to the questions. This was the beginning of a good business relationship.

After the first year of mailing out demo tapes, sending monthly, bimonthly, or quarterly reminder postcards, and making telephone calls, the frequency of promotional materials can subside. With that much time and attention spent on marketing, name recognition should be high. During the second year, the bombarding with materials and phone calls can drop back to only two or three times a year. If you have landed several jobs during the past year, which better represent your improved voice-over expertise than the current pieces on the demo tape, the second year would be a good time to assemble a new tape. This offers an excuse to bring your name to the forefront again. In a promotional nontape mailing, announce that you are working and possess new and improved abilities. By the third year, if you've intensely focused on improving your voice-over skills and followed the aggressive promotional guidelines outlined earlier, your career should show healthy signs of life. If satisfied with the results, you can actually drop promotional mailings back to once or twice a year.

Amazingly, the heavy promotional attention spent in the early years of an actor's career carries a lingering effect. People naturally lose perspective of time; the longer an actor works in the same market, the more likely it is that producers will think the promotional gimmick mailed three years ago was only received three months ago! Use this to your advantage. Three years or so into the career, when things (hopefully) start clicking and you are into the sporadic mailing schedule, use your work flow to gage when to generate new mailers. If the job market is supportive and provides a steady supply of work, promotions may be unnecessary. When things slack off, increasing promotion is a good way to induce more work. You could send a holiday greeting card, capitalize on recent successes, talk about your vacation, or create a "spoof" ad about yourself. Tap into your creativity! There are endless ways of promoting yourself.

PROMOTIONAL IDEAS

The main ingredient in promotions is simplicity. Remember the old adage, K.I.S.S.— Keep It Simple Stupid. Information provided in promotional pieces should be light, fun, entertaining, and easy to read. Do not use vulgarity, tasteless innuendoes, or dirty pictures (unless you know the producer extremely well). In mass mailings, more people are offended by poor taste than impressed. It is best to keep it clean.

Postcards are very effective. Any copy is immediately seen and they make a statement when they land on someone's desk. In addition, there is a significant postal rate reduction as compared to letters and oversize postcards; just stay within the required mailing guidelines of 4 1/4 by 6 inches. There should be a continuity that ties all the promotional material together. It could be a specific color, logo, graphic design, writing style, slogan, or photo. On every item, your name should be prominently featured. New information should be provided with each mailing. For instance, the initial demo tape mailing could include a postcard that describes voice traits and lists contact telephone numbers. The second mailing could be a postcard with a pop-out Rolodex-type file card displaying a newly acquired agency telephone number. After booking some work, a new mailing could be sent out listing your accounts and voice-over job titles, the advertising agencies credited with the campaigns, station call letters where the spots are currently airing, and, when known, actual air times so any prospective employers can tune in and listen. Next, an inexpensive promotional pencil featuring your name could be mailed along with a clever postcard that says something like, "Pencil me in for your next job or audition."

There are numerous ways to create interesting and imaginative postcards. The simplest, but most time-consuming, is to buy a bulk supply of scenic tourist-type postcards and handwrite a note on each one. When selecting postcards, the picture on the front does not necessarily have to pertain directly to voice-overs. For instance, if the picture is a beautiful tropical beach, your note could say, "I'm not in Hawaii yet, but I could be if you book me in your next commercial! Call 555-3456 today. The swimsuit and suntan lotion are packed and ready to go." For photography buffs, do-it-yourself black-and-white photo postcards can be purchased at specialty photography stores. At present, the cost is approximately $25 for 100 card-stock postcards with emulsified photo paper on one side. A photo of your choosing is printed on the front. On the flip side, type written information can be printed either on a home printer/computer set-up or at a local print shop. Another inexpensive way to create your own postcard is to purchase pre-stamped postcards from the post office. This saves money in paper since the cost for each postcard already includes postage.

For people who prefer putting their photo on postcards, there are numerous low-cost headshot duplication facilities around the country. Two such companies are: Anderson Graphics, Inc., 6037 Woodman Avenue, P.O. Box 969, Van Nuys, CA 91408-0969, (818) 909-9100 or (310) 278-9100, and ABC Pictures, Inc., 1867 E. Florida Street, Springfield, MO 65803-4583, (417) 869-9433. Write or call for a brochure. There are various layout styles available.

Many paper supply catalogs sell beautifully designed four-color postcards that can be printed on laser or laser-like printers. Four or six postcards are laid out on each sheet and separated by perforated lines for easy removal. You must have access to a computer and printer, but once the printing is complete, the postcards are easily torn apart and ready to mail. Often, these paper supply catalogs and stores sell matching business cards, letterhead, envelopes, and brochures so that all the promotional materials match. One disadvantage of using these generic products is the likelihood of another actor using the same design or paper stock. Nonetheless, the text would always be unique to each person. Another disadvantage to this type of postcard is the paper; often the paper stock is lightweight and doesn't hold up well in the mail. What starts out looking great can end up on a producer's desk looking like it was wadded up and run over by a truck. Therefore, it is better to use lighter paper stock products inside the envelope with the demo tape rather than as stand-alone mailers.

Although some of the aforementioned ideas sound more cost-effective than the traditional printing press, consider this idea: print the J-cards, postcards, and business cards at the same time. Only four J-cards fit on a standard sheet of paper. The leftover paper is thrown away. Utilize the full sheet (minus the $1/4$-inch margins) and arrange all three items on an $8\,1/2$-by-11- or $8\,1/2$-by-14-inch piece of paper. For instance, if a letter-size sheet is selected, the original art printing arrangement could include three J-cards, one $4\,1/4$-by-6-inch postcard, and one business card. Or, an alternative placement could be two $4\,1/4$-by-6-inch postcards, one J-card, and two business cards. Using this method, the colors, paper, and printing quality all match! Perhaps a little more paper is required for printing, but a theme has been created for a nominal additional expense. The printer only charges for one plate, rather than the three required if you intend to print the business cards and J-cards separately. A slight additional cutting fee may be incurred.

For people with slightly bigger promotional budgets, specialized cards are great. The front cover might feature a humorous photo of the actor in a voice-over or character pose. It could be a generic photograph used all year long for thank you notes and promotional mailings, or reflect a season: Christmas, Thanksgiving, Valentine's Day, Easter, and so on. The actor might be in costume or in a precarious or unusual situation. The inside of the card can either remain blank for handwritten messages or contain a typeset sentiment or note.

The Christmas card is a simple and traditional way to keep in touch with producers once a year. Since Christmas cards can get lost in the holiday shuffle, a memorable approach is to send cards during unconventional holidays. Halloween cards offer numerous opportunities for creative expression. Independence Day cards can get into the patriotic spirit. Thanksgiving cards can be a visual feast and double as a Christmas card owing to its proximity to the holiday rush.

Whatever promotional ideas you choose, keep them unique and original. Old, rehashed ideas have little or no impact and inspire immediate comparison to the original. Keep your ideas fresh!

DEVELOPING A MAILING LIST

Developing a mailing list is a long, arduous process, but a task that is absolutely necessary. It constitutes another business side of the artistic voice-over pursuit. After all, finding, building, and maintaining a list of talent agents, casting directors, and producers is the foundation for getting auditions and jobs. For actors fortunate enough to have a computerized database system, the process is somewhat simplified. The information still has to be input into the computer, but once it is there it can be manipulated in various ways. Mailing labels can be printed, personalized letters and postcards can be "mail merged," and neatly printed lists can be formatted into a variety of styles. Handwritten or typewritten card files and lists do not offer that immediate flexibility. Additionally, computerized mailing lists make additions and deletions to the list a breeze. Each category can to be divided into specific groups, for example, agents, advertisers, producers, and casting directors. Database programs offer a quick reference guide, too. At the touch of a few keys, the company and contact's name appears, along with the demo tape mailing date, the name of the last job in which you worked together, and other pertinent information. As time wears on and the memory fails, technology saves the day!

An actor has several source options when developing a mailing list. There is the ever faithful Yellow Pages telephone directory that lists advertising agencies in the area. Once a year the advertising trade magazine, *ADWEEK*, publishes an excellent national resource guide called the *ADWEEK Agency Directory*. It lists over 4,300 agencies, public relations firms, and media buying services across the country. If unavailable at the local library, the book can be purchased, although it is pricey at over $200. The weekly edition of *ADWEEK*, is an excellent magazine for staying abreast of advertising news. It is broken down by regions so that you get targeted information about advertising account acquisitions and losses, agency mergers, and recent advertising trends. For information on these two publications call the Los Angeles, New York, Chicago, Atlanta, Dallas, or Boston *ADWEEK* offices; their numbers are listed in the phone book. *Breakdown Services, Ltd.,* publishes a book on casting directors and talent agents in the

New York and Los Angeles areas. To purchase a copy, write to them at P.O. Box 69277, Los Angeles, CA 90069 or call (310) 276-9166. Carried in many libraries is the *Red Book*, an annually updated directory of advertising agencies. Actors' trade magazines such as *Daily Variety*, *Back Stage*, and *Hollywood Reporter*, although geared more toward on-camera and stage acting, offer occasional insights into the voice-over world.

Regardless of the source, a mailing list is useless unless it contains the names of the people within the organizations who are responsible for hiring voice-over talent. It may be the writer, producer, director, creative director, owner, production manager, or somebody else. Without this vital piece of contact information, the demo tape and marketing materials are wasted, destined to float aimlessly around the ad agency with only a remote chance of winding up in the appropriate person's hands. Therefore, before mailing anything, call each number on your list and verify address, contact names, correct spellings, and titles. Advertising is a very volatile field. As accounts are acquired and lost and moneys increase and decrease, contact names, addresses, phone numbers, and even the names of the ad agencies change. In fact, don't be surprised if 30 percent of the list requires updating in a short three- to six-month period.

The easiest way to keep track of changes—in addition to keeping up with the trade magazines—is to include the phrase "address correction requested" on all promotional mailings. Rather than the post office automatically forwarding the information to the new address or new person, the mail is returned with a sticker containing the updated information.

Figure 16-6 is an example of how to format this information on the back side of a postcard.

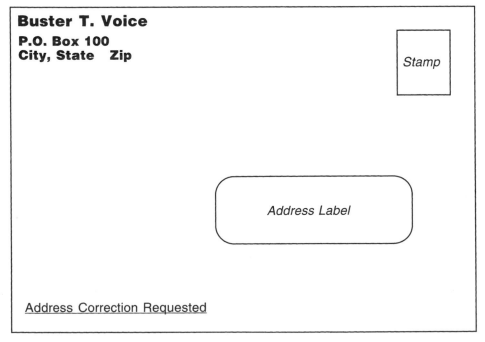

Figure 16-6. Sample postcard back.

To recap, marketing and promoting your talents constitutes a large portion of your career. It is an area in which you must take an active part and coordinate with your agent to broaden the scope of job opportunities. Promotion and a good demo tape can get you the first job, but your talent will get you the repeat business. If the marketing materials are excellent but the actor can't deliver the goods, the money is wasted. Always strive for self-improvement and excellence.

Chapter 17

Staying on Top of the Business

The telephone rings. The voice on the other end of the line says, "Are you available to record a voice-over?" Butterflies flutter in your stomach. Your jaw drops open in disbelief. At last, the time and money invested in training and marketing materials have paid off! Someone wants to hire you. Completely overwhelmed with excitement you stammer, "S-s-sure!" As if on autopilot, questions spill forth from your mouth in rapid succession: When is the session? At what time? Which recording studio? Where is it located? Is this a radio or TV commercial, narration, infomercial, interactive game, cartoon? Will this be under the SAG or AFTRA contract, or is it a non-union job? Are you a union signatory? Do you know how much the job pays? Does the budget allow an additional ten-percent commission for my agent? May I have your telephone number in case I need to contact you later? You finish the inquisition and gingerly hang up the phone so as not to shatter the delicate balance between work and unemployment and jump 10 feet in the air. Now you are part of the Business. Oh, what a feeling it is to be a working professional!

GETTING THE JOB

When that all important "booking" call arrives, it is important to keep a level head. No matter how smart you think you are, do not rely on your memory to get you to the job on time. Make a habit of noting the logistical *who, what, when* and *where* information in your handy dayplanner or portable computer organizer. Information written on scraps of paper is easily misplaced or discarded.

When dressing for the job, remember to wear quiet clothes. Remove any clanking jewelry or loose coins in your pocket before the recording session. Refrain from wearing heavy perfumes and colognes, especially if you are going to be in the recording booth with several actors. If the ventilation system is turned off to minimize sound, the air in the room can get pretty thick. Avoid eating or drinking dairy products, or spicy and salty foods within one or two hours prior to the session. Finally, take a few minutes at home or while in transit to the job to properly warm up the voice.

Plan to arrive at the job from 10 to 15 minutes early. This minimizes commuter stress and allows ample time to get acclimated to the new environment, relax, use the rest room, and grab a glass of water. Being calm and "grounded" before the session is especially helpful when the director, producer, and client burst into the studio frantically at the last minute. Rather than getting swept up in their frenetic pace, you are better equipped to remain a composed observer.

Upon entering the studio, you must alert the people at the front desk of your arrival. They will either instruct you to take a seat and wait until further notification or direct you immediately into the recording room. Ask if there is a script available. If instructed to go directly to the studio, quickly read through the copy as you walk there. Otherwise, sit down and spend some time analyzing the script. If the script is a multiple, check to see if the other people are also waiting in the lobby. Introduce yourself to the other actors and suggest that you read through the copy together. Ask the other actors if the director has given them any information about the copy. While waiting, make script interpretation choices but remain open for a change in direction. Being flexible allows the director the opportunity to mold the performance.

When the opportunity arises to meet the director, whether it's in the lobby or console room, introduce yourself, shake hands, and be cordial. If you enter the console room and there is an entourage of people, prepare yourself. You'll be left unaware and in the quiet recording booth for long stretches of time between each take while they confer. It's amazing how it can be "too big, too small, too fast, too slow, too soft, and too animated" all at the same time. Jokingly, voice actors suggest that their pay rate should increase relative to the amount of people in the room—after all, the more heads, the greater the chance for mistakes and dissent—but, unfortunately, that is not the case. Therefore, it is best to concentrate on the director's suggestions and filter through the peripheral remarks.

The best time to ask questions about the script is before you are separated by a pane of glass. Find out script and character requirements and build a rapport with the director while you are face-to-face with him or her. For instance, if the script appears overwritten, suggest that you read it once for "time." Then, if the director realizes that the script needs trimming, you can be a part of the process instead of twiddling your thumbs in a soundproof room, waiting for something to happen. However, offer suggestions only if it looks like they need help. If the script can be read a number of ways, ask the director and writer how they envision the part played. Give examples of some of your voices to convince them of your interpretation. Taking a few minutes to clarify the script before entering the booth can shave valuable recording time and, hence, money off the session. If you save the client money, you are likely to be hired again.

Once you are in the recording booth, remember to enjoy yourself. Voice-overs should be as much fun as you can have with your clothes on. Do your work, and don't be in a rush to get out. Concentrate on the script, make choices, and live the part. Listen to the direction, whether it's for timing, interpretation, or word punctuation, and adjust accordingly. Embrace direction as your friend, not your enemy. Performing voice-overs is a team effort. Just because you have to repeat the script a dozen times doesn't mean you are awful. Chances are the producer needs a variety of reads to cover all the bases should the client have a different vision and not want to use the selected take. Even if the director thinks you got it right on the first take, you may have to read the copy 15 or 20 times—so be prepared!

It is important during the session to listen. Some voice actors, in an effort to seek approval, nod mechanically and agree to each word of direction as it is given. What then happens is that the brain hears the direction but doesn't process it, and the body and voice do not respond. Therefore, it is better to be quiet, not show how understanding and agreeable you are, and listen and feel the direction as it shifts to the appropriate places within the body, ultimately affecting the voice. For instance, if an actor has to play the part of a sinister beast, the approval seeker's mental choice might be to furrow the brow and force the voice to be angrier. This would indicate that the character is mean, but would not be thoroughly believable. Instead, if an actor allows the direction to be absorbed into the body and soul, a complete shift in persona, breathing, and voice placement should be experienced. The focus should always remain on the performance, and not how much the people on the other side of the glass like you.

In your dealings in the voice-over world, you are going to encounter all types of directors. Some offer very clear and concise direction, while others give vague and verbose suggestions. Sessions where the director is also the writer are especially frustrating and confusing because he may insist that you sound the way he does when he hears his "award-winning" copy rattling around in his head. To say the least, this is a losing proposition, because no matter how well the actor delivers the material, it will never be to the director's satisfaction. Fortunately, over time this syndrome becomes recognizable and less challenging. Keep in mind, too, that, generally speaking, directors are not actors. For the most part, they do not understand the processes an actor goes through in the recording booth to make the copy come alive. Therefore, much of the direction given to an actor is technical: speed up the line, punch that word, hang onto that "m," add more smile. The actor, in turn, has to interpret these requests in a manner that does not sound technical. The director's job is to tell you *what* to do, and your job is to figure out *how* to do it.

Contrary to popular belief, voice actors are not just talking heads. It requires a tremendous amount of energy to deliver a successful voice-over. Therefore, it is best to conserve energy and clear the head during breaks when the director and his entourage confer. Find a chair and sit down. Open the door and let some fresh air into the booth. Grab another glass of water. Go to the rest room. Walk around and relieve any tension that may be building up. After the break, you'll feel renewed.

During the recording session, be prepared for directions to flip-flop dramatically. Polar directorial advice is a technique used to test the range of an actor's abilities in an effort to uncover the desired voice and copy interpretation. Don't let this confuse you. Although it may feel schizophrenic at the time, it is an effective exploratory process for the director. During this creative process, be prepared to abandon the direction from the previous take, listen to new direction, and give an entirely different reading based on the latest information.

If during the session it becomes especially difficult to say a word, repeat it slowly a few times until it fits naturally in your mouth. Also, look at the sentence giving you trouble and see if there is a different way to dissect it. A well placed pause or change in emphasis can alleviate word problems.

Once the most effective voice, character, and interpretation is agreed upon, another directorial technique will be employed, so be aware of the switch. The director will no longer want you to keep creating new and diverse characters. Instead, a specific style of reading or blending of two or three elements from previous readings will be requested. The voice actor must now stay focused on the one direction and hone in on the desired sound until the director gets a winning take.

With studio time and money a primary concern, rarely does the director elect to randomly play back past takes to help the actor to "get it" (understand what is missing from the take). It is the director's job to be the ears of the project and the actor's to be the voice. Only when a director has difficulty in drawing an actor out of a slump is the tape played back. The hope, then, is that the actor will finally hear the missing elements and correct the performance accordingly. Beginning actors, who have not acquired the fine art of listening to a director and taking direction, love to have their work played back. Don't let this become a habit. It eats up valuable time in the studio. Reserve the "playback time" for the end of the session when the director plays the winning recording and asks the actors for their final input. If the actor believes there is a minute detail that can be corrected in the selected take, a final, subsequent reading can be recorded at this time.

After the director feels that the desired take is in the bag, the actors may be given free reign to read the copy any which way they choose. Slang for this direction is "let loose," "play with it," or "have fun." Once the pressure of delivering a "buy-able" take is removed, actors sometimes give their most brilliant and memorable performances. Often these takes are the ones used on the air. The previously accepted spot is then used as a back-up.

Remember that, occasionally, spots are miscast, and the director tries to salvage the project with the talent on hand. I witnessed an example of this when I was cast opposite a talented actor with an older, gravelly voice. The night before the session, the writer decided to rewrite the man's part into that of a 25- to 30-year-old. The next morning the older fellow (who was to play my father) arrived and was required to sound like my husband. Try as he might, he could never sound 30 years younger. Finally, dejected, he was relieved of duty and asked to sign his AFTRA contract. It was not his fault that he couldn't deliver the part; he was miscast! Of course he knew this, but still felt bad. As fate would have it, the session was saved because an actor with the right sound just happened to walk out of a studio down the hall and got whisked into the recording booth.

Reminders, Tidbits, and Advice

When you get behind the microphone, the engineer will ask you to *read for level*. Always read the copy as you intend to read it during the recording! Remember that time is important and that this request is not an idle remark; the engineer must hear how you are going to read the copy in order to set recording levels. If you speak in your regular voice during this test and then shout once the tape starts rolling, the levels are going to be off and the recording will be totally useless.

When recording, always wait for the *slate* before beginning. (This is different from "slating your name" at an audition. There is no need to slate your name at an actual booking; everyone already knows it.) Slating each take (Take 1, Take 2, Take 3, and so on) is a numerical system used by the engineer to keep track of each recording. Winning takes are marked so that they can be easily found later during the edit. Because there is a discernible click after the engineer or director depresses the "talk back" button, it is important for the actor to pause a second or two after the slate before speaking. Beginning too soon can result in the first few words being cut off or inaudible.

Keep the volume consistent. While on stage, it is absolutely acceptable to fluctuate between quiet and loud, but in voice-overs the actor's voice should always remain relatively level so listeners don't have to adjust their volume dials. Treat the microphone like a person's ear. Rather than yelling directly into the microphone to display anger, turn off-mic or internalize the intensity. Playing with your proximity to the mic gives you the freedom to be an inch away from it for close and intimate scenes or to step back for loud and boisterous dialogue. Of course, the further away from the microphone you get, the more audible the room ambiance becomes.

If the director says to *throw it away,* this means to not add undue importance to a word or phrase. Quit thinking about how to say it cleverly, and just do it!

When a reading style has been selected, *stay in character.* Don't drop in and out of character. Consistency is the name of the game.

Tempo is the speed at which the recording should be read. Typically, expensive luxury items are read slowly while limited-time offers and less-expensive items are read more quickly. The amount of words, needed to fit into a designated time period, determines the tempo. A change in tempo may be used to add interest to a reading.

Rhythm is the cadence or pattern of the words. In developing a character, it can be used as a distinguishing characteristic.

Warm it up simply means to be friendly, smile, and act like you're talking to someone.

Billboard it is directorial slang used to alert the actor to add emphasis and stretch out key words so they stand out clearly as major points of interest.

"We'll *wild line* it" simply means that it is necessary to record a single line over again. Rather than re-recording the entire piece, the one line is picked up and cut into place during the editing process. Lines and sections from various takes are often spliced together as a means of achieving the best complete read.

It's a buy! is the sweetest phrase in the voice-over vocabulary. It means that the actor's job is done and the money is forthcoming.

The Follow-Up

When the session is complete, it is good form to thank the person who hired you, the engineer, and any other people in the room who had a part in the completion of the project. After the congratulations for a job well done die down, it is time to sign contracts and take care of finances. If you want a copy of the recording for posterity or use on your next demo tape, this is the best time to ask. At the end of the session, the director can easily make an extra copy as the tapes are being dubbed for distribution to the TV or radio stations. (Remember to always ask for DAT or reel-to-reel.) When the session is over and all the paperwork is in order, you can leave. Recording sessions are divided into two sections: recording and editing. Once the actor's words have been recorded, the director and engineer have extensive editing and magical mixing work to complete. Hanging around to chitchat eats up valuable time and easily becomes annoying, so don't overstay your welcome.

Whenever you work with a new director or producer, it is also a good idea to mail a thank you note. It doesn't need to be long, just an appropriate note card, personalized stationary, or postcard. Comment on the good directing, the hobby the two of you have in common, or the fun you had at the session. Speak from the heart, but don't gush insincere praise. Ingratiate yourself to the director, and you may be hired again. Acknowledgments are often rewarded.

THE BUSINESS

The primary goal of all actors is to work. Some actors are willing to give away their services for free just for that opportunity. Luckily, the union is there to snap some sense into these people and help them acknowledge their contribution to the business. SAG and AFTRA establish minimum pay rates, referred to as *scale*. Actors, especially those in demand and with established track records, can be paid more than scale, for example scale and a half, double scale, triple scale, or higher, but never less. Non-union actors, on the other hand, have to figure out the rate the market will bear for their services. It could be anywhere from $50 to $300 or more. Like bidders at a silent auction, nonunion actors must second-guess how much to charge. It is up to the performer and producer to agree on an appropriate rate.

To better understand the financial picture, this section has been divided into two parts: union and nonunion. SAG and AFTRA union performers are considered the top working professionals. In addition to guaranteed decent wages, they also can benefit from pension plans, health insurance, dental coverage, on the job safety guidelines, and job payment schedules. Nonunion actors must fend for themselves in these areas. Although not governed by strict rules and regulations, nonunion work offers actors an excellent training ground to learn their craft before competing against the established union pros.

Union

Currently, SAG and AFTRA are separate entities. The Screen Actor's Guild handles all film. The American Federation of Television and Radio Artists has exclusive jurisdiction over video- and audiotape, broadcasting, news, soap operas, talk shows, disc jockeys, and radio sound recordings. Commercials on film fall under SAG's jurisdiction while commercials on tape can be either under SAG or AFTRA contract. (Film is a more expensive, high-quality means of visual recording used exclusively in movies and also in some television commercials and made-for-TV movies, corporate industrials, and TV shows. Videotape is a less-expensive, magnetic recording process.) Sometimes the two unions negotiate contracts together, such as with the Prime Time TV agreement. The two unions share jurisdiction in the field of nonbroadcast industrials.

SAG is a national union with branches around the country. It has one initiation fee and one dues structure. Conversely, AFTRA is a series of local unions joined together into a federation. Each "local" has its own initiation and dues structure. Anyone can walk into an AFTRA office, pay the initiation and dues fees, and become a member. An open door policy does not exist with SAG. To join SAG, one must first be hired as an actor on a SAG job or be a member of AFTRA for one year who has performed at least one principal role in an AFTRA production. The Taft-Hartley Act (a Congressional Act passed in the late 1940s applying to all union businesses) allows union employers (signatories) to hire people who are not in the union. The person is allowed to work under that union's jurisdiction for 30 days without joining. If the person gets union work anytime after that 30-day grace period, he is required to join the union. This principle applies regardless of whether an actor gets another job 31 days or several years after the first union job. If the actor does not get union work immediately following the grace period, he has an option to join the union or remain nonunion. The obvious structural differences between the two performing unions makes it difficult for the two unions to merge. Fortunately, negotiations between SAG and AFTRA continue. It is projected that, in the near future, the two unions will merge.

There are about five different SAG, and 400 AFTRA, contracts across the country that dictate an actor's pay rate. These contracts are subject to change and are negotiated on a continual basis. Also, as technology changes, new contracts are created. Of the union contracts, those for commercials are the most complicated. There are an assortment of categories—wildspots, seasonal spots (spots to run only during holidays), dealer spots, regional or network program spots, local spots, tags, and promos. Units and usage dictate how much money an actor gets paid for a spot. This system is based on the number of viewing households in an area of dominant influence (ADI). New York, Los Angeles, and Chicago are considered major markets and so they garner more money for an actor. The word "national" brings dollar signs to an actor's eyes because of the wide scope of unit coverage. The medium—network television, cable, radio— also has a direct bearing on earnings.

Commercial payments are divided into four categories: session fees, use fees, residuals, and holding fees. The session fee is based on the actual recording time. The 1995 radio-commercial rate is approximately $180 for up to one and one-half hours in the studio, and television voice-overs pay approximately $330 for a maximum of two hours of recording time. However, the rate could be higher or lower depending on the intended market for the commercial. The actor is paid for each commercial or program regardless of whether it was recorded in less than the allotted time. A use fee is paid when the commercial airs. Payment should be postmarked within 15 days of the beginning of the use cycle. Actors who voice national commercials receive additional money every time the commercial airs. Thirteen-week cycles dictate the residual payments. In radio the cycle starts at the commercial's first airing; in television it begins on the recording session or "use" date. The actor receives a residual payment for radio at the beginning of every 13-week cycle in which the spot airs. With SAG commercials, the actor gets the residual payment at the beginning of every 13-week cycle and a comparable holding fee if the client elects not to air the commercial continually but to hold it for future use. Seasonal spots, by their very nature, are often held over. During the inactive cycles, the SAG actor is mailed a holding fee as compensation for not performing for a competitive product. Once the client decides not to air the commercial any longer and the actor is released from the contract, the holding payments cease, and the actor is free to work for the competition.

Tags can bring an actor additional money when they are added onto multiple commercials. When voicing tags, you should be aware of the difference in the unions' use of the word. It is a much more stringent definition than the examples used in chapter 6. Technically, short sentences at the end of a commercial and slogans do not constitute tags. A tag is an incomplete thought or sentence, such as "Today, only $14.95." It signifies a change of name, date, or time. The reason for this differentiation is financial. Complete thoughts and slogans are categorized as commercials and paid accordingly. Tags, when they are attached to multiple commercials, have their own sliding pay scale. Since the term *tag* is used freely, it is best to discuss the script containing a tag with your agent or the union office before the session or to keep a copy of the script for discussion after the session.

Promo rates are negotiated individually by television stations in each city. The union acknowledges the volume of work generated by the local television stations and a scale acceptable to both parties is agreed upon. Often, the station is allowed to count three or four promos toward one fee.

Unions have the constant challenge of keeping up with technology. San Francisco, because of its close proximity to Silicon Valley, is often aware of changes long before other areas of the country. The site of many of the first infomercials, the San Francisco office recognized the need for an infomercial agreement. Although subject to change, an actor gets paid approximately $1,000 for the first day's work in an infomercial and about half that amount for each additional day. In 1994, the unions created the first interactive agreement. Presently, an actor can contribute up to three voices for the half-day rate of approximately $500. The cartoon animation agreement has a similar policy. Industrial narration rates (for Categories I and II) are in the $300 to $400 range for an hour's time in the studio. Additional half hours are paid at a slightly lower rate. Should any job be canceled less than 24 hours before the session, the union actor still gets paid.

"Plus 10" is a term commonly used in union contracts. It signifies that the producer agrees to add an additional 10-percent commission for the talent agent. That amount is automatically tacked on to the actor's AFTRA job. In SAG jobs, agents have to request that the commission be added on top of the actors pay. Otherwise, the commission comes out of the actor's earnings or the agent doesn't get paid.

The union also regulates payment schedules—how soon an actor must be paid. At the end of the recording session, the actor and producer both sign a member report. (The actor is responsible for supplying this form, but many recording studios and producers provide contracts.) The actor then mails the original to the appropriate union, keeping a copy for himself. The employer also retains a copy for himself and one for the payroll company. Payment must be received in the AFTRA office no later than 12 working days after the date of employment. Payments for SAG jobs can either be sent to the union or directly to the actor. The actor receives additional money for late payments. If the actor agrees, payment can be sent to the agent. In this case, the agent cashes the check, deducts the commission, and issues a new check to the actor. Payroll companies came onto the scene in the 1960s due to the swift payment requirements. State and federal laws allow a middleman to act as signatory and accept payroll responsibility for union contracts.

One of the luxuries of being a union actor is not having to negotiate your fee, since a reasonable minimum is already established. When in doubt, an actor just calls the union or a payroll company to double-check the rate. Collecting payments is not a problem either, since, if necessary, the agent and the union can play "bad cops" and collect back fees. This allows the actor to avoid uncomfortable financial situations and concentrate on acting. Union actors are expected to be the top professionals; it is assumed that their knowledge and efficiency in the recording studio will save the producer time and money. This perpetuates the need to hire union actors. As long as the members of the union are strong, the union remains strong.

Nonunion

Unlike SAG and AFTRA work, every nonunion job is considered a "buy out." The actor has no established recourse for additional money, even if the spot is aired indefinitely. While the few hundred dollars for the job may seem adequate at the time, it can cause hair-pulling and teeth-gnashing if the nonunion spot continues to play and preempts a future opportunity for the actor to perform a union job for the competition which might pay thousands of dollars more! The best way for nonunion actors to protect themselves against being taken advantage of is to create a contract for the producer to sign. In addition to the amount of money due for the job, it should clearly state airplay time limits. At the end of the contracted time, the producer can either negotiate another payment for the actor or retire the spot and record a new one.

Many producers ask nonunion actors their fee prior to hiring. This sends many actors into a panic. If the actor is new and hungry for work, the rate might be $50, whereas if the actor has years of experience the rate may be $200. The simplest way to determine the fee is to base it on the comparable union scale. Networking with fellow actors is another method of establishing the going rate.

Prior to accepting a job from a nonunion producer, the payment method and schedule should be agreed upon. Will the fee be paid immediately following the session or several weeks later? Should you submit an invoice or does the company have their own contract stating pay rate and schedule? Without some sort of verbal or written agreement, nonunion talent is at the mercy of the producer. Although the majority of the producers are reputable, a few will delay payments or refuse to pay entirely, but 99 percent of producers will pay within six weeks. Two to four weeks from the session date should allow ample time for payment. As insurance against that untrustworthy one percent, nonunion talent should come to the session with an invoice for the agreed sum and payment due date, should small claims court be the only recourse for retrieving the money. Make two copies, one for the producer and one for yourself. If the producer does not have a check or a company contract at the end of the session, you can pull out your invoice for the producer to sign and date.

Chapter 18

Epilogue: The Pep Talk

This book is intended to open up your mind to the world of voice-overs. Using chapters 6 through 14 to practice, record, and evaluate your work should help to expand your realm of creativity and inspire you to think about new and unique ways of delivering the written word. You, as an actor, must make the two-dimensional words on the page appear three-dimensional. Begin by testing the boundaries of your abilities. Develop and explore your voice range. Learn to relax and breathe properly. Boldly go where no other voice actor has ever gone before!

SUMMARY TIPS

1. Pay attention to the trends in voice-overs. This requires periodic television viewing and radio station switching. Are the commonly heard voices quirky, real, or announcer-y? Do they have "wrinkles," "sand," or a brightness in them? Learn to adjust to the changes in voice and acting demands as they occur. Remain vocally and stylistically flexible. This will allow you to continue working throughout your life.

2. Don't let other actors' egos interfere with your performance. Trust your work and forget about their need to stay on top.

3. Learn from your mistakes as well as your successes. Personal growth comes through experience. If you find yourself doing a better job in your car driving to the audition, analyze the situation and figure out ways to improve for the next time.

4. Get to know your agent and the voice-over casting directors. This will add a comfort level to your performance and reduce audition stress.

5. Develop a strong stomach. Every session is different. You might be the star at one session and cast aside as second best at a session two hours later. Understand that whenever money is on the line, emotions and tensions are apt to run high. Every producer handles high-stress situations differently. Divorce yourself from the problems in the room, and concentrate on doing the best voice-over job possible. Performance quality and professional behavior will dictate whether or not you are hired again.

6. Learn to "read the room." Are you the first to perform or the last actor at a 10-hour session? Just because you joked around and chatted with the producer at the last session, doesn't mean that this same joviality and time freedom exists at every job. As the day progresses, schedules often get backed up. Don't add to the problem or overstay your welcome. Unless the signals are otherwise, thank the people in

the console room and leave. Don't fish for approval and, in doing so, ignore the physical or verbal signs that the clock is ticking and the producer must resume working.

7. Don't be self-conscious about your facial or body movements. No one is judging your dexterity. The important thing is to bring the words to life. Stand on your head if it helps you to give your best performance!

8. Don't get discouraged. Voice-overs is a freelance profession. It takes time, commitment, and talent to succeed. Even though you may get work immediately, it often takes three years to become established. Continue studying, take acting classes, and perform on stage. This will expand your repertoire. After 10 years, you'll be surprised at the complexities of your voice and your understanding of subtle nuances which eluded you in earlier years.

9. Prepare yourself for lean times. If you need a paycheck every two weeks, freelance work may not be the business for you. There may be times when you work a lot and other times when the work temporarily dries up. Keep focused, make phone calls to stir up more work, and above all don't get discouraged. It may help to set a goal for yourself, such as trying to double your income every year.

10. When you act, never become *less* than what you are. Keep the dimensions of your personality alive. Feel the power from your gut. Trust the intuition and creativity that comes from your head. Accept the playful feelings of the child who lives inside your heart.

11. Strive for your ultimate goal: to execute wonderful voice-overs *reflexively*. That is the fourth level of learning, where information is so integrated into your persona that you no longer have to spend hours analyzing ways to bring the material to life. Your verbal masterpieces are created effortlessly.

Practice, commitment, and trust are the keys to your success. When you open up your imagination and let the words come alive, the real fun begins!

Glossary

AFTRA   American Federation of Television and Radio Artists. A union for actors.

animatic   A demo-commercial used in-house by advertising agencies to pitch an account or a proposal.

announcer spot   The most traditional style of radio or television commercial that typically features an impersonal voice announcing an item and its price.

articulation   Clear enunciation.

billboarding   To highlight or emphasize a specific word or phrase in the script. As in, "Billboard it!"

body   The main, informational section of the script that answers the *who, where, what, why,* and *when* questions posed in the set-up.

booking   The job. As in when your agent says, "You have a booking tomorrow at 12:00."

booth   The soundproof recording studio where the actor speaks into the microphone.

branching   Scripts recorded with multiple answers that are electronically inserted into the appropriate open-ended sentence. Voice mail systems utilize branching.

button   A single scripted or improvised word, phrase, or sentence at the conclusion of the spot that clinches the commercial without introducing additional copy points.

buy   The recorded take that will be used as the commercial. As in, "It's a buy!"

cans   The headphones used by the actor while recording to hear his own voice and any music, special effects, or comments from the director and engineer. Also referred to as earphones or just phones.

CD-I   Compact Disc-Interactive.

CD-ROM   Compact Disc-Read Only Memory.

color	The subtle nuances of speech that make the words interesting and meaningful.
control room	The room where the director and the engineer sit during the recording session. It houses the recording and mixing equipment.
copy points	The essential pieces of information in the script, such as the client's name, key words or phrases, slogans, sale items, dates, times, and locations.
cross talk	When copy spoken into one actor's microphone is picked up by another mic. The sound is said to "spill over" or "bleed" into the other actor's mic.
DAT	Digital Audio Tape. High-quality audiotape used in sound studios.
demo tape	A voice actor's audio résumé containing representative samples of his recorded work.
donut	A tag that occurs in the middle of a commercial. The body of the spot "wraps around" this announcer hole.
edutainment software	Entertaining and educational computer programs.
improv	An abbreviation (of improvisation) for any unscripted and spontaneous copy performed by the voice actor to enhance the script.
infomercial	A long commercial structured like an actual television program.
intention	The tactic used by the actor to get his character's need met.
iso booth	The isolation room within the recording studio.
J-card	The paper insert that slips inside a cassette box.
level	The recording volume level set by the engineer to match the volume of the actor's voice.
milking	To stretch the words out and give them as much emphasis as humanly possible. As in, "Milk it."
mixing	The engineer's job of combining the actor's recorded voice with the special effects and music to create the finished recording.
motivation	The prior event or emotions that stimulate and give logic and context to the present action and dialogue in the script.
multimedia	Computer software programs that combine the use of text, sound, and graphics.

need	The driving force behind the actor that inspires his deepest desire in the script.
off-mic	The area to the side of the microphone's diaphragm. As in, to speak words off-mic so that they are not recorded as loudly.
over-the-top	An instruction to make the copy sound larger than life. This can be either desirable or overdone, depending upon the script and direction.
personalizing the message	Speaking into the microphone as if talking to a specific, familiar person in order to add realism to the written words.
plosive	The sudden explosion of air as it exits the mouth and hits the microphone's diaphragm. Also referred to as a pop.
plus 10	A contractual agreement in which the producer agrees to add an additional 10 percent to the actor's payment to accommodate for the agent's commission.
pre-life/pre-scene	The previous history an actor invents for his character in order to enhance his own interpretation and performance of the actual script story line and dialogue.
promo	A promotional commercial spot used by television and radio stations to increase audience awareness of upcoming programming.
PSA	Public Service Announcement. Commercials produced to raise the public's awareness of current issues, such as drug abuse, illiteracy, the environment.
real person spot	A commercial utilizing a voice that sounds like a regular person, rather than a professional actor paid to endorse a product.
resolve	The conclusion of a commercial in which all the elements of the script come together in the final restating of the crucial copy points.
resonance	The full quality of a voice created by vibrations in resonating chambers, such as the mouth and sinus areas.
rhythm	The cadence of the words.
SAG	Screen Actors Guild. A union for actors.
SASE	self-addressed stamped envelope.
scale	The minimum wage a union voice actor can earn for a recording session.
set-up	The attention-getting opening statement (or statements) of the commercial copy.

SFX	The abbreviation for "special effects."
shell	The plastic cassette casing that holds the tape in place.
sibilance	An unwanted *s* sound that sometimes occurs in speech and can be minimized electronically by the engineer.
slate	To speak your name or a take number at the start of a recording. Used either at an audition (a name) or a recording session (a take number), the slate helps the director and engineer identify and keep track of the actors and the various takes.
spokesperson	A voice actor who is hired on a repeat or contractual basis to represent a product or company.
substitution	The mental replacement (by the actor) of the written situation with something from his own past to create a personal, emotional connection with the spoken words and therefore achieve a greater sense of reality in the delivery of the copy.
sweeps	The television and radio rating periods during which the total viewing or listening audience is estimated.
tag	An incomplete thought or sentence placed at the end of a commercial to signify a change of name, date, or time.
take	The actual recording of copy and also the number assigned to each recording. As in, "Take 1, take 2. . . ."
tempo	The speed at which copy is delivered.
"Throw it away."	The direction to play down and not add undue importance to a word or phrase.
trailer	A commercial that highlights a new or upcoming movie release.
"Warm it up."	The direction to smile and lighten up the vocal delivery.
wild line	A line of copy that is recorded separately from the rest of the script and then inserted into place during the editing process.

Index